CELTIC IN

CW00339230

This book is dedicated to Jackie and to baby Joseph,
who arrived on 26 May 2003.

MAINSTREAM / SPORT

CELTIC IN EUROPE

FOUR DECADES OF FLOODLIT DRAMA

GRAHAM McCOLL

MAINSTREAM
PUBLISHING
EDINBURGH AND LONDON

Updated and Revised, 2004

First published in Great Britain in 2003 by
MAINSTREAM PUBLISHING (EDINBURGH) LTD
7 Albany Street
Edinburgh EH1 3UG

ISBN 1 84018 777 8

Reprinted 2004

A catalogue record for this book is available from the British Library

Typeset in Avant Garde and Garamond

Printed in Great Britain by
Cox & Wyman Ltd

Acknowledgements

I would like to thank the following, all of whose help has been indispensable in my work on this book: Alec Boden, Liam Brady, Tommy Burns, Bobby Carroll, Elaine Cooper, John Divers, Wolfgang Eichler, Tommy Gemmell, Peter Grant, David Hannah, David Hay, John Hughes, Andy Jackson, Mike Jackson, Jimmy Johnstone, Michael Kelly, Hans Krankl, Peter Latchford, Bobby Lennox, Eugene MacBride, Murdo MacLeod, Brian McClair, Billy McNeill, Ger Mallen, Lubo Moravcik, José Mourinho, Betty Murray, Charlie Nicholas, Neil O'Donnell, Eddy Pieters Graafland, Iain Spragg, Doctor Acacio Valentim, Tristan White, Evan Williams, www.icons.com.

Special thanks also to all at Mainstream, especially Bill Campbell for giving my idea for this book the go-ahead, Tina Hudson for her work on the cover design, and Graeme Blaikie for editorial coordination.

Contents

PREFACE

An electric air of anticipation crackles round Celtic Park on every European match evening. Four decades of thrilling encounters with exotic opponents have cultivated a taste among the supporters for the rich fare that is provided by European football. Sometimes, the thrill is the mystery of facing unknown opponents from far-flung corners of the continent. On other evenings, the hope among the supporters is the anticipation of one of European football's great giants – a club such as a Real Madrid or a Juventus – being brought crashing to earth at partisan Parkhead. The occasions on which that happens live for a lifetime in the minds of the supporters.

The drama is heightened by European matches always being played in midweek, when the green rectangle of the football pitch, the focus of so many lives, is framed and thrown into sharp relief by the floodlights. The turf looks lush and inviting, the green and white hoops on the Celtic shirts take on a special, glossy sheen under the lights and the cut and thrust of the game heightens the value of every action on the part of the players. Nervous tension fills the air – one act of inspiration or one terrible slip can tilt the balance of a top tie for or against Celtic. The drama of it all is as much akin to some lavish stage production as it is to the football that is at the heart of everything. On these evenings, the grit and grind of routine Scottish League matches seems far away.

This is the first time that the tale of Celtic's jousts in the European arena over the past four decades has been told in full. It is a story that will engage every Celtic supporter who has ever enjoyed that special tingle of anticipation in the days and weeks leading up to a European match.

Most of the great names in European football have visited Celtic Park for a European tie at one time or another. Real Madrid, Juventus, Internazionale, Milan, Ajax Amsterdam, Barcelona, Benfica and Valencia are among the plethora of great names to have strutted the turf in the East End of Glasgow. Clubs with more modest reputations have proved to be equally accomplished opponents, such as Ujpest Dozsa, Vojvodina Novi Sad and Basle, all of whom have provided that essential element of surprise that is such a vital ingredient in making European evenings suspense-filled occasions.

Away from Glasgow, Celtic's European adventures have been equally, if not more, eventful as at home. The club's earliest days in European competition produced all sorts of unexpected mishaps, as players and management came to terms with the logistics of taking a trip abroad to play a midweek match. Soon, under the leadership of Jock Stein, European trips began to go more smoothly and Celtic became a name to be feared by all opponents whom they encountered on their travels. Maintaining such a reputation is of vital importance to Celtic – playing in the Scottish League means that it is only in European competition that the true standing of the club can be measured and Celtic's achievement of reaching the 2003 UEFA Cup final against Porto has re-established Celtic's reputation as one of the leading clubs in Europe. That evening in Seville provides a suitably dramatic denouement for a book in which some of the greatest players in the history of the world game sway in and out of the pages: top achievers such as Alfredo Di Stefano, Giacinto Facchetti, Sandro Mazzola, Wim van Hanegem, Johan Cruyff, Santillana, Alessandro Del Piero, David Trezeguet and Deco. Celtic have also had players in the same bracket, including Jimmy Johnstone, Bobby Murdoch, Bobby Lennox, Kenny Dalglish and Henrik Larsson.

The action described in the following pages captures in intense detail how European competition has unravelled for Celtic and it focuses closely on the major events that have shaped the club's progress through each of the European competitions. It is a tale that features magical triumphs, unexpected victories, severe frustrations and a cast of enormously colourful characters. It should provide a fascinating read for anyone interested in Celtic and European football.

ONE

The Fun of the Fairs
VALENCIA 1962

The stars looked down on Celtic's representatives abroad as they gingerly took their first steps into the realm of European competition. It was two o'clock in the morning as the Celtic party descended from the aircraft that had transported them from Glasgow to Valencia. Emerging from the hermetically sealed atmosphere of the aircraft after their six-hour journey, their senses were immediately violently assaulted by reminders that they were now in an alien atmosphere. A wave of heat buffeted them as they left the plane, to emphasise that even though it was the middle of the night, and late September, they were now on Mediterranean shores. The heat was accompanied by rolling thunder and lightning and the whole tempestuous scene was offset by the pungent smell of oranges mingling with the rain from the storm. The sounds and smells that greeted them on their arrival on the east coast of Spain were as dramatic and striking an entrance to Europe as Celtic could have expected, and they were still almost 48 hours away from kick-off in their Fairs Cup tie with Valencia. It was a reminder that they were involved in something new and something very different.

There were 40 people in the Celtic party that travelled to Valencia that autumn of 1962. A total of 21 players made the trip, far more than were required at a time when substitutions were not permitted in competitive matches. It meant a total cost to the club of £1,800, a substantial sum in those days, and it reflected the feeling on the part of chairman Robert Kelly that it was his responsibility to broaden the Celtic players' horizons. Taking part in the trip was also a reward for the young group of players known as the Kelly Kids, who had been doing very well for the club in the reserve league. Kelly was accompanied by fellow directors Desmond White and Tom Devlin; Celtic manager Jimmy McGrory; his assistant Sean Fallon; and trainer Bob Rooney. The remainder of the Celtic party was composed of their tiny band of well-heeled travelling supporters – foreign travel was well beyond the resources of the vast majority of people in the early 1960s.

'For us it was a massive game,' says Mike Jackson, one of the players in that party, 'because it was our first-ever venture in Europe at a competitive level. So we didn't know what to expect and going abroad was new then, so we were excited.'

The party made their way to the Hotel Recati, 18 kilometres south of Valencia. The players were billeted three to a room, where they were to sleep on bunk beds, while the directors and management enjoyed the luxury of taking up residence in individual chalets in prime locations, close to the beach but part of the hotel annexe. When dawn arrived, Robert Kelly and his fellow chalet inhabitants stepped out of their doors and into three feet of water: a temporary approximation of a bubbling, flowing, brothy burn had formed down the side of the hotel as a result of the heavy rain from an overnight storm. This slapstick comedown for the elite provided the players with their first good collective belly laugh of the trip.

The Scottish press were also accommodated at the same hotel and one of the newspaper reporters on the trip also had a watery mishap, running a bath whilst so inebriated that he fell asleep and flooded the floor of the hotel in which he was staying. The same reporter was so incapacitated again later in the trip that some Celtic players had to telephone his report from Spain home for him.

The Celtic party spent the Tuesday, their first full day on Spanish soil, relaxing into their stylish surroundings. These included an American bar and 'Mini Golf International' – the hotel's name for crazy golf – with the latter amusement proving a compelling attraction for the

Celtic players. The players were also allowed to find relief from the searing heat by refreshing themselves in the hotel pool. They were out mucking about at the pool that Tuesday afternoon when they were alerted to the predicament of two young Swiss boys who had been washed out to sea. The youngsters had been floating in an inflatable dinghy when they had been carried off. Their father came running up from the beach to inform the Celtic party of this and when players and officials rushed to the beach they could see that the boys were getting further and further away from land.

Sean Fallon, who had been a lifeguard in his native Sligo and who was a strong swimmer, immediately plunged into the Med and swam out to sea to bring the boys back to safety. They had been close to 300 yards from the shore and had almost disappeared over the horizon. Celtic's assistant manager had saved their lives.

As the hours ebbed away, the minds of the players began to turn more and more towards the business end of their trip. Those who were to be involved in the match on the Wednesday night were allowed only very brief exposure to the sun before being told to go indoors and go to bed. John Fallon, the back-up goalkeeper, was messing around at the pool with his fellow squad members when, mid-afternoon on that Tuesday, he was called away and told to get into his bed quickly to rest. First-choice goalkeeper Frank Haffey had taken ill and would miss the match.

The Inter-Cities Fairs Cup was the oldest of the three major European tournaments that were in existence during the early 1960s. The European Cup was for the league champions of each European country and the European Cup-Winners' Cup was, as its title suggested, for each country's cup winners. The Fairs Cup, which had been in existence since 1955, had originally been a competition restricted to cities that held trade fairs but by the early 1960s that restriction had been quietly set aside. Now those clubs who had won neither their domestic cup nor their domestic league – clubs who were among the best of the rest from each country – entered the Fairs Cup. Celtic's high ranking at home had won them their entry – they had finished third in the Scottish League in 1961–62, their best showing since an impressive set of crane-like floodlights, visible from miles around in the East End of Glasgow, had been installed at Celtic Park in 1959 to make midweek European evenings a viable proposition. The club's lack of domestic success in the late 1950s and early '60s had led to their late entry to European competition, seven years after Hibernian had been Scotland's first entrants, but now that Celtic were finally in Europe the players intended to make the most of their chance.

Bobby Carroll, Celtic's centre-forward for the first leg, recalls arriving at Valencia's Mestalla stadium on the evening of the match and being awestruck by the steepness of the gradient at which the Spanish stands rose above the pitch. In Scotland at the time, terraces and stands ran back from the pitch at a much gentler incline. At Valencia, the stands and terraces angled sharply upwards, allowing the home spectators both a spectacular view and the opportunity to get on the backs of their team's opponents.

'We had never seen a stadium like that before,' says Carroll. 'It was something else. The atmosphere was amazing. There were several tiers on the terraces but the supporters were so close to the park that they seemed to be towering above you. It was a terrific stadium and I felt that their fans were actually quite receptive to us. Once the game starts, though, on an occasion like that, you get excited and you forget about the crowd. There could be 80,000 or 8,000. You forget they are there. You only heard them shouting at you when the game stopped for a throw-in or whatever but once the game was moving again you forgot about the crowd. I don't remember them chanting the way the continentals do now; at that time, it used to be more of a roar that got louder as the play got nearer the goal. The other thing we found about the stadium was that there were no stairs in it. Theirs had circular walkways going down in the way our modern stadiums have now – they were way ahead of us at that time.'

The foreignness of the entire experience of visiting Spain, then an underdeveloped country, had been brought home to Carroll a few hours before the match, when he got the sensation that he might be an extra in a spaghetti western. 'I can remember on the Wednesday, on the morning of the game,' he says, 'Charlie Gallagher and I had a walk because we were fed up remaining in the hotel. We had a walk along the main road and turned up in a wee town, which looked like it was out of one of those cowboy films, with the old fellows sitting outside the bar. There was a wooden platform about three feet high all the way along the side of the street – it must have been liable to flooding, I take it – where the shops were, and the butcher shop's window was open, with flies everywhere. Charlie and I walked into this village and you could see these old-timers sitting with their pipes and their drinks and they looked up at us as we went past. It was as if we were two strangers moseying into town. Other than that it was just lazing about until it was time to go for the game.'

The draw for the Fairs Cup first round could hardly have been more cruel to Celtic. At the time of Celtic's visit, Valencia were still basking in the success of becoming the Fairs Cup holders after their first entry into European club competition and they had won the trophy only a fortnight previously. In those early days of European football, arrangements for the staging of matches were less rigidly controlled than today and the 1961–62 Fairs Cup final had taken place a few days before the beginning of the 1962–63 Spanish season.

The first match of the two-legged final, on 9 September 1962, had seen Valencia defeat Barcelona 6–2 in the Mestalla. Inside-left Vicente Guillot had netted a hat-trick in that match and he had also contributed Valencia's goal in the 1–1 draw in the Nou Camp three days later that had secured the Fairs Cup for Valencia.

There were three changes to the Valencia side that took the field for the match with Celtic on 26 September 1962 from the one that had taken the Fairs Cup just two weeks previously. There was a glimmer of hope for Celtic in that one of the absentees was Brazilian centre-forward 'Waldo' Machado da Silva, although Vicente Guillot, the goalscorer *extraordinaire* from the final, was in place at inside-left. Valencia had started the Spanish League season with two defeats but they had never lost to British opposition.

The Celtic team showed five changes to the side that had lost 2–1 at home to Aberdeen the previous Saturday. Such fluctuations in the Celtic line-up were entirely the norm during the early 1960s. Jimmy McGrory had enjoyed the title of manager since 1945 but it was well understood inside Celtic Park by players and staff that it was the

chairman, Robert Kelly, who selected the team. He would chop and
change the line-up on a whim, without argument, and the players
simply had to get on with it. This lack of a settled team contributed
greatly to Celtic's fluctuating fortunes – by that autumn of 1962 it had
been five years since the club had won a major trophy.

Even those players who survived from one match to the next found
things to be less than settled. Bobby Carroll had played on the left wing
against Aberdeen, but for the Valencia match he was pitched in at
centre-forward. He replaced 19-year-old John Hughes, who had
struggled to make an impact in a friendly match against Real Madrid a
fortnight earlier. Carroll had come on for Hughes at the beginning of
the second half that evening and had done well. It appeared to have
resulted in Carroll getting the nod for the match against Valencia,
although it was always dangerous to try to deduce any logic from Kelly's
team selections.

'You hardly played in the same position from one week to the next,'
explains Carroll. 'I would be outside-right, then centre, then outside-
left, then inside-right. Stevie Chalmers was the same – in fact, everybody
was getting switched about. It wasn't very professional, to be quite
truthful, at that time. The players were all well aware that Robert Kelly
was picking the team but at the end of the day what could you do? They
were the guys that picked the team. We never had any tactics in those
days. Nobody ever went to see the opponents playing. You just got told
you were playing and that was it – away you went out and you played.
There were no tactics at all. They'd give you your strip, Jimmy McGrory
would read out the team and then give you a wee pat on the back as you
were going out of the door and that was it.'

Billy McNeill, who had been made Celtic captain in 1962, led out
the following team at the Mestalla: John Fallon, Dunky MacKay, Jim
Kennedy, Pat Crerand, Billy McNeill, Willie O'Neill, Stevie Chalmers,
Mike Jackson, Bobby Carroll, Charlie Gallagher and Alec Byrne. It was
a young team, brimming with talents such as the quick, skilful right-
back MacKay, precision passer Crerand, intelligent inside-forwards
Gallagher and Jackson and the rapier-sharp Chalmers, playing at
outside-right. Chairman Kelly, in advance of the Valencia tie, had
earmarked Stevie Chalmers as the 'key man against continental
opposition. We will certainly try to field him in all our European

games. His style must click.' Bobby Carroll, centre-forward on the night, possessed the versatility to switch, on demand, from the left or right wing in one match to target man in another. 'At Valencia we were excited,' he says. 'We were desperate for the game.'

Carroll himself is in no doubt as to who was the most impressive player in that Celtic team. 'Big Billy was an inspiration, even at that time,' he explains. 'Billy had been the captain for a while even though he was young. He was a ball-winner, a competitor. Paddy was a great player as well, a bit slower, but he could pass a great ball and he would also be shouting all the time.'

The match kicked off at 10.30 p.m. on Wednesday, 26 September, and Valencia began confidently, as might be expected of the holders. 'They were a bit harder than we had experienced,' states Bobby Carroll, 'and they were fast; stronger than us. They were big, bulky guys; the defenders were, anyway. They were a big, fit, strong team but a sporting team. I seemed to get more room against them, more time on the ball. I don't remember their defenders ever coming too far up the field. I don't remember ever being played offside – they never played that tactic. They seemed to hold their line and let you come to them. It was very warm, it was roasting, and that probably took its toll on the players. The heat never bothered me – I don't seem to sweat so I don't remember it bothering me, but it was very warm.'

After nine minutes Celtic conceded a corner and, when the kick came over, Valencia outside-left Luis Coll buried the ball in the Celtic net. Midway through the first half, further Valencia pressure led to a free kick for the Spaniards and Coll used the advantage to score Valencia's second. Heat, dehydration and the sharpness of the Valencia players appeared to be taking its toll on the Celts, but after 28 minutes, and just two minutes after Coll had made it 2–0 to Valencia, Bobby Carroll scored Celtic's first goal in competitive football in Europe.

'Somebody has got to score the first goal, right enough,' he says, modestly. 'It just happened to be me. Some reporters said it was an own goal but what I remember of it would suggest it wasn't. The ball came across from Mike Jackson and I hit it. I beat the goalkeeper, who was just off his line. He had a defender behind him and the defender tried to stop it with his foot but he couldn't stop it and it went in. The defender was on the line and I would probably be just inside the six-yard box because Mike crossed it from the byline. I was right in the centre in front of goal and I just hit it first time past the goalkeeper. The lad who was on the line tried to stop it and he deflected it into the net. He was in the middle of the goal – it wasn't as if the ball was going wide – and he sent it into the net. It was going in and he just couldn't stop it. If a goalkeeper goes to block it and it goes in, it's not an own goal; it's the same with a defender.'

It had been the Valencia left-back, Manolo Mestre, who had been attempting to block the ball and he would later be credited by some with netting Celtic's first goal in Europe. The confusion as to who should be credited with the goal arose because of the Spanish tradition that a goal is given as an own goal if a defending player gets any sort of contact on the ball on its way into the net. The Scottish tradition is that it should only be given as an own goal if the defender plays a decisive role in putting in the net a ball that would otherwise not hit the target. As such, Carroll deserves the credit for Celtic's first counter on the continent.

There was no time for the Celtic players to concern themselves with such niceties as they battled both Valencia and the draining late-night heat and humidity in the brightly lit bowl that was the Mestalla. Two minutes after Carroll's strike, Valencia restored their two-goal lead through Vicente Guillot. The Spaniards now began to dominate and the Celtic players were relieved to return to the dressing-room at half-time only 3–1 down. Their relief lasted only slightly longer than the interval. Two minutes after the restart, Guillot pounced to make it 4–1.

A rout began to look ominously possible, although McNeill and Jim Kennedy were defending like demons in the face of the clever, fast-moving Valencia forwards. Slowly but steadily the tide of attacks was stemmed and ten minutes after Guillot's goal Stevie Chalmers had the ball in the Valencia net. It was disallowed for offside, despite loud and long protests from the Celtic players. Celtic continued to press and after five successive corners Bobby Carroll planted the ball in the Valencia net for a second time. 'Both the goals were the same,' says Carroll. 'For both, Mike Jackson cut the ball back low from the byline. The second goal was almost a replica of the first one. He got to the byline and cut it back for me and I hit it home from the edge of the six-yard box.'

Mike Jackson remembers the events of that evening well. 'They had hit us like a whirlwind at the start. They were quick and it was hot and they had a couple of big Brazilians playing for them and they played one-touch football and their passing and movement was superb. It was great to watch and in the first half we watched a lot of it! I was playing in the middle of the park with Paddy Crerand and at times in the first half we couldn't get a kick, couldn't get a touch. They were fabulous on the ball; they were playing a different game from us. Our fans here like the ball to get played forward as quickly as possible whereas they're patient. They'll play it one-touch rather than touch, touch, pass. They were just better footballers. They played a better game than us.

'It probably took us the best part of the first half to get into the game and get our second wind and settle down and start to get the ball. There was no air; it was one of those balmy, hot nights and it took us about half an hour to get acclimatised to the heat. Once we did that and then started winning the ball and getting closer to people and started playing, the game started to come for us, whereas early on we were sluggish, we couldn't get a breath. Everything was laboured and they were just flying by us. Once we settled down and got our game going, passing it and playing, I thought we did well and in the second half I thought we played really well. By the end we could say that we had given them a game. It was a great experience.'

The remainder of the match saw Celtic pushing hard for more goals and Valencia pressed back. Two Celtic penalty claims were dismissed by the referee and, in the final minute, Alec Byrne had a good opportunity to score but lost his balance. It ended 4–2 to Valencia, a result that Bobby Carroll is gracious enough to admit the Spaniards probably deserved. 'I think they did,' he says. 'On reflection, we must have been under quite a bit of pressure defensively. They were a good team; although not as good as the Real Madrid team that we had played against a fortnight previously. We were a young team. That was probably part of our problem as well; there were not enough experienced players to help you.'

Bobby Lennox, 19 at the time, was one of the youngsters who had been taken out to Valencia to experience the game and he recalls how magnificent the stadium looked lit up at night. The match itself did, as Robert Kelly had hoped, help add to Lennox's footballing

education. 'They had a lad played for them and he never came back
past the halfway line,' recalls Lennox, 'one of the first players that I
had seen do that. Watching him, I remember thinking that he was
terrific and that it would be great to be like him and be able to play
that way.'

The team's flight back from Valencia was not scheduled to leave until
5.35 p.m. on the Thursday so the players spent that day bathing in the
Mediterranean and buying presents and souvenirs of Spain. As they
prepared for their flight home, the Celtic party collected a supporter
who had hitch-hiked from Barcelona for the match and made him part
of their trip; a gesture typical of the relaxed informality of the Celtic of
the early 1960s. The players broke the monotony of the journey by
taking trips to the flight deck until their plane landed at Lourdes
Airport to refuel. They disembarked to have coffee in the airport lounge
and were amused by one of the French porters, who scooped up a large,
black beetle and began stroking it lovingly. As he was doing so, Pat
Crerand came up behind him and brought his hand down on the beetle
to flatten it. The angry porter gave chase to provide further amusement
for the players. Another large beetle appeared on the floor of the bar
and Sean Fallon stood on it accidentally.

It was a content Bobby Carroll who arrived home late that Thursday
evening. 'I thought I did all right in the game,' he suggests. 'I thought
I linked up well and I was in position to get the two goals.' The player
had scored Celtic's first two goals in Europe, against top-class
opposition. It was a fine achievement but instead of providing the
overture for the player to go on to do great things for Celtic, it instead,
and quite shockingly, would prove the beginning of the end of Carroll's
career at the club. Carroll turned up at Celtic Park on the Friday
morning, with the memories of Valencia fresh in his mind, to discover
that he had been omitted from the Celtic team that was to face Raith
Rovers at Stark's Park on the Saturday. Also missing from the line-up
was Mike Jackson, the player whose skilful play had provided the
groundwork for both of Carroll's goals.

'I scored the two goals that night and Mike Jackson laid them on,'
says Carroll. 'He got to the byline and crossed and I put them away. The
defence lost four goals and yet it was Mike and I who were dropped.

Nobody said anything to you and told you that you hadn't done this or that. You were simply dropped. That was it. I can remember meeting Mike and walking up to the park for the reserve game on the following Saturday and the two of us moaning about being dropped. We [the Celtic Reserves] beat Raith Rovers 7–1 that day. Mike and I between us got the two goals in Valencia and for us to be dropped when the defence let four in was a wee bit disappointing.'

It was not as though Carroll and Jackson were among a number of changes for the Raith Rovers match. Only one other change was made to the line-up that had faced Valencia and that was the restoration of first-choice goalkeeper Frank Haffey, who had missed the Fairs Cup match through illness, in place of John Fallon. The omission of the two players who had created and scored the goals that gave Celtic a lifeline in the Fairs Cup was an inexplicable, baffling decision but one that was all too typical of a time when chairman Robert Kelly would tinker and toy with the team and the careers of the Celtic players as if they were mere playthings for him. 'I thought I did really well in Valencia that night,' says Jackson. 'I made the two goals for wee Bobby. I got along the byline and provided two cut-backs and Bobby stuck them away and the only two guys that weren't playing at Kirkcaldy on the Saturday were Bobby and me. What did we do wrong? The team selections were so inconsistent it was laughable. I was sick about missing out on that game against Raith Rovers.

'I must have done something in Valencia that Robert Kelly didn't like but we didn't get up to anything really. The only thing I got up to was to go in for a swim on the Thursday morning with Desmond White. The hotel we were staying in was outside Valencia, on a beach. It was a bit like Seamill Hydro, and I was always a good swimmer. I loved snorkelling and Desmond White gave me a shot of his snorkel; he did a lot of diving. Desmond and I were the only two that had gone in for a dive in the sea. I walked back up from the beach with Desmond White and when I got up to my room I found that the boys had taken all my gear. So I came down the stairs, soaking wet, covered in sand, and with only a pair of Celtic pants on, and the bus was getting ready to go. Sean Fallon, who was in charge, started shouting at me. I said, "What do you want me to do? I've been in swimming with Desmond White and have come back and found my room empty." So Sean went on the bus and as usual big Billy and Crerand had all my gear. So the bus was delayed, but they surely wouldn't have left me out of the next game because of that.'

The Celtic first team won 2–0 at Raith Rovers that Saturday and then Carroll found himself restored to the team for the three other League matches prior to the home leg of the tie with Valencia. Carroll seized the opportunity to score two of Celtic's four goals in those three games. It seemed of little account to chairman Kelly. Worse was to follow for Carroll, when, on the very day of the return with Valencia, he was dealt the final, crushing blow in his career at Celtic Park. With the minutes ticking away before the Valencia tie, the Blackburn Rovers player Bobby Craig was rushed to Glasgow and signed by Celtic for a £15,000 club-record fee. Craig was immediately pitched into the line-up for the Valencia match and Carroll found himself despatched to the stand to watch the game as a spectator. 'I would have expected to be in the team,' says Carroll. 'I was a bit disappointed but that's football. It's up to the manager.' Carroll would never appear in a Celtic jersey again. Mike Jackson did not make the team either; he too had also played his final match for Celtic.

A 45,000 crowd had been drawn to Celtic Park for the first competitive European match at the ground and the team that lined up for the return with Valencia showed several changes from the first leg. It was: Frank Haffey, Dunky MacKay, Willie O'Neill, Pat Crerand, John McNamee, John Clark, Stevie Chalmers, Bobby Craig, John Divers, Charlie Gallagher and Alec Byrne. Spurred on by the crowd, the Celtic forward line went at the game with some brio but despite showing some nifty skills they lacked the precision to put the ball in the net. Their first chance of note arrived after 18 minutes when John Divers was tripped inside the Valencia penalty box and tumbled to the turf. John Clark took the resultant penalty but his kick was aimed too high and the chance had flown.

At half-time Valencia looked to be sitting comfortably on their tidy 4–2 first-leg lead. Three minutes after the interval the Valencia right-back Manuel Verdu attempted to clear the ball and instead sliced it wildly into his own goal. Verdu was so upset by his mistake that he plunged to the turf and pounded his skull with his fists, so distraught that he was in tears. A member of the Valencia backroom staff was allowed on to the turf by the Dutch referee to attend to the player in a bid to restore his equilibrium. Verdu probably felt a good deal better when Guillot, whose intricate ball skills had posed a serious danger to Celtic all evening, struck back with the equaliser in the 63rd minute. The tie was now slipping beyond Celtic and, with ten minutes remaining, Waldo Machado da Silva hammered a magnificent drive high into the Celtic net. There was enough time left for Pat Crerand to score a similarly striking goal and salvage a draw for Celtic but the final result of 2–2 meant that Valencia eased through to the next round. Other than Crerand's scoring effort, Celtic had managed just one shot on goal all night. It had come from Craig who, otherwise, had had a less than impressive Celtic debut. Craig's signing would prove to be a dreadful mistake; he would go on to become something of a troublemaker inside the club and made little impact at Celtic Park before being transferred to St Johnstone in the summer of 1963.

Celtic's 6–4 aggregate defeat was no disgrace. Valencia would go on to retain the Fairs Cup that 1962–63 season, defeating Hibernian and Dunfermline Athletic, managed by Jock Stein, on the way. The Celtic players had learned enough to make sure their next tilt at a European tournament would be more successful. They would be more adept at dealing with diverse opponents. A more pertinent question would be whether the Celtic players could achieve success in Europe whilst Robert Kelly was pulling the strings like some crazed puppet master behind the scenes.

TWO

Semi Darkness
MTK BUDAPEST 1964

Trips abroad were something to be savoured by Celtic's 1960s footballers, but visits to Eastern Europe usually proved the exception to the rule. Grim-faced people and grey surroundings loomed over every journey that Celtic took to that part of the continent during that decade. So when the Celtic players found themselves Hungary-bound in the spring of 1964, they expected another dose of the severe austerity that they had experienced on all of their previous visits to communist Eastern Europe. To their utter surprise, the Celtic party were treated to some unexpected glimpses of grandeur on their arrival at Hungary's national stadium, the magnificent 100,000-capacity Nepstadion, for the second leg of their European Cup-Winners' Cup semi-final with MTK Budapest. The players were pleased to find sumptuous armchairs, chaises longues and big easy chairs awaiting them in their dressing-room and, when they took the field, they were equally impressed by the sight of two massive, glowing, ultra-modern, electronic scoreboards overhanging the terracing behind each goal, timekeeping units far in advance of anything to be seen inside stadiums in Scotland during the early 1960s. The clocks on those impressive scoreboards showed the game ticking away minute by minute, but they would become less pleasing on the eye for the Celtic team as the match progressed.

Celtic had completed the first leg of the tie with MTK at Celtic Park with a momentous 3–0 victory that had looked sure to be enough to carry them into the Cup-Winners' Cup final, but in Budapest an Istvan Kuti goal after 11 minutes rapidly brought the Hungarians back into the tie and the Celtic bench began to glance anxiously up at those gigantic clocks. Bobby Lennox, a substitute in Budapest, recalls: 'I remember we went over there and I was sitting on the bench with Dunky MacKay, a super player who was before his time, and Dunky said, "Och, there's no danger." He said that to me at half-time, even though it was 1–0 to MTK. Then they scored again and we looked up at this big clock and saw that the first minute of the second half was not even out and Dunky said, "We're in trouble now!"'

The match with MTK was the culmination of Celtic's first extended run in European competition, which in that 1963–64 season had seen them score 16 goals and concede just 2 in dismissing from the Cup-Winners' Cup FC Basle, Dinamo Zagreb and Slovan Bratislava. The team's visits to Zagreb in Yugoslavia and Bratislava in Czechoslovakia had served as primers for the semi-final in Budapest. Yugoslavia and Czechoslovakia were, in common with Hungary and other eastern European countries, satellite states of the communist Soviet Union, which had Russia at its heart. The Soviet Army, as allies of the USA and Great Britain in the Second World War, had swept west during the conflict with Germany and, post-war, the Soviets simply colonised the countries through which they had marched on their way to Germany. Life was generally grim for the populations of those eastern European countries that, after 1945, were trapped behind the Soviets' grey 'iron curtain', where one-party, puppet-Soviet states presided over poverty-stricken populations who had been cowed into subservience by secret police. A stifling lack of individual freedom was accompanied by such grim realities as an ongoing lack of basic foodstuffs, largely brought about by state inefficiencies.

Bobby Lennox recalls the first taste of the type of food on offer in Eastern Europe when the team ventured there in that 1963–64 season. 'That was a bit of a hoot to start with,' he laughs. 'The first time we went, the grub was really rotten and after that we decided to travel with our own stuff. So the next time we went we took hamper-loads of grub: cornflakes, steaks and so on. At the first meal, the grub came through and it was stinking. It was rotten. They had taken our stuff, put it away and given us their stuff! So Jimmy Steele and Bob Rooney went through and stood over their chefs in the kitchen until they had made our meals and brought them out to us.' Steele, the physiotherapist, and Rooney, the trainer, were vital to the upkeep of morale on Celtic's away trips in Europe.

The visit to Zagreb for Celtic's second-round tie had been packed with incident on and off the park. Celtic had been invited by their hosts at Dinamo Zagreb to visit Mount Sljeme, a 3,000-ft-high peak on the edge of the city and the Zagreb officials had arranged for the Celtic officials and team to be taken out to the mountains and put on a cable car to enjoy the mountainous scenery. 'I don't know why they thought this would be a good idea, because it was the middle of December,' says John Divers, a Celtic forward who featured prominently in the ties with Zagreb. John Hughes did not enjoy the journey by cable car so when he reached the top he was given permission by Sean Fallon, the Celtic assistant manager, to make the return journey on foot, with John Divers accompanying him.

From the cable car the players had been able to see a road zigzagging its way down the mountainside, so Divers and Hughes thought they could simply follow it down. As they were doing so, they became alarmed when they began to hear gunshots ringing out around the nearby mountains – some locals were out shooting bears. As the players were manoeuvring their way down the mountain, they saw the cable car, lit up against the gathering gloom, gliding down to the bottom again and soon they heard the howls of bears to accompany the gunshots. Their slow progress in following the road made Hughes and Divers quickly decide that it would take too long to travel down by tarmac so they instead opted to try to take a short-cut across the mountain terrain, crossing the winding mountain road only occasionally. At one point, on reaching a section of the road, John Hughes made to jump onto the road surface only to tumble into a deep pile of leaves, lose his balance, hurt his ankle and end up spread-eagled across the icy road, skinning his elbow and muddying his club blazer and trousers.

At that point the duo spotted a car, with its headlights on full, approaching them. Out stepped two Yugoslavian police officers, guns at the ready, so Divers and Hughes frantically showed them the Celtic club badges on their blazers. The officers, aware of who they were, then proceeded to take them back up the mountain. 'At one point the car broke down,' says Hughes, 'so they parked it and got out. I was sitting in this wee Fiat and I was saying to JD, "We're going to be in big trouble now!" I then turned round and looked out of the window and down and there was nothing there!' The policemen had parked on the very edge of the mountain and there was a sheer drop into oblivion on the side of the road from which Hughes was looking. The two Celts were eventually taken back up to the top of the mountain by the police and up came the cable car, all lit up, in which they were sent back down on their own. 'When we got back down they were all sitting on the bus,' says John Hughes. 'They had been waiting on us for two hours. You can imagine how popular we were when we got back on the bus!'

Celtic went out to attack on the afternoon of the match at the Dinamo Stadium in Zagreb; it was a matter of pride and policy on the part of Robert Kelly that the team should not adjust its approach even in the toughest of European ties away from home. For the players it proved to be a difficult afternoon on an icy playing surface. The Zagreb players, on home terrain, knew how to deal with the conditions and had cut away their studs to the metal to give themselves a better grip on the treacherous surface. It worked and their extra hold on the game gave them a 2–1 victory. It was not enough to overturn Celtic's 3–0 advantage from the first leg but of the two sides Celtic had been under the majority of pressure and felt some relief at passing into the next round.

The most dramatic part of Celtic's eventful visit to Zagreb was still to come, as John Divers recalls. 'Zagreb had no floodlights,' he says, 'and we played them in the afternoon. I remember it was really dark, the stadium wasn't well lit and everything was dark round about it, although there was a big crowd there. The game finished late afternoon in darkness and Zagreb won 2–1. We had to go back to the hotel to pick up all our gear and then go from there to the airport in Zagreb. The airport in Zagreb was a small, Nissan hut-type place then and, when we arrived back at the airport, heavy snow had come on. In those days you had to walk out onto the runway and get on the aeroplane, carrying your luggage, even in that really heavy snow. I can remember there was only one other aircraft in the airport other than the Celtic charter flight and that was a French jet, a Caravelle. Word got out that the Caravelle couldn't take off because the snow was too heavy and might get sucked into its jets, but there was a chance that our Aer Lingus aircraft could take off because it was a turbo-prop.'

Five years previously, in February 1958, a British European Airways Elizabethan Class AS 57 aircraft, a turbo-prop, carrying the Manchester United squad back from a European Cup tie with Red Star Belgrade, had left Yugoslavia before making a scheduled stop at snowbound Munich, Germany. The pilot, after refuelling, had then made two attempts to take off along the slippery Munich runway before screeching to a halt on both occasions when he realised the aeroplane was not going to make it into the air. Snow had been falling heavily and it was still drifting down from the sky as the pilot, Captain Kenneth Rayment, made his third attempt at lifting into the sky the BEA Elizabethan carrying the United party. Again he failed, but this time the plane had picked up such speed that Rayment's efforts at applying the brakes were in vain. The Elizabethan skidded across snow and slush to collide with a tree, a house and a hut. Twenty-three people, including eight Manchester United players, lost their lives.

'Let's not forget,' says John Divers, 'that Manchester United had come back from Belgrade, which is in the same part of the world as Zagreb, and that, of course, was in people's minds that December with the cold and the heavy snow. On the aircraft were the team and all the officials and also some press and once we got on it everyone sat talking nervously before the pilot came on the intercom and said, "Would you all move to the front of the plane."' The Aer Lingus pilot had been informed that Europe was fogbound and engulfed in heavy snowstorms and so he had taken on a full load of fuel to compensate for being unable to land at Frankfurt, Germany, to make his scheduled refuelling stop. Instead, he would fly on to Manchester before refuelling and hopping on to Glasgow. Everyone on board had to move to the front of the aircraft to counterbalance the weight of the full load of fuel at the rear.

More echoes of Munich bounced around the players' minds when the pilot took the plane halfway down the runway in an attempted take-off from Zagreb before applying the brakes heavily and sliding to a halt. With the players and officials now bunched together down at the front of the aeroplane and hunched tightly in their seats, there was a real feeling of apprehension among a Celtic party that, as with the Manchester United squad in 1958, included several young stars-in-the-making, such as Tommy Gemmell, Billy McNeill, Jimmy Johnstone, Bobby Murdoch, Stevie Chalmers and John Hughes. 'You could feel the wheels weren't gripping,' says John Divers, 'and halfway along the runway the brakes got slammed on and the plane slid to a halt, circled around and went back to the top of the runway again. I think it was the fourth time we went down the runway that we realised, "He's not going to brake this time." Then we shot off the runway and into the darkness.'

Fear gripped the players as they were taking off and it was only when their Aer Lingus flight had been airbound for several minutes that that fear was replaced by relief. Meanwhile, in Glasgow, it was the turn of friends and relatives of those in the Celtic party to feel real trepidation. The word on the ground was that the plane had gone missing: confusion had arisen at Frankfurt when the Aer Lingus flight that had left Zagreb had failed to land in Germany to refuel. The atrocious weather had led those at Frankfurt to believe that the Aer Lingus flight might have succumbed to the conditions. Friends and family were delighted to find that their fears had been misplaced when the Celtic players and officials came strolling through passport control.

Another peek behind the iron curtain was Celtic's reward for defeating Dinamo Zagreb when the quarter-final draw paired them with Slovan Bratislava of Czechoslovakia. A 1–0 home victory left Celtic perched precariously on the edge of elimination as they travelled to Bratislava. The second leg remained finely balanced at 0–0 until, five minutes from the end, John Hughes took possession of the ball inside his own half and set off on a powerful run. Jan Popluhar, Czechoslovakia's centre-half in the 1962 World Cup final, was the last of several defenders who tried to block the way as Hughes raced towards goal, but the Celt swayed round him and was soon bearing down on Viliam Schroif, Czechoslovakia's World Cup goalkeeper. A quick flick from Hughes sent the ball past Schroif and Celtic into the semi-finals. It had been one of the great solo goals in Celtic's European history.

Hughes had, pre-match, enjoyed some sprinting practice that had served him well in preparation for his goal. Having gone out for a walk around the murky streets of Bratislava with John Divers, the two players suddenly became aware of two soldiers following in their footsteps. They walked and walked with the soldiers still on their tail before eventually turning round a street corner and bolting – at that time, in the Cold War, westerners were the enemy to the defenders of communist states and the two Celts were genuinely worried that they would be shot at. 'It was *The Spy Who Came In From The Cold* type of thing,' comments Divers.

'Bratislava was some place,' adds John Divers, as he recalls sampling the type of luxuries afforded to only the very privileged in communist Czechoslovakia. 'I can remember the hotel at which we stayed in Bratislava. It was a huge mausoleum-type place with marbled floors and marbled halls and a guy playing the piano. We were the only people, as far as I remember, who were staying in this hotel. There was a huge dining hall, with marbled floors and big, marbled panels and you had all these guys from the west of Scotland sitting there in this cathedral-like dining hall and a man playing the piano. You had the sound of the piano playing and everybody was feeling very awkward.

'People wanted to do some shopping to get presents and I remember getting taken on a bus to a big store that they said they would open up for us. This was the only place in Bratislava, 40 years ago, where you could shop and buy trinkets. In the city there were only the occasional streetlights; it was very dark, very dismal. It made Glasgow look like Las Vegas.'

The eastern European thread that had run through Celtic's 1963–64 European Cup-Winners' Cup adventure would continue into the semi-finals and their meeting with the Hungarians of MTK Budapest. It was a rainy Glasgow that greeted the players of MTK for the first leg, but that appeared hardly to concern the Hungarians: in training they proved hugely impressive as they whipped the ball around from foot to foot. They showed similar skills from the start of the match at Celtic Park, but it was Celtic who went ahead shortly before half-time. John Clark's shot was blocked close to the goal-line but not properly cleared by the MTK defence and Jimmy Johnstone nipped in to scrape the ball over the line. Midway through the second half, Jim Kennedy, in outstanding form, fed Stevie Chalmers and from the corner of the penalty area Chalmers' shot glided into the net. Ten minutes from time, a Bobby Murdoch cross eluded the Hungarian cover inside the penalty area to find Chalmers hovering for a header that pinged off the post on its way into goal. The 3–0 victory was as good as anyone could have expected and the Celtic players, some in their stocking soles, re-emerged from the dressing-room to satisfy the relentless chants of their supporters, who had demanded a lap of honour to acknowledge the quality of the team's performance.

The air of innocence that surrounded Celtic's trips abroad in the early 1960s was still very much present as they travelled to Budapest for the return with MTK a fortnight later in that April of 1964. The second leg with MTK offered Celtic the opportunity to clinch a place in their first European final but there was a light-hearted approach to the entire business, as exemplified by chairman Kelly's insistence that the players should include a bit of tourism in the trip. Manager Jimmy McGrory, always fully compliant with the wishes of his chairman – this was Celtic's own version of a puppet dictatorship – went along with the scheme. 'In the early '60s,' explains Bobby Lennox, 'when we went to places like Budapest, where we played MTK, Robert Kelly would arrange a bus on the Tuesday and would take us sightseeing. That was when I first found out that it was Buda and Pest, the two parts of the city on each side of the river.

'The directors thought they were doing the right thing by us; they weren't being smart. They just thought that the boys might want to see the place. The first two or three times we went abroad we did a bit of sightseeing on the Tuesday. Now that would maybe sound great at the time, but the Celtic players weren't interested in that. That eventually got put to the side; that only happened three or four times because the players were only interested in the game. The directors and the club doctor would be interested in going to see the cities. That was fine, but it was better that they went and did that and allowed us to get to our beds. It was just a thing you didn't want. It wasn't so much that it would tire you out, it was more of an irritation when you were really there to focus on playing an important football match. It seemed a nuisance to be sitting on a coach on the Tuesday when we were playing a big game on the Wednesday night.'

A heatwave had been engulfing the Hungarian capital on Celtic's arrival in the city and it continued into the Tuesday, the second day of their stay, when they were conducted on that sightseeing tour of Budapest by the British ambassador to Hungary. Some shopping was also on the agenda and in the afternoon the players were conducted on a tour of the Nepstadion by the sharp-featured MTK manager Antol Bakos. He was only too happy to provide that diversion for the Celtic players, fully kitted out in shirts, ties and blazers as they were led around that vast bowl of a stadium and fully exposed to the glaring sun. There would be no training for the Celtic players that Tuesday, not even a light, limbering-up session. Meanwhile, 16 miles outside Budapest, the MTK players were being kept in seclusion at their training base, where they would remain until two hours prior to kick-off, focusing fully on football as they limbered up for their tie with Celtic. On the Tuesday evening, as the MTK players relaxed after a light meal together, the Celtic squad were attending a reception at the British Embassy in Budapest.

There is a strong suggestion that an atmosphere of complacency had entered the minds of some of those connected with Celtic prior to that return match with MTK in the spring of 1964. Club secretary Desmond White, for one, already had his mind on the final and was suggesting that he would soon be contacting UEFA (the Union of European Football Associations) who ran the tournament, to suggest that the venue for the final should be changed. The European Cup-Winners' Cup final was scheduled for neutral Brussels, but White believed that the game should either be played home and away over two legs or that a toss of the coin should be employed to have the match played on the home ground of one of the finalists. As soon as the winners of the other semi-final between Olympique Lyon and Sporting Lisbon had emerged, stated White, he would contact them to discuss his plan for a change of venue for the final. It seemed unlikely that White would be doing so for the benefit of MTK Budapest. The implication was clearly that White felt Celtic would be involved in the final. The Celtic secretary even told John Divers, who had been injured for the first leg, that he was not to travel to Budapest for the return and that the player was to concentrate on getting fit and to save his energies for the final.

MTK had been without their outstanding player, outside-right

Karoly Sandor, for the first leg. He had been absent from the MTK side for five months with a knee injury but Bakos, the Hungarian side's manager, had stated before the tie at Celtic Park that even if his team lost 2–0 they could win the return with Sandor playing in that game. Sandor, capped 68 times by his country, and several other Hungarian internationals, including the fine midfielder Istvan Nagy, lined up against Celtic in the Nepstadion. Now they had to pull back three goals, not two. Facing those players was no mean prospect for the Celts: the Hungarian international team was one of the strongest in the world in the 1950s and '60s but that was of little consequence to Robert Kelly as he stepped up to address the Celtic players in the dressing-room during the moments prior to the match, as John Hughes recalls. 'I remember Bob Kelly slapping his glove into his hand before the game and saying, "Och, we beat them over there in Glasgow – we can beat them here as well. Just go out and play." That was the attitude – there was no, "Let's go out and try to hold them for 20 minutes." There were no thoughts of soaking up pressure.' On the evening, it would be Sandor and his teammates who would fully enjoy the opportunity afforded to them by Celtic's tactical plan to 'just go out and play'.

A 35,000 crowd was in the stadium for the second leg between MTK and Celtic, a smaller figure than might have been expected, but the match was being televised live in Hungary. MTK had scored only eight goals in their eight Cup-Winners' Cup matches prior to the return with Celtic, but it took them just 11 minutes of their home leg to add another goal to that tally. Sandor streaked past Tommy Gemmell on the Hungarians' right wing and crossed. John Fallon came for the ball, appeared to slip, and Istvan Kuti stuck out a foot to jab the ball into goal. The Nepstadion – the People's Stadium – had been built only a decade previously, constructed by a people's army of 10,000 volunteers, and prior to this match, MTK had appeared to be facing a similarly Herculean task to turn round the tie, but that task was made considerably easier when they went 2–0 up shortly after half-time, through a penalty from Mihaly Vasas. It was a goal that had resulted from a handball on the Celtic goal-line when Tommy Gemmell had punched a net-bound shot over the crossbar.

The Hungarians now began to motor. On the hour, Sandor, from six yards, eluded several challenges, kept his balance, and lifted a delicate shot over Fallon to make it 3–0 to MTK on the night and level the aggregate. Celtic were now under incessant pressure from the Hungarians and their best hope was to hold out for a play-off, scheduled, if required, for Rotterdam. MTK, though, had the bit between their teeth and, with 20 minutes to go, Istvan Kuti got his second of the night, latching on to the ball close to goal and nicking it into the net. That goal, MTK's fourth, obliterated Celtic's hopes of reaching their first European final at only the second attempt. Back in Scotland, commentary on the game, on the BBC's Home Service, had faded out with the score at 3–0, to make way for a speech by the Prime Minister, Alec Douglas-Home. It left Celtic supporters in some distress as they awaited news of the fate of their team.

'They got a hard time of it over there, the boys,' says Bobby Lennox. 'Once MTK went 2–0 up there was no way back for us. Maybe it was because of a lack of experience; just trying to play the game as we would normally play it back in Glasgow. A 3–0 lead was a great advantage to have, but once MTK got on top over there, they were very good. There are a lot of teams in Europe whom you will play at home and think they are all right, nothing more. Then you get them over at their home ground and they'll be great once they get going. I think back then, in the earlier days of European competition, home advantage was really important. I don't know if it is just as important now. Later on, when you spoke to opponents from those teams, you found out from them that they didn't want to come to Glasgow because they felt it was a hard, hard place to come to. Our European nights were great. The place was always full and really, really noisy and the fans got behind you from start to finish. So I felt home advantage was great for us, but when you went to their place a team that might have looked ordinary in Glasgow could look like an entirely different side altogether.'

The Celtic team was identical for both legs against MTK: John Fallon, Ian Young, Tommy Gemmell, John Clark, Billy McNeill, Jim Kennedy, Jimmy Johnstone, Bobby Murdoch, Stevie Chalmers, Charlie Gallagher and John Hughes. The Celtic players complained after the second leg that the Austrian referee, Dimitrios Wlackojanis, had clamped down too heavily on their robust tackling, but the team was undone more by the lack of proper preparation for the tie and by the policy, imposed from above, of Celtic attacking strongly regardless of the score.

A flippant definition was once offered to suggest that a Hungarian is someone who can enter a revolving door after you but manage to leave it before you. The Celtic players certainly knew that feeling in the spring of 1964, but their defeat owed as much to Celtic's own muddled internal affairs as to the sharp wits of the Hungarian players and management. Celtic, though, would soon have on board a wit the equal of anything that the most sophisticated Europeans might possess.

THREE

Breaking the Ice
DYNAMO KIEV 1966

A web of intrigue was spun around every one of Celtic's matches in European competition during the 1960s. There was little television coverage of football at home or abroad during that decade, so the clubs that Celtic faced were almost always unknown quantities right up until kick-off and supporters would turn up for each match ready to be surprised by a mysterious set of players and a different approach to the game of football. This was never more true than when Dynamo Kiev of the Soviet Union arrived at Celtic Park for the first leg of their 1966 European Cup-Winners' Cup quarter-final with Celtic.

The communist Soviet Union was a state that was shrouded in secrecy and mystery. It was, by the mid-1960s, in the midst of its Cold War with the capitalist West and, in particular, the USA; a duel for dominance backed up by nuclear weaponry that would last four decades and one that was being fought out through bluffing, spying, secrecy and subterfuge. It meant that the footballers of Kiev carried with them even more of a mystique than most of Celtic's European opponents. These representatives of the secretive Soviet Union, one of the world's two superpowers in the 1960s, were sure to be strong, daunting opponents since the Soviets had invested heavily in their sportsmen as a means of earning prestige. Kiev were the first representatives of the Soviet Union to have been released into European competition by the Soviet authorities, so they had to be good to be exposed to external forces by the secretive Soviets. The Celtic players were assumed to be on the brink of facing super-athletes, primed and conditioned to the maximum peak of physical fitness.

One man remained completely undaunted by the spectre of the Soviets. Jock Stein had been appointed Celtic manager one year previously and, as the Kiev squad trained on the Celtic Park pitch on the day before the game, the shadow of Stein suddenly loomed over them. His bulk and his presence meant he was a man who could not be ignored and he quickly got his message across to the Kiev coach that his players would be allowed just five more minutes on the pitch before they would have to wrap up their session. The reason given by Stein for his intervention in Kiev's training session was that he wished the Celtic groundsman to have the chance to fork up the pitch in order to guard against the overnight January frost setting in and leaving the turf in an unsatisfactory condition. As with so many of Stein's moves, his action also had a dual purpose. It showed the opposition that Stein was calling the shots and as a piece of psychological combat it would have done any Cold War operative proud. It was a pricelessly wily move in the battle of nerves that often surrounds major European ties. Stein could have shown double agents a trick or two.

Tremendous anticipation surrounded the tie and on the night of 12 January 1966 a crowd of 64,000 flooded into Celtic Park to get a look at the Soviets. It was the highest attendance up to that point for a Celtic match in Europe, and the crowd were to be presented with exactly the type of spectacle that they had anticipated. Celtic found themselves facing a team that mixed athleticism with ability and it was Kiev who dominated early in the match. Almost half an hour had passed before Celtic made their first dramatic intervention, when left-back Tommy Gemmell powered on to the ball 35 yards from goal to send it streaking past goalkeeper Viktor Bannikov. It was Gemmell's first goal in Europe and it turned the tie Celtic's way. From then until the end, Kiev were under siege. Celtic added to their tally when Bobby Murdoch drove deep into the Kiev penalty box to pelt the ball between Bannikov and his near post to make it 2–0. Murdoch, thriving in a new midfield role under Stein, then saw a shot bounce back off the bar but he later had the considerable consolation of sidefooting home his second of the night six minutes from time to give Celtic an impressive 3–0 victory over formidable Dynamo Kiev. The Celtic team that night was: Ronnie Simpson, Jim Craig, Tommy Gemmell, Bobby Murdoch, John Cushley, John Clark, Jimmy Johnstone, Charlie Gallagher, Joe McBride, Stevie Chalmers and John Hughes.

Some supporters left the stadium with their natural elation tempered by the memory of the match with MTK Budapest less than two years previously, when Celtic's 3–0 lead had melted away in the heat of the away leg. This time, under Stein, there would be no mistakes – unlike in Budapest, the team's attacking style at home would be tempered to fit the requirements of defending a healthy lead away from home. For the away leg with Kiev, Stein tinkered tactically to try to ensure his team obtained the right result and the most significant move by the manager was to add steel to his side by replacing Charlie Gallagher with Billy McNeill. Centre-half McNeill would strengthen the Celtic side by playing alongside Cushley and Clark in a five-man defence. It proved to be a tight, tense, violent encounter with a player sent off from each side – Craig being the offending Celtic player – and with only one goal for each of the teams. The Celtic goal was another long-range effort from Gemmell and it helped put Celtic into the semi-finals of the tournament for the second time in three years. The club had previously enjoyed several handy victories in Europe but Kiev were by a distance the most prestigious European opponents to have thus far fallen to the Glasgow club.

'They were the first teams we encountered that kept the ball,' says Bobby Lennox as he thinks back to encounters with clubs such as Dynamo Kiev and Barcelona during Celtic's infancy as competitors in Europe. 'A Scottish team getting a free kick would knock the ball forward; these guys would come and knock it back just to keep it. We would start games in which, if the opposing team centred the ball, you might not get a touch of the ball for a minute or so. That was especially true of the Latins. Now, you could have let that get to you, but big Jock told us not to be worried by that because that is how they play. They would knock it about and you would say to yourself, "Are we going to get a kick here?" Once you got it – great – but then they would get it and keep it again. They were great at keeping the ball, which was completely different from us. Our football was about getting it forward and getting into the other team's box. They were all about, "Give us the ball and we'll keep it." They were different from us. We played blood and thunder and they just played deeper.

'Over the years, we just got better as players and better as a team. I suppose big Jock moulded us. He liked to play with his back four and his four in the middle and his two up front and he liked his two wide men to get up and down. We never really changed in that respect. He came and changed our system and then we just sat with that.

'He always wanted me just to keep running across defenders, running behind defenders and keep working them off the ball. I have come in from games where people have thought, "You didn't do that well tonight, wee man." And big Jock would come and cuddle me and say, "You moved every defender in their back four. You were great for us tonight." The people sitting in the stand or standing in the Jungle would maybe think, "Oh, he was just all right tonight." Jock always felt that football wasn't entirely about the man on the ball.'

The concept of regular, midweek, cross-continental clashes in European competition had been made possible by improved air transport and footballers were among the pioneers in regularly criss-crossing the continent using a form of travel that was still in its early days and that retained a sheen of glamour because of its sheer exclusivity. Many Celtic players made their first journey by aeroplane with the club and the airports and airlines of Europe in the 1960s were often seen as synonymous with sophistication, wealth, status and luxury. Flying was one of the bonuses of being a top footballer but it did not seem like that to the Celtic players as they made their way back to Glasgow from the city of Tbilisi in the Soviet Union following the return match with Dynamo Kiev. The game had been switched from Kiev in the Ukraine to Tbilisi in Georgia because the annual snowfall in Kiev that gripped that city during the winter made it impossible to play a match there during the month of January.

The post-match reception after Celtic's 1–1 draw in Tbilisi had been a rollicking affair – no one in Tbilisi appeared to have heard of soft drinks and the players were plied with plenty of potent refreshments as they listened to speech after speech from the Soviet side's officials. One prominent Celtic player, bored by the incessant speeches and infused with the free-flowing drink, began to get louder and louder in his exhortations to his teammates until he was stopped in mid-sentence by a heavy clip round the ear. The player turned round to confront his attacker only to find that it had been Jock Stein himself who had dealt the blow. 'Shut up,' was Stein's curt instruction.

It was a bleary-eyed Celtic party that arrived at the airport in Tbilisi the following morning only to find that the air-crew, who had also been at the reception, were still in their hotel beds sleeping off the effects of the night before and that the aircraft, a BAC 1-11, which was far too small for such a journey anyway, had still to be refuelled and prepared for take-off. Soviet bureaucracy meant that the aeroplane had to be routed from Tbilisi via the capital of the Soviet Union, Moscow, and then on to Stockholm in Sweden, where the Celtic players and officials were told to disembark and embark again several times before it was agreed that an overnight stay in the Swedish capital would be necessary that Thursday evening. A combination of freezing weather and technical problems with the aircraft meant that the BAC 1-11 had to be replaced, which had delayed take-off from Sweden by 24 hours until the Friday evening. The Celtic party finally arrived home at Prestwick Airport late that Friday night, expecting to be ordered to go straight home to obtain as much rest as possible before their Scottish League match on the Saturday afternoon, against Hearts in Edinburgh.

John Hughes remembers that episode well. 'You would think he would have said, "Go home to your beds." What did he do? He took us to Parkhead for a training session in the early hours of the morning and took us out on the park under floodlights with all the press there. We eventually lost 3–2 to Hearts but we had been on the road since early Thursday morning and the Scottish football authorities had refused to postpone the game. They should have postponed it but they said, "No". He would never do what everybody thought he was going to do. He was trying to show people that that was what we were doing at three o'clock in the morning to prepare for a game on that afternoon at three o'clock, having just arrived back from the Soviet Union after two days' travelling. I think one of the reasons he did that was just to make the Scottish football authorities look a bit silly, to get at them, which I think he did do because there is no doubt they should have postponed the game – but that's just the way they work.'

A dire performance in Europe against Barcelona the previous season had helped pave the way for Stein's appointment as manager. After a 3–1 defeat in Spain, a disorganised Celtic side had capitulated weakly at Celtic Park, finding themselves thoroughly outclassed in front of a 43,000 crowd early in December 1964. 'It looked 0–0 from the start,' says Bobby Lennox of the second leg of the Fairs Cup tie. 'We didn't get many chances.'

It was just one of a series of poor results that had resulted in chairman Robert Kelly eventually deciding that, after 20 years with Jimmy McGrory at the helm, the time was ripe for a change of manager. McGrory was the manager who, on a tour of the USA in the 1950s, had gone into the shower room to remonstrate with centre-half Jimmy Mallan, who had been sent off in a friendly with Fulham, only to discover that Mallan's response was to drag his manager by the lapels into the shower. Such was the lack of esteem in which McGrory was held by his players.

No such liberties could be taken with Stein and the new manager had restructured the Celtic team to place pace, skill and quick thinking as the foremost requirements in his players. He also took full responsibility for team selection. Bobby Murdoch was one of the finest examples of Stein's radical reconstruction of Celtic. The player had been deployed in the forward line prior to Stein's appointment but almost as soon as he arrived at Celtic Park the manager moved Murdoch back into midfield to open up an entirely new vista for the player. Now in a new playmaking position, Murdoch had the game spread out in front of him and, as Stein had surmised, the player thrived on the opportunity to prove himself as a master passer. He was still allowed to roam forward when the time was right and, as witnessed by those who attended the Kiev match, Murdoch made a considerable goalscoring contribution to the team, often in the most spectacular style.

A new surge of energy was now coursing through the body of the Celtic side. The manager had restored confidence in his players and particularly in winger Jimmy Johnstone, who had suffered particularly badly from the inconsistent team selections that had been made when chairman Kelly had been picking the Celtic side. Another to benefit was John Hughes. As with Murdoch, Stein had transformed him through a change of position. Hughes had been switched from centre-forward to the left wing although, as with Murdoch, the player was still encouraged to get into the box and get goals as often as possible.

Inside him on the left flank, Hughes had Bertie Auld, who had asked Birmingham City for a transfer in August 1962, shortly before Celtic first entered European competition. Auld had appeared in the 1961 Fairs Cup final for Birmingham, but had not been granted his wish of a transfer until 1965, when he had embarked upon a second spell as a Celtic player. Auld too had benefited from a change of position, Stein having shifted him from the wing into midfield where his sharpness and accuracy with the ball were deployed to better effect. Similar stories abounded throughout the side of Stein working magical transformations in players' styles and instilling a refreshingly positive attitude in each and every individual in his team. 'There was plenty of ability at Celtic Park,' says Tommy Gemmell, 'but we required guidance from somebody and Jock Stein was that somebody. Everybody was asked to do what they were good at doing and when you get a chance to express yourself, the best comes out in you. Apart from all the individual ability, we had the ability to gel together as a team. We were very friendly off the park as well as on the park and that makes a big difference. That helps everybody to pull together, and when you pull together it is like having an extra man.'

Stein's first full season in charge of Celtic, 1965–66, had seen the club re-establish itself in the Scottish competitions, but Stein was always a man in a hurry and he had been unwilling to wait for a gradual growth in stature for Celtic in Europe. He wanted to win all the Scottish trophies and the European Cup-Winners' Cup in that first season. Even so, he had had to remain patient before obtaining his first crack at the big time in Europe: his debut European tie with Celtic, four months prior to the explosive encounter with Kiev, had taken place in one of the game's least intimidating settings, the Adelaarshorst stadium in rural Deventer, Holland. It was home to the quaintly named Go Ahead club, who were participating in their first-ever European tie that September of 1965.

'Before the tie, the Deventer manager had actually wanted to sign me and take me to Holland,' remembers Bobby Lennox as he looks back on a match that Celtic won comfortably. 'We went over there and because Deventer is a small place we walked to the ground and when we got into the ground we found it was mobbed an hour before the kick-off. The gates were shut. They had welcoming banners and were singing songs such as "Daisy, Daisy, give me your answer do". The atmosphere was unbelievable; terrific, a really friendly atmosphere. We beat them 6–0 and I scored my first ever hat-trick for the club. Their manager met me after the game and said to me, "I told them you were the danger man." It made his night as well! Deventer was a very pleasant night. It didn't give you the satisfaction of qualifying against some of the greater teams, but I enjoyed it.'

Victories over Aarhus of Denmark and then the 4–1 aggregate victory in the classic triumph over Dynamo Kiev put Celtic into a Cup-Winners' Cup semi-final against Liverpool and the 80,000 crowd was an official record attendance for a midweek match at Celtic Park. 'We played really well in Glasgow and made quite a few chances,' recalls Bobby Lennox, who scored Celtic's goal in their 1–0 win at Celtic Park. 'We should have put the tie beyond them and didn't. It was a nice night in Glasgow; the park was quite hard, quite firm. Down there it was the complete opposite. The pitch was heavy and they probably played better against us. They got their two goals within a few minutes early in the second half. The first goal was a free kick which just took a deflection – it clipped the side of the wall.' That 60th-minute Tommy Smith strike was followed by a scoring header 5 minutes later from Geoff Strong. It remained 2–0 to Liverpool when, close to full-time, Bobby Lennox darted on to the ball and, sharp as ever, turned it into the Liverpool net. It was a goal that would have levelled the tie at 2–2 and forced a play-off but referee Josef Hannet of Belgium disallowed it for offside. The referee would later admit, after scrutinising the 'goal' on television, that he had got that decision wrong.

'We were all raging,' recalls Lennox of the aftermath of that incident. 'Everybody was raging. Loads and loads of bottles came on to the field from the Celtic supporters. Thousands came on and the referee stopped the game for a while. There was also a lot of shouting and bawling in the tunnel at time-up, handbags and things like that – it was just emotions running high. We got the "goal" late on, which everybody remembers. We should have been in the final really. We should also have beaten them convincingly in Glasgow so we were unlucky not to be in the final.'

Tommy Gemmell also remembers that tie well. 'We beat Liverpool 1–0 at Celtic Park, going on four or five. We gave them a real going over and just couldn't put the ball in the net. They beat us 2–0 at Anfield, but Bobby Lennox scored a perfectly good goal, which was ruled offside when there was no way it was offside. We should have buried them at Celtic Park; we played very well apart from putting the ball in the pokey hat. Going to Anfield had never held any fears for us because we knew we were as good as them, if not better.'

Celtic were, by the time of that Cup-Winners' Cup semi-final, en route to their first Scottish League Championship title for 12 years, thanks to the expert guidance of Stein. It would afford them entry to the European Champion Clubs' Cup for the first time, but that did little to mollify the players' desperate disappointment at missing out on a European final by the narrowest of margins for the second time in three years. The Cup-Winners' Cup final of 1966 was to be held at Hampden Park, Glasgow, and the Celtic players knew that they would never have a better chance to take the trophy. One lingering question, though, is whether victory in that tournament might have left the players less hungry for further success in Europe the following, 1966–67, season. It is a suggestion that Bobby Lennox is keen to refute.

'There was the Cup-Winners' Cup and the European Cup,' he explains, 'which stands on a plateau above everything else, obviously. I can't see it having been a good thing us not winning the Cup-Winners' Cup that year. I don't see where the complacency could have come from, especially with the manager we had. If you had become complacent he would just have said, "There's the door, son." Every game we came to, we wondered if we would win it. I don't think there was any game where we thought, "Oh, we'll beat this mob." Every game was going to be a really hard, tough game and you were up for every game.

'We all loved to be in Europe, playing against the best. It was absolutely great. We would leave for a European match on the Monday morning, arrive at lunchtime, go to our beds and train on the Monday night. We were in bed a lot of the time. The next morning we would go for a walk – we were the greatest team in the world for going on walks. Neilly Mochan would always take us for a walk. We would then probably go to bed on Tuesday afternoon and then on the Tuesday

night we would go to see the stadium. We would be in bed a lot in
between times. We would be in our beds but we wouldn't be asleep all
the time; we would be lying resting. A lot of the time, the boys would
instead sit and have a cup of tea and a blether.

'We would have a late breakfast on the Wednesday, a nice relaxing
day on the Wednesday, a team talk, go to bed in the afternoon, and play
the match and go back and get to our beds and fly home on the
Thursday. If we had had a good result the boys would have a couple of
beers after the match, but nothing more than that. It was great to get
up the next morning, have breakfast with the guys and fly into Glasgow
at lunchtime the next day. Nowadays teams tend to fly back from
Europe immediately after the game but I liked the camaraderie of
having a relaxing breakfast with the boys the next morning before flying
back. I think it was good for us. That was the way big Jock liked to do
it and it worked for us. We always felt that with the European Cup it
was a full week – you went away on the Monday and came back on the
Thursday.' There would be many more opportunities for the Celtic
players to enjoy lengthy midweek breaks in the great cities of Europe
during the years to come.

FOUR

The Peak of Perfection
LISBON 1967

Seven minutes of the 1967 European Cup final had passed when Sandro Mazzola placed the ball on the penalty spot in the National Stadium in Lisbon. It was a moment loaded with poignancy for Internazionale of Milan's great goalscorer. Eighteen years previously Sandro's father Valentino had, at the age of 30, been a key member of the Torino team that had played against Benfica in the same stadium. It would prove to be the final match for that Torino team. On the following day, the aeroplane carrying them home to Italy had crashed into a hillside at Superga, just outside Turin. Valentino and 17 other Torino players – the pride of Italy and the bulk of the national side – had been among the 31 victims of the crash.

Sandro Mazzola had at the time of that disaster been just six years old but now, in 1967, the 24-year-old Italian had finally been granted the wish he had cherished in his heart throughout his boyhood and into early manhood: to score on the ground where his father had played the final game of his short life. The lean, moustachioed Mazzola took stock of the situation: standing tall, he then hovered on his toes before beginning a gentle run at the ball and gradually accelerating before making graceful contact and brushing the ball low to his left with all the assurance and style of a quality player. The Celtic goalkeeper Ronnie Simpson had moved slightly in the opposite direction to the ball and it gently drifted into the corner of the Celtic net. Inter were a goal ahead in the 1967 European Cup final and few of those watching the match on television around Europe were in any doubt that Mazzola and his fellow Inter players were firmly on course to take hold of the greatest prize in club football for a third time in four seasons.

The Celtic players themselves were fully aware of just how much ability their opponents possessed. They had not envisioned themselves being able to live with such luminaries as Inter when they had begun their first-ever European Cup fixtures back in September 1966. It was one thing to cope with the challenges of the skilful sides that were to be encountered in the Fairs Cup or the Cup-Winners' Cup but the European Cup was a different matter. The Celtic players believed, as they entered that tournament for the first time, that it was only the stuff of dreams to believe that they could match the greatest clubs on earth and take the trophy. 'We thought it would be impossible,' confirms Bobby Lennox. 'We had seen Real Madrid and all those teams play, the Milans and all those, and they had looked magnificent.'

It may have been Celtic's first bash at the European Cup but the Celtic team were no surprise package to their opponents: they were already highly regarded across Europe as a result of their engaging exploits around the continent in previous years. 'People who were drawn against us that year,' continues Lennox, 'would know that we had reached the semi-finals of the Cup-Winners' Cup two years before, when we met MTK, and the previous season, when we had played Liverpool. So we were building up a reputation. People tend to think we were unknowns, but although it was our first year in the European Cup we had done well previously in the Cup-Winners' Cup.'

Celtic had not erected floodlights until 1959 so there was still a real novelty value involved for the Glasgow club's support in being able to attend evening games during the 1960s, and the club's participation in the new sphere provided by European football added extra spice to the experience of attending those evening fixtures. Floodlit football seemed to heighten the drama of the game. The crowd on those evenings would be blacked out in the background, highlighting, in sharp relief, the green turf, enabling everyone to focus fully on the ongoing spectacle of the game itself. On those evenings, the drama inherent in sport seemed to be heightened and for those in attendance, midweek games, especially glamorous European Cup ties against illustrious opponents who might be paying their one and only visit to Scotland, had an element of the theatrical spectacle about them that was far removed from the routine business of league fixtures against familiar faces on Saturdays.

'Everybody loved European nights at Celtic Park,' says Tommy Gemmell. 'Two weeks before the game you couldn't get a ticket – almost every match would be a 75,000 sell-out – and 15 minutes before kick-off there would be no queues at any turnstiles. We'd go out to loosen up three or four minutes before we normally would, just to soak up the atmosphere, which was always incredible, and the reception we got when we came out would frighten any side. The Celtic supporters were out of this world: I've still to find supporters to better them.

'I loved playing at night, especially when the ground was dewy and wet. You could fire the ball around and it was great for long-distance shooting because the goalkeeper was always liable to fumble things and inevitably Bobby Lennox would be there to tap the ball into the net. He scored some great goals from two yards. The ball would come off the keeper's chest, or it would cut across the goalie, and there would be wee Bobby, two yards out, flicking it in. I don't think wee Bobby scored too often from outside the six-yard box. He was brilliant at seeing things happen and his timing in making runs to the near post was perfect. I knew that if I made an overlap to the goal-line, and was firing the ball back, that Bobby Lennox would be coming in late to that near post and I would fire it across and nine times out of ten there he would be, just arriving, and he would stick it in or have a goal attempt anyway.'

There was a gentle introduction to the European Cup for Celtic when they were presented with a home match against Zurich of Switzerland for their debut in the competition. The crowd of 50,000 witnessed a fractious tie that failed to flow smoothly, chiefly because of the gamesmanship and spoiling tactics employed by the Swiss players to hamper and hinder their opponents. Thoughts of advancing to face the European elite were pushed firmly to the backs of minds as Celtic and Zurich went into the dressing-rooms at half-time at 0–0. Midway through the second half a moment of inspiration turned the tie in

Celtic's favour, and it came from Tommy Gemmell, the Celtic defender who was beginning to make a name for himself as an expert at cracking open the safety codes used by continental teams' defences.

Gemmell was one of those who was thriving greatly under Jock Stein. Prior to Stein's arrival, the left-back had been told by the Celtic managerial and coaching staff that he should restrict himself to working as a defender inside a few square yards on the left side of the Celtic defence. Under no circumstances was he to cross the halfway line and he was told in no uncertain terms that if he did so his position in the team would be in jeopardy. Those were frustrating instructions for Gemmell, a pacy player with an explosive shot who had begun his career as an outside-right for amateur team Meadow Thistle. Stein, on taking control at Celtic Park, had swiftly reversed Gemmell's previous instructions, telling him to get forward as often as sensibly possible and to try his luck with long-distance shooting. Now, as Zurich grew ever more confident of escaping from Glasgow with a draw, Gemmell eased into position 35 yards from goal and as the ball was nudged leftwards towards him, he flew at it to send the ball streaking high into the Zurich goal. The Swiss, weakened and made uncertain by the loss of the goal, conceded a second goal five minutes later; this time a close-range effort from striker Joe McBride. It ended 2–0, but the Celtic players wondered among themselves whether it would be enough.

'At that point we had no thoughts of winning the European Cup,' says Bobby Lennox. 'In fact, it was a big thrill for us just to go to Zurich because we had never been there. I remember our team talk in Zurich – everyone was crowded into this small hotel room and big Jock said, "They'll play exactly the same and we'll do this, that and the other." He was saying that they would play exactly as they had done in the first leg. One or two of the lads suggested that they thought he was wrong and said that they thought Zurich would change their style and come out and have a go at us, but big Jock said that Zurich had been at their best in Glasgow and that they couldn't play any better. He said that they did not have the ability to change their game or to play any differently to how they had done in the first leg. He said, "They haven't got the players to have a go at us. We will play exactly the way we played in Glasgow and we'll get a result." I don't think the guys doubted him, really. They just kind of asked whether he thought Zurich would change and he just said that they wouldn't.' The hotel where that meeting took place was the Dolder Grand, a magnificent edifice perched in its own extensive grounds that looked more like an Alpine castle than a hotel and the perfect setting for Stein to organise a hilltop summit designed to emphasise his vision and leadership qualities.

Stein, who was to turn 44 on the day after the return with Zurich, had an immeasurably high reputation amongst his players, a reputation that stemmed to a large extent from his three-year-long stint as Celtic's reserve-team coach in the late 1950s. Players such as Billy McNeill and Bobby Murdoch, teenagers at that time, had greatly enjoyed the progressive manner in which he had worked with them. They had then seen him go off and do great things as a manager at Dunfermline Athletic and Hibernian but Stein, in a way, had staked his reputation all over again on his assessment of Zurich as a limited side who would be unable to offer much more than they had shown in Glasgow. If he was to be proved wrong and Zurich were to give Celtic a fright, it could have the effect of weakening his authority as Celtic manager.

There was an element of the unexpected about Zurich as they took to the field for their return with Celtic. The Swiss side showed three changes from the one that had lined up at Celtic Park and their selection for the home tie featured one of the greatest names in European football: Ladislav Kubala. The forward had been part of the great Hungarian national team of the 1950s and of a Barcelona side that had won five Spanish championships and he was once described by former Barcelona manager Helenio Herrera as 'the greatest player I have ever known'. Kubala was now player-coach of Zurich, but he was 39 years old and it was his first appearance in the Zurich first team for months. It would prove to be a game too far at the top level for the once-mesmeric attacking player.

It did not take long for the prediction by Jock Stein to ring true: his assertion that the return with Zurich would mirror Celtic's first game against them quickly showed itself to be correct. Midway through the first half, Tommy Gemmell pounced on the ball 35 yards from goal to send it streaking into the roof of the Zurich net; an identical strike to the one with which he had opened the scoring against the Swiss in Glasgow. A second Celtic goal, scored by Chalmers before half-time, ended the tie as a contest and Gemmell rounded things off by scoring from a penalty kick three minutes after the interval. 'We were hungry for success,' says Gemmell of that emergent Celtic team, 'and once you start winning things it becomes a habit. You don't want to stop winning. We had players who had a high pain barrier and who wanted to play. They had the fear of death of being left out through injury because they might not get back into the side. We were winning and everybody wants to be a winner.

'I scored three goals in the two games. I scored a 35-yarder at Celtic Park and an identical goal over there in Zurich. You would have thought the goalkeeper would have been geed up and clued up from the first match. The goal in Zurich was from exactly the same distance and exactly the same angle as at Celtic Park and still he wasn't ready for it. There was nothing flukey about it. Every day in training we worked on hitting the ball from that distance. Everything we did was worked at, every day of the week. I can assure you that we did not play the game off-the-cuff, although you would get off-the-cuff stuff from wee Jinky; we didn't know what he was going to do next. I don't think he knew what he was going to do next, so what chance did we have and what chance did the opposition have? We gave Zurich a going over and that set us up for the next round.'

The players now waited to see whom they would face next. 'A big part of the fun of European football for us, being all young guys,' says Bobby Lennox, 'was the excitement of the draw. Who are we getting next? The draw was normally made on the Thursday or the Friday after the game. They would run a big foamy bath at Parkhead and all of us would be sitting about in the bath after training and waiting for someone to come in and say, "We're away to . . ." or "We're at home to . . ." I remember the excitement of the draw as much as anything – it was great just to find out where we were to go and who we were to play. I remember the excitement of the draw as much as the excitement of the games.'

The name out of the hat to face Celtic in the second round of the 1966–67 European Cup was Nantes of France: a challenge that appeared a grade higher than that offered by Zurich. 'They started over there like champions against us – maybe that was because they were the champions, of France!' states Lennox. 'They started really well. They got in front, but then we just wore them down. We played well in both games against them. Over there, wee Jimmy got on the ball a lot and he roasted them. In the second half he just kept the ball and kept doing his thing.' It was this match that led the French press to label the elusive Johnstone as 'The Flying Flea' as a result of the manner in which he had managed to get repeatedly under the skin of the French players.

'The biggest thing about Jock,' says Jimmy Johnstone, 'the biggest thing he used to do, was that he made you feel that you were the best team in the world. He made us believe in ourselves and I think he knew the potential that was there. That year, Jock used to say, "Do you know something? You could be the greatest team in the world." He never ever said, "You are the best team in the world." It was, "You could be . . ." Especially when we were in Europe he would say that regularly because I think somehow, somewhere, the big man had the feeling that it was going to happen for us. I think it stood us in good stead that we never, ever thought we were the greatest. On the park we were confident, cocky, but we never got bigheaded about it; we never went overboard. We knew within ourselves our own ability and we started to believe in ourselves but we never, ever thought for one minute that we would win the European Cup.'

Celtic reached full time in Nantes winning 3–1, and won again, by the same score, against the French at Celtic Park in early December 1966 to push on into the quarter-finals of the European Cup. The opening two rounds had enabled the Celtic players to acclimatise gradually to the demands of the European Cup against useful opposition, but opposition whom they had been able to grind down gradually through Stein's careful guidance and their own superior ability. Now, in the quarter-final of the tournament, Celtic would face a team that were their equals: Vojvodina Novi Sad of Yugoslavia.

Vojvodina could not claim to be one of the great names in European football but they were going through the greatest period of their own history. Such clubs are as much a part of the rich fabric of European football as those whose financial resources enable them always to be strong, such as Real Madrid or Milan. The Vojvodina players, typically of those from central Europe, possessed an excellent mastery of the game and they pooled their individual resources for the benefit of the team. The club had also been able to hold on to their talented players long enough to mould them into a tight-knit outfit: young Yugoslav footballers traditionally emigrated to the better-rewarded European leagues, particularly that of France. Vojvodina were to be respected but they were experiencing difficulties in the approach to the game. The first sign of the inevitable break-up of their team had come with the defection of Silvester Takac to Rennes of France. The midfielder's last act for Vojvodina had been to score the goal that had won the tie for Vojvodina against Atletico Madrid in the previous round. The Yugoslavs had also had two of their first-choice forwards dismissed in the match against Atletico in Madrid and Vojvodina would be without them for the first leg of their quarter-final with Celtic, in Novi Sad. It did little to detract from Vojvodina's all-round strength; their teamwork would compensate fully for the absences of those three key players.

'I thought Vojvodina were a really good team,' says Bobby Lennox. 'They had good players and they were so strong all round. They were really tight at the back; really, really good. We played well over there, I must say. We made a mistake for the goal over there, which was unlike our boys, but we made a mistake and it cost us a goal and that could have put us out.' That goal, 20 minutes from time, was the only score of the first leg, but it did nothing to knock Stein's confidence in his team as he looked forward to the second leg. 'I feel we have the players fit to wear the mantle of champions of Europe,' he said. 'I have told them so. Now they know it's up to them. I believe our boys and our style are good enough to win this match and win the European Cup, with which nothing else compares.'

Vojvodina, back to full strength for the second leg, continued to give Celtic problems at Celtic Park. The Yugoslavs smoothed their way through the first half, speeding up and slowing down the game at will and coming close to scoring on a couple of occasions. There was little hint that Celtic, even with the backing of a packed crowd, would be able to make progress in the second half, but it was at half-time that Stein often did a lot of his best work and on this occasion he made an alteration to the balance of his team that he hoped would unbalance the Yugoslavs. As Celtic lined up for the restart, both wingers, the diminutive Jimmy Johnstone and the giant John Hughes, could be seen on the right wing, a tactical switch that forced Vojvodina to reorder their defence. Johnstone, at five feet four inches tall and nine and a half stones in weight, perfectly complemented Hughes, who was six feet two inches tall and thirteen and a half stones in weight. Johnstone would tease defenders out of position, twisting and turning his markers so much he would leave them searching for their centre of gravity. Hughes, nicknamed 'Yogi Bear', would use his power and pace to run directly at a defence. It meant that the left side of the Yugoslav defence now became overworked in trying to cope with two different wingers' contrasting styles simultaneously.

After an hour of the match, Stevie Chalmers took advantage of continued defensive confusion on Vojvodina's part to nudge home a goal that levelled the tie on aggregate, but Vojvodina settled again and adjusted to the new demands being made on them. The prospect of a play-off in Rotterdam began to loom ever more clearly as each minute ticked away and the score remained the same. As the match entered the final minute, and Celtic made one last, desperate push for the winner, Charlie Gallagher took a corner from the right. He went to play it short, but had that option cut off when a Yugoslav defender raced out to cover. Instead, Gallagher floated the ball high into the penalty area. Stevie Chalmers moved towards the ball, drawing two defenders with him, and Billy McNeill rose above the remaining defenders to smack a header high into the net. It was the most dramatic way possible in which to clinch a semi-final place. 'Stevie scored with half an hour to go in Glasgow; there was a bit of a scramble and he put it in,' says Bobby Lennox. 'Then Billy got the winner. I'd say by that time we were thinking about the third game.'

Tommy Gemmell is in no doubt that the closeness of that match with Vojvodina reflects clearly the calibre of the Yugoslavs. 'We thought Vojvodina were the best side we played in the European Cup that year. They had class, the Yugoslavs. At that time their international side was doing really well and every one of the Vojvodina players looked comfortable on the ball. They had good teamwork; they knocked the ball around well, held possession well. Those were two very difficult matches against them and I think most of the guys would agree that they were the best side we played in Europe that season. Vojvodina were the hardest nut to crack. They really made life hard for us.'

Another technically accomplished eastern European side, in the shape of Dukla Prague, presented themselves at Celtic Park for the European Cup semi-final in April 1967 and it would prove another exhilarating evening in Glasgow. Five minutes had passed when Stanislav Strunc, the Dukla outside-right, shuffled through the Celtic defence, but goalkeeper Ronnie Simpson leapt into action and stretched out a hand to divert the ball away from his goal. Simpson was another of the Celtic players to have been re-energised by Stein's arrival at the club. He had actually been transferred from Hibernian to Celtic by Stein in 1964 but, on arriving at Celtic, Stein had given Simpson another chance to prove himself and the 36-year-old was now enjoying a balmy Indian summer with Celtic at the end of an illustrious career.

Jan Viktor, Simpson's opposite number on the night, had less success when faced with the talents of Celtic's outside-right, Jimmy Johnstone. One of Johnstone's favourite ploys was to move from wide on the right wing into the inside-right channel to obtain a better angle to score. Now, after almost half an hour of the game against Dukla, Johnstone did exactly that as he chased a spinning, swirling ball that bounced into the air just inside the corner of the Dukla six-yard box. Johnstone used his pace to get to the ball and nick it over Viktor as the giant, fearless Czech came rushing towards him. Viktor could only claw at the air helplessly as the ball flew over his body into the net. Johnstone had shown real bravery to get to the ball in the face of the goalkeeper advancing threateningly towards him.

Dukla's cultured, classy passing style continued to pose a threat for Celtic and shortly before half-time the Czechs cleverly worked the ball through three Celtic defenders on the edge of the penalty area directly in front of goal. This time, Strunc evaded a challenge from Billy McNeill to shuttle the ball past the defender, making just enough space for the winger to curve the ball into the corner of the Celtic net for the equaliser. At half-time, Stein told his players to press up ever more tightly on the Czech defence. On the hour, Gemmell played a quick, high pass that whirled over the heads of the Dukla defenders and, as they re-established their bearings, the ball sat up nicely for Willie Wallace on the edge of the penalty area. The forward expertly and economically volleyed the ball past Viktor to put Celtic ahead again. Celtic continued to exert exceptional pressure on the Czechs and a desperate handball outside the Dukla penalty area gave Celtic a free kick in a threatening position. A Dukla defender held on to the ball until Viktor was entirely sure that his defensive wall fitted together flawlessly. They had reckoned without the cunning of Bertie Auld. As he prepared to take the kick, the Celtic midfielder walked forward to where the ball sat, as if to adjust its position. He bent over it but instead of walking back again, as would have been orthodox, Auld, from a crouching position, swiftly swiped a short pass to his right where Wallace again showed quick reactions to whisk a fiercely accurate shot past the stationary Viktor who looked pleadingly at his defensive wall as if to ask where the shot had come from. 'That was Willie's transfer fee paid for already!' says Tommy Gemmell.

Wallace was the most expensively acquired member of that Celtic team, having been signed from Heart of Midlothian for £30,000 in December 1966. Stein's plan had been to pair Wallace with Joe McBride as his twin strikers, but in only their second game together McBride had suffered a cartilage injury that would, ultimately, cut short his career at Celtic Park. An administrative mix-up meant that Celtic had failed to register Wallace for the European Cup quarter-final with Vojvodina, which could have proved a costly error, but all was well for the semi with Dukla, in which Wallace made his European debut. He was forming an effective partnership with Stevie Chalmers, the player who would have been sidelined had McBride not suffered his injury. Wallace was sometimes underrated by supporters because of his straightforward, economical style but he was fully appreciated by his fellow players, who realised just how effective and integral to the team he was.

Celtic's 3–1 win gave them a healthy lead for the second leg but players and management had seen enough from the Czech champions to know that they would be more than a handful when the two teams came together again at the Juliska Stadium in Prague. Stein, the arch-pragmatist, decided on a 4–5–1 formation, featuring Stevie Chalmers alone up front and a heavily fortified five-man midfield in front of the usual four-man defence. 'Dukla were a really good team, with Josef Masopust,' says Bobby Lennox. 'They gave us a hard time over there. They pushed us back over there. People were saying that Celtic played a defensive game, but what actually happened was that they just pushed us back. Stevie seemed so isolated, doing his thing so far up the park, by himself, and wee Jimmy seemed to be beside Jim Craig for a lot of the game. I can remember standing beside big Tommy Gemmell for most of that game. I remember just before half-time one of their players hitting one that went past the two of us and I thought it was in – then I heard it hitting the railing behind the goal. I thought, "We have had a real escape there – this might be our night!" It was backs to the wall but that was because of their ability – not because of our deficiencies. We didn't go out to play defensively; it just happened. I think there's a natural thing in football that if the ball comes up the park and bounces as it is coming towards you when you are in front in a big game, your natural tendency is to take a step back rather than to take a step forward. If you are needing a goal you would instead take a step forward. It's just human nature – you take a step back. I think that was what happened that night in Prague.'

Gemmell, the left-back, whom Lennox was pushed back alongside in that match, recalls how Celtic's strategy in Prague made them play a game unnatural to the team. 'Over there was the one and only time we were ever asked to play defensively by Jock Stein. We put the shutters up. Stevie played on his own up front and everybody else played at the back of midfield. We just filled the middle of the park and Ronnie Simpson had a tremendous match. We got away with a 0–0 draw but they had chances to bury us. When I say they had chances, they never had any glaring chances, clear-cut chances, but they had a lot of half-chances. All they needed was to pop one away and they would have hit us like a ton of bricks. We just kept firing balls to the corner flags and Stevie held on to them until he got a bit of support. He didn't want to go anywhere and didn't want to try to score goals. We would just hold on to it for as long as we could and then it would be everybody back again. Big Jock, hands up to him, said afterwards, "We'll never play defensively ever again." We had got the result but, oh, it was fingernails stuff.

'Dukla were almost as good as Vojvodina but they had a lot of players coming to the end of their careers, like Josef Masopust, for example, who was a magnificent player for Czechoslovakia and for Dukla. In the return match in Prague he took the game by the scruff of the neck, but in the last half-hour he tired and as soon as we snuffed him out, it snuffed them out. They had a lot of players that were getting to the stage where they were past their best, put it that way, but they could knock the ball around. We had so many bodies in the box or outside the box that it made it very, very difficult for them. You could fill your box with 11 schoolboys and the opposition would find it difficult to score. It was a nerve-racking afternoon and we all got pissed on the flight back. I think it was through relief rather than anything else because we had created history in doing something that had never been done before by a British side, reaching a European Cup final. Basically, that meant the load was off our shoulders. We had done something no other British side had done. So that was a first. We were going to be complete underdogs against Inter in the final, and that suited us fine.'

Most of the Celtic players had little opportunity to dwell for long on the significance of having reached the European Cup final. Their timetable was far too busy to allow them much pause for thought. On the Saturday after the semi-final first leg, for example, several Celts had travelled south with the Scottish national team to face England in a Home International Championship match that doubled as a European Championship qualifier. It ended in a 3–2 victory for Scotland at Wembley Stadium, the first defeat any country had inflicted on England since they had become world champions the previous year. Ronnie Simpson won his first Scotland cap, at the age of 36, in that game. Bobby Lennox scored Scotland's second goal and Willie Wallace was a vital component in a smooth-moving Scotland side. After the second leg against Dukla, Celtic had a Scottish Cup final to play against Aberdeen and then, on the following Saturday, 6 May, a League decider against Rangers at Ibrox Stadium. From there, seven Celtic players joined up with the Scotland squad for a friendly match against the Soviet Union and two days after that international, Celtic rounded off their league fixtures with a home game against Kilmarnock on 15 May. After that, there were just ten days remaining before the game with Internazionale in Lisbon, Portugal. It proved the perfect preparation for the European Cup final.

'As soon as we beat Dukla in the first leg,' says Bobby Lennox, 'four or five of us went straight down to Wembley with Scotland and we got a good result there. With games like that to play, it meant that although we had the prospect of playing in the European Cup final and were due to play it a few weeks later, it felt a million miles away. When we went back to Celtic Park after the second leg, I don't think the final came into it because you had to try to keep playing and winning your place in the team, first and foremost. After everything was finished, though, and we could start to think about Lisbon, the build-up was great.'

The Cup final with Aberdeen ended in a 2–0 victory for Celtic and a dramatic 2–2 draw at Ibrox enabled Celtic to bag their second Scottish League title in a row. Stein had chosen an identical line-up for three of the most vital matches of Celtic's season until that point – the second leg against Dukla in Prague, the Scottish Cup final with Aberdeen and the title decider against Rangers – and he would go with the same 11 for the European Cup final. 'After the 0–0 draw over in Prague against Dukla,' says Bobby Lennox, 'and when the same team got the draw against Rangers, I think that team was going to be the team. With big Jock, you didn't know for sure who would be playing until the team was actually picked, but I think most of us thought that that would be the team.'

Celtic flew into Lisbon on 23 May, two days before the final. Stein had done all he could to get his players in a relaxed frame of mind in advance of the match. They had spent four days at Seamill Hydro on the Ayrshire coast, combining hard training with golf, card games and watching films of great football matches. A lot of it had been a lot of fun. The players had then spent the weekend before the match with their families and were now tension-free as their bus wound its way through narrow Portuguese streets to the exclusive Hotel Palacio, one of the world's most prestigious hotels, in Estoril, a pleasant coastal town situated to the west of the Portuguese capital.

'When we got to Estoril,' says Billy McNeill, 'the hotel was absolutely magnificent. It was perfect, with a beautiful swimming pool and beautiful gardens, but the big fellow gave you half an hour or so in the swimming pool and then said, "Right, get out of the sun, because the sun will tire you." Whether the sun would have tired us or not is one thing but I think what he was always reminding us of was the fact that it was extreme luxury, really the top end of the market, so therefore he was showing us, "This is where you are now. You are at the top end of the market but don't lose sight of the reason why we are here. We are not here just to relax and enjoy ourselves. We're here to appreciate these luxuries that we are getting access to because of the level at which we are now playing, but we got here through hard work, through being diligent, and we'll stay at this level through remembering we're here to play a game." He planned everything to perfection.'

There were plenty of light-hearted moments to help release the inevitable tension surrounding the occasion, as Bobby Lennox explains. 'Our boys enjoyed each other's company,' he says. 'No matter where you were, the banter was great, the patter was good and you got a laugh. We trained in the National Stadium on one of the days before the match and Milan watched us. Big Jock knew Milan would be watching us so he said, "Billy, go and play centre-forward. Jimmy, go and play centre-half. Don't play in your own positions." It was just a wee bounce game. It was a bit of fun. Then we trained on another wee pitch on the other day. The sun was shining and it was great but as soon as training was finished big Jock would make us stay in the shade.' The players were not kept in isolation from those who had travelled from Glasgow to lend them their backing. 'We stayed in Estoril,' says Lennox, 'and people came wandering in from time to time. We didn't exactly mingle with the supporters, but we didn't ignore them either. If they were there we would speak to them, and there were a few floating about the hotel.'

The day of the final dawned and several Celtic players began the morning in prayer. 'I remember it was a Holiday of Obligation,' recalls Bobby Lennox, 'and we all went to Mass in a wee room in a hotel – we walked from our hotel to another hotel – and a Scottish priest said Mass in a room; the quickest Mass ever. The priest said the Mass and then wished the players all the best in the match. Then we went back into our beds for a wee while.'

During that rest period prior to the match, every set of room-mates discussed how they thought the afternoon's match might unfold. Jimmy Johnstone was rooming with Bobby Lennox and Johnstone began listing the famous names in the Italian side, players with daunting reputations such as Giacinto Facchetti and Sandro Mazzola. 'I thought we were going to get a doing,' says Johnstone. 'We had watched them; they had been World Club champions twice and at that time they were the best defensive side in the world. They would just score one goal at home and say, "That's enough." That was because they knew that in the second leg the other team would have no chance of scoring. We still thought we should go out and give it a go anyway.' Bobby Lennox countered Johnstone's opinions by listing the qualities of Johnstone and the other Celtic players and suggesting that they would be a match for the Italians. 'I think we were quite a confident bunch of guys,' he says. 'I don't think we went into the game thinking we were going to win the European Cup 4–0 or 5–0 but we didn't go into the game thinking we were going to be beaten. We thought we could beat them. I thought that that Celtic team could have beaten anybody on the right day.'

The setting for the 1967 European Cup final was like none before or since. Most of the major European grounds were hemmed in tightly in built-up inner cities, with floodlight masts visible from miles around – the ability of clubs to light up the night for midweek matches from the 1950s onwards had been one of the major reasons why European football had begun to catch on so quickly. The National Stadium in Lisbon, though, was without floodlights in 1967, which meant the final would have to begin in the late afternoon, at half past five, to ensure that, in the event of extra-time, proceedings would be complete before night descended on Portugal.

Unlike its city-central counterparts across Europe, the National Stadium was situated in deep woodland six miles outside of Lisbon itself, and anyone seeking the stadium found that it was hidden to the eye until they were right on top of it. There seemed to be an almost mystical quality to this setting, and even the construction of the stadium made it decidedly different. It was a three-sided entity – one touch-line did not even have terracing of any description behind it, although for the European Cup final a tiny, temporary stand that was only five seats deep and stretching only a few yards either side of the halfway line had been installed. Trees dotted the background, dwarfing this stand. This was where the press and a few privileged others would be stationed for the match, along with the two teams' benches and numerous members of the Portuguese militia; the country at that time being ruled by a dictatorship. The strangeness of this backdrop was completed by a neatly trimmed hedge, which would not have been out of place in a suburban garden, running alongside the touch-line on that side of the stadium.

The other three sides of the ground, in contrast, were grand and imposing, consisting of steep terraces of smooth stonework fashioned into rows and rows of elongated benches, which curved gracefully around each end of the ground: the National Stadium was an all-seated arena, a rarity for the 1960s. The stand that ran along the opposite touch-line from the hedge-bordered one could not have been more different from its ramshackle counterpart: the main stand reached an imposing pinnacle in a set of marble pillars that rose from a marble rostrum which towered high above the halfway line. It was from there that the various dignitaries, including the president of Portugal, would watch the match and it was there that the European Cup would be presented to the winning captain. This woodland glade seemed the perfect setting for the conclusion of Celtic's fairy-tale progress to the final.

None of these details mattered much to the players as they prepared for the game. They were there to do a job and, as true professionals, were not about to be distracted by their surroundings. 'We didn't even look out of the windows,' says Bobby Lennox of the team's journey to the grand ground. 'We just got into the coach, had a wee sing-song and a laugh and a blether and someone said, "There's the park," and we were there.' The driver of the Celtic team's coach had, on collecting the players and officials from the Hotel Palacio, started out in the wrong direction and by the time he had righted himself and finally reached the stadium, it was within an hour of kick-off. It seems strange that a Portuguese driver would not know how to reach the National Stadium and would instead head from Estoril out towards Cascais and the other seaside resorts of the Portuguese Riviera – since that is the only alternative to heading back towards Lisbon. It was a bit like a Scottish driver leaving Seamill and heading towards Ayr and Troon rather than towards Glasgow. Machiavellian minds might suspect that he had been 'persuaded' to do so by someone with an Inter connection. If it was a ruse, it failed. Instead, it actually worked in the Celtic players' favour as it meant that they had less time in which to wait for the game to start. There was just enough time for them to have a look at the pitch, get themselves changed, enjoy a warm-up and listen to a few words from Jock Stein before they were called into action.

'It was a very good surface,' says Bobby Lennox. 'The pitch was great. There were no problems at all. We were a wee bit late coming to the game because we got lost a bit and that didn't do us any harm either. We got ready and walked on to the field, got back into the dressing-room, changed and got on with the game. So there was no sitting about for ages and ages, which was quite a good thing. I think we got there about 50 minutes before the kick-off. Normally we got there a good bit before that. So by the time we had had a look at the place and had got ready it was time to get out. So that was really good.'

The Celtic and Inter players were billeted in L-shaped dressing-rooms, which meant, unusually, that, as they changed, Celtic players were split up from each other in the two parts of the dressing-room. As they left the dressing-room, the teams crossed a small courtyard behind a corner of the stadium and from there they descended into an underground tunnel that led down into half-light and then up towards the playing surface. A brief pause ensued as the two teams lined up alongside each other in the tunnel before trotting out onto the pitch together. 'I remember,' says Jimmy Johnstone, 'wee Bertie, with the Maryhill humour, having a laugh in that tunnel before we went out. We were standing right beside the Italians, so close we were breathing on them and you could smell the Ambre Solaire off them, and wee "Ten-thirty" was shouting, "Wee man! What about this big one?" Then he says to the Italian, "Tell your maw you're going to be late in getting out of here! Your eyes will be burling!" The Italian boys were all looking at each other and saying, "Loco, loco!"'

The Celtic players who emerged into a fierce Portuguese sun that afternoon were: Ronnie Simpson, Jim Craig, Tommy Gemmell, Bobby Murdoch, Billy McNeill, John Clark, Jimmy Johnstone, Willie Wallace, Stevie Chalmers, Bertie Auld and Bobby Lennox. Every one of those players had been born within a 30-mile radius of Celtic Park, but they were in Lisbon because of their ability, not because of local sentiment. Inter limbered up as the two teams took to the field together; the Italian players jogging gently or jumping athletically. Celtic simply strolled out. Jock Stein, smart as any Italian sophisticate in his dark suit and shades, made for the bench, along with trainers Neil Mochan and Bob Rooney, physiotherapist Jimmy Steele, assistant manager Sean Fallon and John Fallon, Celtic's reserve goalkeeper, the team's 12th man, who was clutching a lucky teddy bear. Of the 11 players who lined up against Internazionale in the final, 5 had been in the party of Celtic players who had travelled to Valencia for the club's first competitive match in Europe back in 1962: Stevie Chalmers, John Clark, Bobby Lennox, Bobby Murdoch and Billy McNeill. Of those, only McNeill and Chalmers had started the game with Valencia. Others from that party had played a role in the run to the final: John Fallon, Charlie Gallagher, John Hughes and Willie O'Neill. Stein had taken a core group of players from a directionless, under-achieving squad and transformed them into European finalists. Other players from that 1962 squad, such as Dunky MacKay, Mike Jackson and Bobby Carroll, who had left the club prior to Stein's arrival but who had been well regarded by the manager, looked on and wondered whether they might also have enjoyed a similar boost to their careers had they still been at Celtic Park after the arrival of Stein in 1965.

The 56,000 crowd contained approximately 10,000 followers of Celtic and around 4,000 Inter supporters. 'I don't think you could ever be surprised by Celtic supporters,' says Bobby Lennox. 'Everywhere you go there are Celtic supporters – it is just a fact of life. They made you feel at home and the Portuguese were also more or less behind us.'

Helenio Herrera, the Inter manager, had enjoyed a previous connection with Lisbon – he had been, early on in his career, the manager of Belenenses, the club from the south-west of the city that lives in the shadow of the two giants Benfica and Sporting. He had even narrowly avoided death in an air crash near Lisbon shortly before quitting Belenenses to move on and become manager of Barcelona in the late 1950s. One week prior to the match against Celtic, Herrera, with customary thoroughness, had travelled to Lisbon to check that the facilities that had been booked for his club were up to a high standard. He had also used that trip to try to whip up support for his Inter side among the locals. They were not having it. The Benfica supporters still remembered how their team had lost to Inter in the European Cup final two years previously in circumstances that they had considered highly suspicious.

Herrera was one of the great managers in the European game, so much so that football aficionados referred to him simply by his initials: HH. The Argentinian had a reputation as a master tactician, a football grandmaster who employed his players like chess pieces to outwit the opposition. That was to underestimate Herrera's abilities as a man-manager. He had the ability to instil enormous self-belief and confidence in his players, as he had shown at modestly resourced clubs such as Belenenses, Malaga and Sevilla. That man-management was allied to Herrera's exceptional professionalism to create a formidable style of leadership. He would make copious notes on the opposition and supply his players with detailed notes on their opponents. The Inter players had been briefed in detail as to what to expect from Celtic, and Inter had played practice matches against the Italian club's second string with those reserve-team players set up in Celtic's style. Nothing, Herrera was sure, had been left to chance.

It had been defeat to Real Madrid in a 1960 European Cup semi-final, whilst manager of Barcelona, that had spurred Herrera to move to Inter as manager. He resigned after the defeat and the move to Internazionale allowed him to command a salary beyond the dreams of his British counterparts, conjoined with a seemingly bottomless transfer budget, all of which was funded by the club owner, oil magnate Angelo Moratti. On taking control at Inter, Herrera had found the Italian club to be in a state of instability and very much in the shadow of neighbours Milan. Undaunted, Herrera had promised that within three years Inter would be European and world champions. He was a year late in achieving that ambition, when Inter won the European Cup and World Clubs Championship in 1964, but compensated for that by repeating the feat one year later.

Herrera's dressing-room slogan at Internazionale was: 'We win because we are the best.' It was more complicated than that. Self-belief was soldered on to a tactical system that was intended to guarantee the success that Herrera and his team craved. The Inter manager had perfected the *catenaccio* system, through which his team's defence would be bolted firmly shut. A sweeper was employed – in the 1967 final this would be Armando Picchi – to sit behind four defenders to provide extra security in the event of a forward breaking free of his marker. The use of this extra man in defence meant that Inter were often characterised as a defensive side, but that was only half the story. Herrera required cast-iron defending but only if it could create a springboard for swift goalscoring breaks out of defence. Opponents would become tangled in Inter's defensive web and then find the left-back, Giacinto Facchetti, swiftly turning defence into a counter-attack by breaking free and using his speed and athleticism to provide the extra man in any breakaway move. Facchetti would carry the ball, at speed, to midfielders and forwards, such as Luis Suarez and Sandro Mazzola, and would then provide the extra man in attack; he also had the pace to return to his position in the Inter defence as quickly as possible. It meant that Inter were at their best when turning defence into attack and the better the opposition, the better it worked.

Attacking players facing Inter would be lulled into thinking they were doing well as the Inter defenders, seemingly under irresistible pressure, dropped back deeper into defence. This would encourage the opposition to flood forward in ever-greater numbers until Inter would suddenly burst free, turning defence into attack in an instant. The key to Inter's success was in enticing as many of the opposition into Inter's own penalty box as possible; a strange match-winning tactic but one that had proved consistently effective. Facchetti, for example, had scored twice in Inter's semi-final against CSKA Sofia. Their tactics meant that Inter disliked facing defensive teams; they preferred to meet attacking teams that took the initiative. As such, Celtic were perfect opponents for the Italians in the final.

It was not only in tactics and transfer fees that Inter had invested during the Herrera era. Decades before British clubs had even thought of self-contained training complexes, Inter had the Centro d'Appiano Gentile, a base with 17 football pitches, swimming pool and sleeping accommodation: here, the first team would go about their tightly controlled preparations whilst young players would be coached and educated in the ways of Inter and brought through to supplement the first-team squad.

Inter would line up for the European Cup final without their Brazilian outside-right, Jair Da Costa, who had suffered a knee injury in Inter's League match with Fiorentina on the Sunday prior to the final. Jair had been an integral part of their European Cup-winning teams in 1964 and 1965, but he had struggled for form in the 1966–67 season. Herrera also lamented the absence of Spanish midfielder Luis Suarez, their playmaker-in-chief and a man whose transfer from Barcelona to Inter in 1961 had been for a world-record fee of £214,000. Suarez, 32, had picked up a thigh strain towards the end of the Italian season. The thrust and thinking power he gave Inter in midfield had guided them through the 1960s. The absence of Suarez was counterbalanced by Celtic being without striker Joe McBride, a longer-term absentee but a player who would almost certainly have taken part in the final had he been fit. McBride had scored a magnificent 35 goals for Celtic that 1966–67 season, all of them before Christmas, but he had suffered a debilitating knee injury at Aberdeen on Christmas Eve 1966. McBride had cost Celtic a modest £22,000 in 1965, but he had been just as important to his team as Suarez had been for Inter. Absences of such great players for key matches are part of the game of football and, to his credit, Herrera, pre-match, avoided using it as an excuse. 'Inter will not be able to count on two of their best players,' he said, 'but the greatest obstacle will be Celtic. This will be a very difficult game.'

Back at Barcelona in the early 1960s, Suarez had been earning £7,000 per year; the Celtic players of the time were on approximately £1,250. Suarez' £214,000 transfer fee in 1961 had been five times the cost of the entire Celtic team in 1967; indeed the £60,000 cut of that fee that Suarez had received for himself was, in itself, more than the entire Celtic team had cost. The Inter team that lined up in Lisbon were, by comparison, the most expensively assembled team in Europe. The absence of their Spanish playmaker may have been lamented by Inter but it hardly made the 1967 European Cup final an unequal contest.

Inter kicked off the match with characteristic confidence and seemed determined to dispose of the threat of Celtic as swiftly as possible. With just three minutes gone, Renato Cappellini streaked down the left wing, flitted past right-back Craig with extreme ease, reached the goal line and pulled a cross back for Sandro Mazzola to head the ball goalwards with exceptional power and precision. The striker's slick header was equalled by the save that it brought in response from Simpson, who reached low down on his line to stop the ball. Jimmy Johnstone was then responsible for Celtic's first good goal attempt and, unconventional as ever, the winger chose to establish Celtic's threat with nothing other than a header – Johnstone climbed into the air to direct the ball at a spot just under the Inter crossbar and it forced Giuliano

Sarti, the Inter goalkeeper, to arch his back and perform a half-cartwheel in mid-air while stretching behind him to save.

The resultant corner was knocked clear of the Inter goal to the right wing, from where it was shuttled swiftly by midfielder Mario Bicicli into the path of Sandro Mazzola, beautifully positioned in the centre of the field. As the striker loped forward, scanning the territory in front of him to see who was available for a pass, Celtic players dropped back and Mazzola, taking advantage of some confusion in his opponents' ranks, sent a piercingly accurate diagonal ball into the Celtic penalty area that bypassed central defenders Clark and McNeill to find Mazzola's fellow forward Renato Cappellini. The Celtic right-back Jim Craig had come across from one wing to the other with Cappellini. Instead of jockeying his opponent, which would have allowed Craig's teammates to regroup, Craig angled his run deliberately to try to ensure that he would block Cappellini and that Cappellini would collide with him. That was exactly what happened and the collision sent the Inter player tumbling to the ground. German referee Kurt Tschenscher immediately awarded a penalty and, after long, loud and increasingly agitated protests from the Celtic players, Mazzola stepped up to smoothly stroke the ball into the net.

'I often think,' says Billy McNeill, 'that possibly the best thing that ever happened to us was to lose an early goal, and to lose it in the manner in which we did, through the penalty, because we felt the penalty was an injustice. It wasn't, as it so happened, but we felt that an injustice had been created. We all thought it was no penalty at the time, but it was definitely a penalty. We would have wanted a penalty kick for that. Them scoring that goal meant that we had no option but to push forward.'

Inter took a great pride in being able to hold whatever lead they had on a football field, but they did not try to sit back on their lead; it is a common misconception to believe that Inter stopped attacking once they had scored their goal. The Italians certainly tried to indulge in some time wasting – particularly at dead-ball situations – and after only quarter of an hour of the match Tschenscher admonished Sarti for spending too long over the taking of a goal kick. Overall, though, Inter still tried to get the ball forward. They still looked to maraud into

Celtic's half and always presented a danger through Giacinto Facchetti's willingness to overlap, through Sandro Mazzola's availability to set up moves from a central attacking position and the pace of the forwards Cappellini and Angelo Domenghini. The Italians posed a serious threat, but it was one that was almost entirely snuffed out because Inter were simply pushed back by the force of Celtic's attacking play. Only rarely in the first half were the Italians again able to muster an attack that put the Celtic defence under severe pressure.

Soon after the Inter goal, Bertie Auld clipped the bar with an angled shot from just inside the Inter penalty area. Then a 20-yard shot from Tommy Gemmell went wriggling into the side netting. The match was only at the midway point of the first half but, as Giuliano Sarti lay panting, spread-eagled on the turf after scrambling across his goal to try to deal with Gemmell's shot, the Inter goalkeeper already looked like a man who felt as though he had done a full day's work.

Still Inter tried to thrust forward, painstakingly working their way through midfield. To the Italians' credit, they almost always tried to work the ball towards the Celtic goal, rarely opting to pass the ball back, even when such a pass was on. Still they found too many Celtic challenges in their way and again and again the Italians conceded possession and had to fall back as Celtic flooded forward. The Celtic tackles flew in too quickly for the Italians: the Celts were usually first to every loose ball, and, when they had possession in midfield, Auld and Murdoch outmanoeuvred their opponents.

'They probably wanted to sit back but we also penned them back,' says Bobby Lennox. 'If you look at the game, wee Jimmy, Stevie, myself and Wispy didn't get many touches of the ball. All we did was keep moving people. Most of the shots came from Tam, Bobby and Bertie – the midfield players – but big Jock thought the movement of the forwards was great during the game and although we weren't on the ball much he thought we played well during the game. We kept them moving so much and they were penned in. That's why the boys could push right in on top of them.'

Stein's pre-match instructions to his forwards had been to make themselves as elusive as possible; continually to push and pull the Inter players in all directions. The Celtic manager knew that the Italians would man-mark his players, so if the Celtic attackers kept moving into space, the Italians would soon be twisting and turning and the Inter defence would become as tangled up as a bowl of spaghetti. 'We were just told to keep moving because the Italians would come and mark us,' says Lennox. 'So we were told to keep moving to move them into areas where their marking was going to be more effective for us. We were told not to stand in front of the goals and be marked in there; we were told just to keep taking them from side to side and move them from one place to another. That would mean our midfielders would get their passes going while we were taking our markers into positions where they didn't want to be. Movement creates room and that's how football players play.

'The Inter players were masters at man-marking. The Italians would keep touching you and all that sort of stuff, which is frustrating for Scottish players. It was not so much that they were pulling your jersey; more that they were just reassuring themselves that you were there by continually touching you again and again, but it wasn't a dirty game.'

A searing volley from Gemmell late in the first half produced another fine save from Sarti, the goalkeeper falling low to his left to touch the ball round his post just as it appeared sure to fly into the net. Then the spectators were treated to a most extraordinary sight. Renato Cappellini went streaking through the middle of the Celtic half in pursuit of the ball and the chance of Inter's second goal. He had only Ronnie Simpson to beat if he could get to the ball and although the goalkeeper, now yards out of his area to meet the challenge, looked sure to get to the ball a fraction ahead of Cappellini, there was the danger that a conventional clearance would result in the ball rebounding off the Italian, as he closed in, leaving Cappellini alone in front of goal. Any attempt by Simpson to dribble the ball back to the safety of his own penalty area was even more likely to result in disaster. As a solution, the experienced Simpson simply backheeled the ball out of Cappellini's path. The Italian went racing past the Scot like a bull charging past a matador's quickly withdrawn cape. Simpson steadied himself before coolly clearing the ball. It was a piece of improvisation entirely in keeping with that cavalier Celtic side.

It remained 1–0 to Inter at half-time but the Italians, despite being in the lead, were now on the back foot. They had found it difficult to cope with Celtic's style. In the Italian League, opponents would tend to pressurise each other heavily only when the ball was in the final third of the field. At the National Stadium, Inter found themselves up against a Celtic side that were forcing the Inter players into mistakes in all parts of the park. Inter were being jostled out of their normally smooth, composed game. The longer the game went on, the more often Inter players would drop back behind the ball to try to stem the flow of Celtic's attacks.

'At half-time,' says Jimmy Johnstone, 'we knew we would do it simply because of the amount of chances we had made; that was even though we were down 1–0. Another thing was the temperature: we had never, ever played in that type of heat in our lives and these Inter guys were used to it, from playing in Italy. It was about 75 degrees! It would have burned a hole in your head! We didn't even think about it because when we got that ball we wanted to run and run at them and skin them. We felt the heat but it didn't affect us. That is another thing that people tend to overlook, but I think it's a major point. I think we were just so carried away by the occasion that neither the heat nor anything else mattered. Everybody was so motivated. It was a great occasion.'

Stein had had to calm his players down in the dressing-room at half-time – they were still agitated about referee Tschenscher's decision to award Inter a penalty, which the Celtic players thought, wrongly as Billy McNeill and others would later accept, had been an error on the official's part. The manager eventually cooled the heated tempers of his players and told them to persist in doing the things that they had been doing so well in the first half. 'It suited us ideally, them getting the penalty kick so early in the game,' says Tommy Gemmell, 'because at that time the Italians' motto was "If we score, get everybody back". They played in the way we tried to play away to Dukla in the return match of the semi-final but there wasn't a side in the world that could afford to give us as much of the ball as they did without being beaten, because if you take out Ronnie Simpson and John Clark, every other player was a potential goalscorer. So we had nine potential goalscorers and they gave us the ball! In saying that, it was one of those days on which we had so much of the ball that you were wondering if anything was going to come from it.'

After 63 minutes Tommy Gemmell advanced deep into the Inter

half. Jim Craig, close to the spot where he had given away the first-half penalty, spotted Gemmell hovering in space on the edge of the Inter penalty area and sent a pass in his direction. Gemmell had made a run from inside his own half and as the ball reached him the left-back showed the type of improvisation present in all top-class players to adjust his body well enough to get a clean, first-time strike on the ball and it went racing high into the Inter net. Gemmell was finishing his European Cup season in the manner in which he had begun it against Zurich, with a long-range goal of the finest quality. The left-back had spent much of the match awaiting the ball on the edge of the Inter penalty area. He had been unlucky not to score with two first-half attempts on goal but now, at last, his patience had paid off.

'I should really have had my backside kicked for that,' says Gemmell of his goal, 'because I shouldn't have been there in the first place. The golden rule was that if one full-back was up the other one was to be round covering in central defence and it was Jim Craig that cut the ball back for me. Now, if you look at that game on film and look at the goal, there is an Italian defender comes out to attack the ball as Jim Craig squares it to me. The Italian stops two yards from me and I knock it in, of course. If that guy takes another pace he blocks that shot and nobody has ever heard of Tommy Gemmell and Celtic might not have won the European Cup. It just shows you how fate plays a part in things. If that guy had taken one more pace he could have changed the whole course of Celtic's history.

'Looking at it hypothetically, if that guy had blocked my shot and they had broken away and scored a goal it would have made it 2–0 for them and I would have got castigated because there is no way I should have been there in the first place. If Jim Craig was up, I was supposed to be supporting our central defence but there was no need because they had one player in our half and that was it. We had John Clark and Billy McNeill back there so it was two against one so there wasn't a problem there. If it had been two against two I would have had to have stayed back.

'The big problem was getting the breakthrough. As soon as I scored the goal you just had to look at all the Italian players to see that their heads were down. They didn't want to know after that because they were aware that the writing was on the wall, and if it had gone to a

replay two days later we would have given them a right going-over. I
think they were only in our half twice in the second half.'

Bobby Lennox agrees with Gemmell that Inter's tactics aided Celtic
enormously. 'By that stage Inter were really penned in,' he says. 'They
couldn't get out. Billy and John had no problems with Mazzola the
longer the game went on, so there was no need for Tommy or Cairney
[Jim Craig] to be back three against one. They did the right thing as
good, thinking professionals. We could get goals from Billy coming up
or Tam coming up, or through Bobby or Bertie. Most of the boys could
get a goal if it was needed.'

Five minutes from time, goalscorer Tommy Gemmell eased down the
left wing to back up the attack yet again. 'The ball was knocked out to
me,' he recalls, 'and a defender came to me and then another defender
went behind him. I just did the wee Ali-shuffle thing and knocked it
back to Bobby Murdoch, who had a shot at goal that was going past
and Stevie slid it into the net. That wasn't an accident. We did exactly
the same thing in training every day of the week; players coming down
either side and cutting it back to midfield players who were supporting
front players. The midfield players would then hit it and the front
players would always try to deflect the ball into goal.'

Bobby Lennox knew when that second goal went in that the
European Cup, gleaming high above the field of play, was as good as in
Celtic's hands. 'On the day, we got on top of them and never gave them
a minute,' he says. 'I think they would have liked to have played the
game slowly but we never gave them the time to do that. The boys
hassled and harried them and worked really hard. Remember, it was
roasting hot as well. When the second goal went in there was no way
back for them. At that point I think every Celtic player knew we had
won the European Cup.' Tommy Gemmell concurs, 'Their goalkeeper
Sarti had six saves that were out of this world. We beat them 2–1 going
on 6–1 and he saved them from a real going-over.' Giuliano Sarti, in
common with Ronnie Simpson, had had plenty of experience on which
to draw: the Italian had kept goal for Fiorentina in the 1957 European
Cup final, against Real Madrid. As in 1967, he had performed
brilliantly but had finished on the losing side.

At the conclusion of the final, there were anarchic scenes when local youngsters joined hundreds of Celtic supporters on the pitch. As Billy McNeill received the trophy, a graceless Inter supporter continuously waved, underneath the plinth on which McNeill was standing, a flag thinly striped with the blue and black Inter colours. It was a gesture that looked cheap in comparison to McNeill standing majestically holding up the great trophy. It was a new trophy too: the Greek-urn-like European Cup with short arms and small, chunky body that had been the prize for the first 11 tournaments had been retained by 6-times winners Real Madrid in 1966. Now, McNeill held aloft a new version of the European Cup, a much bigger, longer-bodied, more graceful trophy, elegantly designed with smooth, elongated, streamlined surfaces that made it distinctly different from the smaller, more ornamental Victorian-style trophies that were the prizes in Scottish domestic competition. It was a magnificent trophy, one that fully embodied the growing importance of the greatest of modern club tournaments, and it belonged to Celtic. 'I thought the best presentation ever was Billy in Lisbon,' says Bobby Lennox. 'It looked terrific: Caesar up there with the Cup.'

McNeill feels privileged in the extreme to have been the man who took possession of that trophy on the winners' rostrum on an afternoon that had afforded him extreme satisfaction. 'Inter played *catenaccio*,' he says, 'and it was something that was very successful for them and helluva difficult to play against. I think when they got the early goal they underestimated the skill and the quality we had in the side. We had players, like wee Jimmy, who could destroy anybody. Stevie Chalmers, Bobby Lennox and Willie Wallace were persistent runners and sharp. Wee Bertie was a great passer of the ball; Murdoch could pass it, strike it, score, he could do the lot. Tommy Gemmell and Jim Craig could go up and down either side all day long. I don't think Inter expected the creativity that was there in our side and it bears testimony to how good they were that it took us so long to break them down. They also carried a helluva lot of luck because we struck the woodwork on so many occasions and missed a chance or two; 2–1 was not a real reflection of the game. It was a victory for progressive and open and entertaining stuff rather than the dull, secure, organised system that they used.

'Before the game they would probably have been dismissive of our claim on the European Cup. So they would have been arrogant about their own chances of winning the trophy. The Italians had taken over from the Spanish as top dogs in Europe and they were an excellent side with fabulous players.'

In the wake of Celtic's victory, some people, including individuals who were on the Celtic playing and coaching staff at the time, suggested that Inter were not quite as good as they had been when winning the European Cup in 1964 and 1965. It seems over-critical to suggest that the Inter side had gone into steep decline in two years. They had, after all, reached the 1967 final and had eliminated the holders, Real Madrid, in doing so. Inter's defeat in 1967 was not so much about their weaknesses as Celtic's strengths and ability on the day to hustle the Italians out of their stride and to claim sole rights to running the game. 'You can only play what is put in front of you,' is how Bobby Lennox sees it. 'Their record stands for itself. They possibly weren't as good as they had been a couple of years before, they possibly were – I couldn't answer that – but if they had beaten us 4–0, people wouldn't have said that about them. We played well on the day. It is true that Vojvodina were a harder team to beat, but that was over the two legs. Now whether Milan would have been a harder team to beat over two legs is another story.

'When that second goal went in they knew they were beaten but that doesn't take away from the great players that they had. You don't do what they did in the European Cup with bad players and a bad team. We played really well on the day. On the day I couldn't have told you who was who in their team. We were too busy playing the game. I couldn't tell you who played well or who played badly for them, but I know who played well for us, because Murdoch and Auld were never off the ball. John Clark was also great for us. A lot of people don't realise how much wee John Clark was on the ball.'

Perhaps the best testimony to Internazionale's quality is that no fewer than four of the Italians who took the field against Celtic – Giacinto Facchetti, Tarcisio Burgnich, Angelo Domenghini and Sandro Mazzola – would go on to represent Italy in the 1970 World Cup final against Brazil. Mazzola, Inter's goalscorer and 24 years old at the time of the European Cup final with Celtic, had had his best-ever season in terms of hitting the net in the 1966–67 season. Aristide Guarneri and Armando Picchi had looked rock-solid in the Inter central defence during their run to the final, especially in that victory over Real Madrid in the quarter-final. These were hardly players who were over the hill. Apologists for Inter would later point to the absences of Jair and Suarez as key factors in the defeat, but both of those players had been in patchy form all season; Inter had had all their best players on the park on 25 May but, on the day, they had not been good enough to resist Celtic's style and substance. Herrera, a football man to the last, admitted afterwards that Celtic were fully worthy victors. 'Celtic's victory was a victory for sport,' he stated gracefully.

At the end of the 90 minutes in Lisbon, the Celtic players found that their dressing-room was mobbed with people but that there was no sign of the European Cup. The pitch had been invaded by Celtic fans, delirious in the aftermath of victory, and the players had made a beeline for the dressing-room. It had been left to captain Billy McNeill to go solo up to the marble rostrum to receive the trophy. 'After about ten minutes in the dressing-room,' remembers Bobby Lennox, 'people were saying, "Where's the Cup? Where's Billy?" Then Billy came in with the Cup – he also came in with a shoe box and handed everybody their medal – we got on the coach and went into Lisbon and up to this lovely restaurant where the two teams were to eat together, but we had to wait for about an hour and a half for Milan coming because they were still in their dressing-room getting a hard time.'

It was a sour and surly bunch of Italians who eventually turned up at the post-match reception one and a half hours late. If they had planned to delay and disrupt the Celtic celebrations by their actions, then they succeeded to some degree. The evening proceedings at that reception proved a bit of an anti-climax for the Celtic players after the natural high of the match in the afternoon.

The Celtic players' wives and girlfriends had flown in for the game and afterwards had gone to a separate restaurant for a celebratory meal. They were scheduled to fly straight back to Glasgow afterwards, so the Celtic players decided to move on to their restaurant, found that they were in the middle of their meal, and joined them for a short while. 'Then the girls were going to the airport,' explains Bobby Lennox, 'so we joined them in going to the airport, which was the worst mistake ever, because there were thousands at the airport, and the girls got squashed. We got into a lounge and the girls' flight was late so we sat for ages there. Then they announced their flight so we had to fight back through the crowd and by the time we got back to the hotel it was about two in the morning. The bar in the hotel was shut and we had just got to our beds when big Jock chapped all the doors to say that the wives' flight had been held up and that they were coming back out from the airport. We sat up most of the night and the girls went away at about half past six in the morning. All of that meant that we never got a proper celebration at all that night.'

The following day, on their return to Glasgow Airport, the players were transported to a packed Celtic Park where an open-topped bus took them round the running track to display the great trophy to the support. Even in victory Jock Stein could not relax, could not cease being the boss, the organiser: the driver of the vehicle was subject to a constant stream of instructions from an animated, at times agitated, Stein. Afterwards, the players made their exits from the Janefield Street side of the ground, opposite the dressing-rooms and main stand, to avoid the waiting throng outside the main entrance to the ground. They sped off home in their cars and back to relative normality. Bobby Lennox, for one, cannot remember the couple of days afterwards to have been anything special in terms of being treated any differently by his fellow natives of Saltcoats. Lennox was due to get married in mid-June; Jimmy Johnstone had become a father in the week of the European Cup final. For all of those young men there was so much living to do that there was little time to sit and dwell on the magnitude of their achievement. Johnstone, Lennox and the other players had one more game to play and then just enough time to enjoy a break with their families before training was scheduled to begin in advance of the 1967–68 season.

'I think that because we were the first British team to win it, it has been remembered,' suggests Bobby Lennox. It is a typically modest statement from one of a magnificent group of players who remain modest about their talents and who were assembled by Stein using the most modest of means. Their task in the coming months and years would be to maintain the peak of perfection they had achieved and their new ranking among the aristocracy of the European game.

CHAPTER 5

A Roll of Honour
MILAN 1969

Celtic earned huge respect and admiration from the west to the east of Europe for winning the European Cup in such magnificent style. It meant that the team was now feared in all corners of the continent and in the years to come they would soon find that all means possible would be deployed to counter their renowned talents. It did not take long for the Celtic players to obtain their first experience of the type of underhand tactics that would be employed by clubs desperate to combat the abilities of the Lisbon Lions. Celtic's first tie after the European Cup win had them facing Dynamo Kiev in the opening round of the 1967–68 European Cup and some state-sponsored gamesmanship would be used by Kiev to try to destabilise their Scottish opponents.

The night before the second leg in Kiev, the Celtic party were kept from sleep by some Stakhanovite Soviet-state workmen digging up the road immediately outside their hotel. Bobby Lennox recalls: 'They were working outside all night. There's not much you can do about something like that. You've just got to get on with it. What should you do? Go out and get battered and not play the next day?'

The off-field tactics employed on behalf of the Soviet side failed to work. At Kiev's Central Stadium the following day, Celtic were at their determined best. The team had lost the first leg 2–1 but were convinced they had the ability to turn the tie in their favour. Their task looked tougher when Bobby Murdoch was dismissed by the Italian referee, Mr Antonio Sbardella, after an hour's play – for throwing the ball down in a fit of temper after one of numerous mysterious refereeing decisions had gone the way of Kiev. Celtic still maintained enough momentum to open the scoring through Bobby Lennox two minutes later.

Celtic's goalscorer that night remembers the tie well. 'We lost two early goals to them in Glasgow,' says Lennox, 'but we played them off the park in the second half at Celtic Park. We got a goal back and we could actually have gone on and won the game in Kiev because over there we played as well as we could play. Billy got a goal chalked off at the back post, which was unbelievable. As well as that, big Yogi raced through the middle, dribbled round the goalkeeper, put it in the net and the referee gave them a foul for dangerous play – for whatever reason.'

Those two disallowed goals kept Kiev level on aggregate at 2–2 but ahead on the away goals rule, which had been newly introduced to European competition at the beginning of that 1967–68 season. Celtic's fate was sealed in the final minute of the away leg when Dynamo Kiev centre-forward Anatoly Byshovets worked his way clear of the Celtic defence to poke the ball into the Celtic net and give Kiev a 3–2 aggregate win. It meant that Celtic became only the second European Cup holders to be knocked out of the competition in the opening round of the following season's tournament.

'It was one of those games where for ages after it I couldn't believe we were out because we didn't deserve to be out,' remembers Bobby Lennox. 'It was 1–1 over there when, in the last minute of the game, we got a corner-kick and everybody, but everybody, went into their box and their centre-forward was on the halfway line. The ball was cleared by them and the boy went right through on Ronnie on his own, with everybody chasing him. It was unimportant, that goal, because on the away goals rule we were out anyway. We played well in Kiev. We shouldn't have been out. I felt really dejected after that. If a team come and give you a doing there is not much you can do, but I thought we should have gone through after that game.'

Jimmy Johnstone is far more forthright about the goings-on in Kiev. 'The referee ruled out two goals and denied us a penalty kick. We beat them hands down over there; it was just that the referee was "got-at", definitely. That's a certainty. That was a wee bit of a let-down.' The defeat was a serious blow to the side. There was enormous pressure to win on the Celtic players of that time. The players were on a moderate weekly wage that would be topped up hugely by victories in European Cup ties and those bonuses would increase enormously with each round through which the team advanced. It meant that the players of the 1960s had to make sure the team remained in European competition to ensure they were well rewarded financially. 'You can't win everything every year,' says Tommy Gemmell, philosophically. 'In '67 we won everything. We won the five trophies that we played for and you can't top that, because there is nothing else left to play for. You've just got to keep pushing yourself and geeing yourself up and getting yourself going and motivating yourself.'

The early exit from Europe did allow Celtic to concentrate fully on winning an extremely tight 1967–68 Scottish League title race and gain entry to the 1968–69 European Cup. Once again, they found themselves presented with a difficult draw. Their opening-round opponents were to be St Etienne of France, a fast-moving, skilful side and, as with the previous season's encounter with Dynamo Kiev, it would prove both an eventful tie and one in which the losing side would feel strongly that there was something suspicious about the method of their elimination.

St Etienne were on a roll. They had won the French Double in 1967–68, giving them their third title in five years, and in the 1967–68 European Cup had lost only narrowly to Benfica, the eventual losing finalists. It meant that the Celtic players found their visit to industrial St Etienne far more testing than their previous trip to France and the coastal town of Nantes, where, two years earlier, the Celts had smoothed their way past their hosts. 'They gave us a hard time over there,' says Bobby Lennox of the match with St Etienne. 'They scored two goals quite early over there and after that I remember one of their boys being clean through and Billy making a great challenge on him to keep us in the game. Then they came to Glasgow and it was really tight up until injury time before half-time.'

French internationals Roby Herbin and Bernard Bosquier were part of that St Etienne side which held out robustly to keep the score at 0–0

until the verge of half-time at Celtic Park. Then Joe McBride fell to the
turf inside the St Etienne penalty area and events started moving
Celtic's way. 'We got a penalty kick just a minute before half-time at
Celtic Park,' says Tommy Gemmell, 'and I was the penalty kick taker at
that time. As I was putting the ball on the spot, the St Etienne players
were throwing clods of dirt at the ball and all that sort of stuff; delaying
tactics. So I was having to go up and take these clods away from the ball
and I said to myself, "You've really got to score this!"' Gemmell did his
usual from the penalty, whacking the ball straight into the middle of the
St Etienne goal with unstoppable power. 'That helped us a great deal,'
he continues, 'because it was a great time to score the goal.'

The French players lost their concentration in the wake of that goal
and began rubbing their fingers together in the faces of the referee and
of the Celtic players in the universal gesture that suggests a bit of
bribery has taken place. They were furious that all their good first-half
work had been undone by a penalty decision that they considered
incorrect. Bobby Lennox was fully aware of the importance of the
timing of that goal. 'We got the penalty kick,' he recalls, 'and it was a
completely different St Etienne team that came out in the second half.
The boys were great in the second half and St Etienne just seemed to
bottle it. In saying that, our boys hassled them and in those days Celtic
Park was a hard place to come and win. We got on top right on half-
time and their good players stopped playing.' The evening ended with
a scoreline 4–0 in Celtic's favour.

There would be less controversy surrounding Celtic's next European tie,
but it would be crammed with even more action and excitement. As in
the 1966–67 season, a meeting with the champions of France was
followed by one with the champions of Yugoslavia, in this instance Red
Star Belgrade. A third-minute goal from Bobby Murdoch got Celtic off
to a fine start in the first leg at Celtic Park but six minutes before half-
time Red Star, playing a powerfully precise passing game, equalised.
Once again, Stein would have to dig deep to deal with the situation,
and this time his half-time solution would show the depths of his
imagination and his masterful timing. As his players milled around in
the dressing-room, Stein took Jimmy Johnstone aside and made him an
offer the player could not refuse.

'I hated flying,' says Johnstone, 'because I had had a fright coming back from America in 1966 when the aircraft I was on fell out of the sky. It was horrific; it wasn't just a wee bit of turbulence. The stewardesses were serving meals to people two seats in front of us – I was flying back early from our tour with Ian Young because we were both being married – and without warning the whole plane fell out of the sky. All the food flew everywhere and there were children thrown into the air. You should have seen the mess in the plane after that. That was the reason I developed a fear of flying and, after that, I had told everyone how terrified I had become of flying.

'So, at half-time in the match with Red Star, and the score 1–1, Jock said to me, "If we win by four clear goals you won't need to fly to Belgrade." I said, "You're joking?" He said, "No, honest to God." So I went out and did the business. That was the spark. I hated flying that much and that was definitely what spurred me. I was everywhere looking for the ball. That was great psychology from Jock, wasn't it?' Only two minutes of the second half had passed when Johnstone pounced on a loose ball inside the box, tamed it with the sole of his boot and skelped a shot high into the Red Star net to put Celtic 2–1 ahead. Three minutes later, Johnstone wound his way deep into the Red Star penalty area and bypassed four Red Star defenders with a low cross, leaving Bobby Lennox with a simple sidefoot to put Celtic 3–1 up. 'I was saying, "What's that? Three? I'm still going for another two,"' says Johnstone. With 15 minutes remaining, Johnstone, again hovering on the edge of the Yugoslavs' penalty area, headed expertly into the path of Willie Wallace, ensuring that the ball sat up nicely for Wallace to swipe a low shot into the corner of the Red Star net to make it 4–1 to Celtic. Johnstone still needed to make sure Celtic got another goal if he was to maintain his part of his pact with Stein. Nine minutes were left when one masterful touch from Johnstone allowed him to duck and swoop past two wrongfooted Red Star defenders inside the Yugoslavs' penalty area and, unhesitatingly, he drilled a low shot into the Red Star net to make the final score 5–1 and ensure that he would not need to dig out his passport for the trip to Belgrade.

Johnstone had not restricted himself to seeking goals in that second half. 'He was magnificent that night,' says Tommy Gemmell. 'With two or three minutes to go, they had a corner-kick on the left-hand side and guess who cleared it with his head? Wee Jimmy! Six yards out, he was up thumping the ball clear with his head. I said, "What are you doing here?"'

The other players had been blissfully unaware of the reasons for Johnstone's supercharged second-half performance. 'Nobody knew about it,' says Bobby Lennox. 'When the fifth goal went in, he was running about shouting, "I'm not going, I'm not going!" Everybody thought, "What's he raving about here?" Then it all came out. What a man! He was great that night, although he was always great anyway.'

Stein rarely let any matter rest if he could extract a little bit more for himself and the club and, the following day, he came up with a clever ruse to try to get Johnstone to fly to Belgrade after all, as Johnstone recalls. 'Things had quietened down a bit and he said to me that the Red Star coach had said to him, "You've got to let the people of Belgrade see Jimmy Johnstone." This was him being cute again! We were 5–1 up and he is thinking we are going to get beaten! I said, "You've no chance!"' Stein tried everything to get Johnstone to travel, even telling the player that the British Embassy in London were requesting that the winger go to Belgrade to strengthen relations between Britain and Yugoslavia. He also told Johnstone that the player had had glowing write-ups in the Yugoslavian press and that there had been numerous telephone calls asking whether Johnstone was going to play in the second leg and that everybody wanted to see Johnstone perform in Yugoslavia. As the match drew closer, Stein tried another tack, telling Johnstone that there were a few players carrying knocks and that the winger would be required to help Celtic retain possession of the ball when under pressure in Yugoslavia. Johnstone was not having a bit of it. 'Before the second game,' the player says, 'I kept out of his road for about three days until they were all safely away!'

Stein relented – had he insisted on taking Johnstone with the team after the player's performance on the back of a promise, the manager might have found it close to impossible to regain the player's trust – but although the manager had dressed up his request for Johnstone to travel to Belgrade with a sugar coating, by appealing to Johnstone's pride as a footballer to show his talents to the people of Belgrade, there was a practical purpose behind Stein's plea. He was well aware that the tie was still far from over and that Celtic would have to travel to Belgrade carrying every ounce of talent that they could take through customs. 'When we got to Belgrade,' says John Hughes, 'all the photographers were there, saying, "Johnstone, where is he?" We said, "We've not brought him." I think they thought we had brought him in one of the hampers! They couldn't believe that we hadn't brought him and they were expecting him to appear at any moment. What other manager would have left his best player behind because he had promised him, "If we win by more than three you don't need to go"? I didn't think he wouldn't take him.'

Stein's apprehension about the return match proved to be justified. 'Red Star were a right good team as well,' says Bobby Lennox. 'Wee Jimmy beat them in Glasgow but when we went over there we got an absolute doing for about half an hour. That was as good a performance as any club put up against us. I'd have said that at 5–1 we were through, but what a roasting we got at the back in Belgrade. Billy and the rest of the boys were diving into tackles, blocking shots, heading the ball away. The boys at the back were great: they just kept them out. I think we scored 20 minutes into the second half – Willie Wallace hit a great shot. Then Red Star scored right on the final whistle. They took a short corner kick when everybody had turned their backs; it was a really stupid goal to give away but by then the game really was finished.'

That defensive performance in Belgrade was just one of Billy McNeill's many outstanding European nights for Celtic. As the cornerstone of the Celtic defence he was unbeatable in the air and an inspirational presence, a man who would encourage and cajole his fellow defenders to give of their very best. Few players in Celtic's history have gone about the business of playing for the jersey with such determination and desire to advance the club's cause. Nor was it only his defensive teammates that McNeill inspired. As captain, he ensured that everyone else in the team was encouraged by his example. 'I felt he was an inspiration to us,' says Bobby Lennox, 'because Billy was always available. Billy was rarely injured and you always looked to Billy to be there. We didn't have the biggest team in the world and any balls in the air, Billy dominated. I thought Billy was great. I love telling him that he was my hero when I was a youngster! I think we had a few guys on the pitch that would talk us through a game – Murdoch and Auld, big Tam, Billy; obviously as the

captain you would look to Billy, but there were a few of those guys
could tell you if you were doing things wrongly.'

The two ties with St Etienne and Red Star Belgrade had provided Celtic
with opposition of the highest calibre. The structure of the European
Cup in the 1960s, as with many of the best things in life, was based on
a simple and straightforward formula and one that gave the tournament
a marvellous aura of democracy. Every nation in Europe, large and
small, was allowed only one representative in the tournament and each
club was the one that had been champions of their country in the
previous season. The only exception to the rule was that the holders of
the European Cup were given automatic entry to the tournament even
if they had not won their country's league competition the previous
season. A lack of seeding meant that, on occasion, the luck of the draw
could mean that two of the most highly rated teams in the tournament
could be paired in the opening rounds, whilst minnows could wriggle
freely into the quarter-finals.

Celtic faced just such a situation in the 1968–69 competition. St
Etienne and Red Star Belgrade were teams of the highest quality and of
the type that could normally be expected to be encountered only in the
latter stages of the tournament. So, as Celtic prepared for the draw for
the quarter-finals, they were entitled to hope that it would deal with
them kindly and offer the team a less taxing route from there into the
semi-finals. Instead, they were given the hardest task possible: a tie
against Milan, champions of Italy. The only bonus for Celtic was that
the first leg would take place away from home. As an attacking side,
Celtic always preferred to be away from home first. They would then
return to Celtic Park knowing exactly what was required to win the tie
in the second leg and, with one of Europe's most partisan crowds
behind them, would be confident of getting as many goals as needed to
see them through. Celtic went to northern Italy in late February 1969
determined to return home with a result that would make their task in
the second leg as simple as possible and, once again, Celtic found
themselves having to counter some underhand methods in their quest
to reach a second European Cup final.

'We went to the stadium the night before the game,' remembers
Bobby Lennox. 'The bus driver, an Italian, took us there, dropped us

off and went away and we found we couldn't get into the ground. We footered about and finally got in to have a look at the stadium. Then we went out again and the bus never came back for ages and ages. The boys were going to kill the driver. I think it was a wee plan on their part. When we had got into the ground we had found that the pitch was just a sheet of white; it had been snowing heavily. The stadium looked huge that night with all the snow on it. On the night of the match it was also snowing, during the game, and they just kept clearing the lines. We played well over there.'

The Celtic team that took to the turf in front of 80,000 fanatics at the San Siro, Milan, was: John Fallon, Jim Craig, Tommy Gemmell, John Clark, Billy McNeill, Jim Brogan, Jimmy Johnstone, Bobby Murdoch, Bobby Lennox, Willie Wallace and John Hughes. Stein had employed one of his favourite tactics of adding a defensive-minded player – in this instance Brogan – to the midfield so when Milan were on the attack they would be confronted by three defenders across the middle plus the two full-backs. John Hughes, the outside-left, was fielded in a withdrawn role to patrol the midfield. Stein's team emerged from the San Siro with a hugely creditable 0–0 draw and, with such a good result to work with, the supporters prepared for victory in the return at Celtic Park three weeks later. Some even went so far as to book flights to Madrid for the final. 'We were the first British team to get a result in the San Siro,' says John Hughes. 'I remember I had been injured and I had been out for six weeks and Jock Stein came to me before the game and told me he needed me to do a job for him in the middle of the park. I said, "Boss, I've not played for six weeks and the job you are asking me to do involves a lot of running." He said, "I think you can do it." He was great at that; at putting his arm round you, telling you that you were his best player, and making you feel that you were important to him and to the team and because of that he made me believe I could go out and do it. That was his forte, not coaching. On the night I played well, even though I should not have been playing and even though I was playing in a position, wide right, to which I was not accustomed.'

Stein had hoped to field the same 11 in the return match, but was forced to replace the injured Bobby Lennox with Stevie Chalmers. After only 11 minutes Jim Craig's throw-in to Billy McNeill put the captain

in trouble and, as McNeill tried to deal with the ball, Milan striker
Pierino Prati eked it out of McNeill's feet with surgical precision and
then went streaking towards goal with the speed of a high-performance
Italian sports car. John Fallon, a replacement for the injured Ronnie
Simpson, had distinguished himself in the match in Milan, making
numerous fine saves, but as Prati bore down on him at Celtic Park he
had little chance of defying the Milan man. Italian strikers are trained
to seize ruthlessly on every rare chance that comes their way in their
defensively disciplined domestic game where, unlike in Britain, a striker
might only see the ball once or twice in a match. Prati made the most
of his opportunity and motored smoothly goalwards, with desperate
Celtic defenders in his slipstream, before despatching the ball into the
Celtic net.

The Italians had been consuming champagne at the Marine Hotel in
Troon on the previous evening, but that had been no premature
celebration. They had simply been cooking their rice in champagne, the
Italian way, to aid their digestion. Now the celebratory champagne
really was put on ice back in Milan; as with neighbours Inter, Milan
were expert at defending a lead. On going ahead, the Italians
concentrated their resources even further on defence, especially as,
under the away goals rule, Celtic needed to score twice to survive. 'We
should have beaten them that night,' says John Hughes. 'We
pummelled them. I was being marked by Karl-Heinz Schnellinger, the
German international, and I remember getting a ball inside the box. It
came to me and I just turned and hit it and it went just past the post.
There were a lot of occasions that night when we got close to a goal.
Apart from their goal, Milan were never in the game. They were still
hard to play against because of their man-marking. They are always
niggling at you and they are dirty, pulling your jersey.'

It was a deeply disappointed Tommy Gemmell who left the pitch
that evening. 'That was a disaster because we had played so well in
Milan and had given as good as we got over there,' he says, 'and, apart
from that error that led to the goal by Prati, they hadn't created any
chances at Celtic Park. Still, you've got to take into account whom you
are playing against and they were a right good side, with Rivera and
Prati and all their other internationalists. Prati had a deadly left peg.'

Bobby Lennox had failed a fitness test shortly before the game and he had a frustrating evening watching events unfold from the stand in Glasgow. 'At that time,' he says, 'Celtic could hold their own against Inter, Milan and Madrid; all those teams. It was always the case that one thing could happen to win the game or lose the game and we lost a bad goal. That happens and that was the only difference between the two teams. There was always a way back for our team and we had our chances that night but the luck just wasn't with us. They went on and won the European Cup, easily, I think, 4–1 against Ajax. So we weren't that far away again.'

It had been a mixed campaign; the progress past pedigree teams, in St Etienne and Red Star Belgrade, to the quarter-finals had made for a journey in first-class style and such achievements seemed due a greater reward than an exit at the quarter-final stage. Defeat to a great Milan team was no disgrace, but the feeling stlll lingered that Celtic could, and should, have beaten them. There would be no such ambivalence about the following season's events in the European Cup as Celtic would find themselves fully rewarded for some fantastic feats by getting within touching distance of the great gleaming trophy yet again.

SIX

The Final Blow
FEYENOORD 1970

Players slid across the marble floor as a street-type scuffle erupted in the grand foyer of the Stadium of Light minutes after Benfica's 1969–70 European Cup tie with Celtic. The brawl inside the Portuguese club's ostentatious atrium took place in front of an ornate backdrop of cabinets filled with trophies and mementos of famous Benfica victories and it was none other than the great Eusebio, Portugal's finest player, who found himself at the centre of events as players from the two teams collided in the aftermath of the match. Minutes earlier, Benfica and Celtic had concluded their second-round tie by drawing 3–3 on aggregate with no away goals having been scored by either side – each having won 3–0 at home. By that 1969–70 season UEFA had abandoned its system of using a play-off on a neutral ground to obtain a winner after a tie had ended level. Now, the geniuses at UEFA headquarters in Switzerland had decided to replace the play-off system with the toss of a coin to determine the winners of any match that had become deadlocked after two legs.

It meant that in Lisbon, coaches and management from the two teams, plus keyed-up, adrenaline-charged players, with their strips soaked with sweat, crowded round Dutch referee Louis van Raavens and team captains Billy McNeill and Mario Coluna as this most unsatisfactory means of arbitration took place. 'We went to watch the toss of the coin,' says John Hughes. 'So we were all gathered around trying to see big Billy and watch what was going on and there was shoving and pushing and that Eusebio was shoving so I grabbed him and said, "Who are you pushing?" Next thing, I turned round and his bodyguard was looming over me.' Studs scraped across the slippery floor as players from these two great clubs clashed, but once things settled down again, all eyes returned to the two team captains and the referee.

'We had beaten them easily over here at Celtic Park: 3–0,' adds Hughes, 'and we went to Lisbon. At the kick-off, the ball was touched to Eusebio, he took one step forward, and he hit the bar! They gave us an absolute roasting, I had never been as tired in all my life, and it was 2–0 to them with a couple of minutes to go when one of their guys was away out wide on the left, going nowhere, and Jim Brogan whacked him; free kick to them and from it they made it 3–3. What a roasting they gave us! You know what these guys are like when they get going; it's bad enough feeling knackered when you are playing well and are on top but it's worse when you don't have the ball and you're chasing and you never get a touch. Benfica were brilliant that night, they really were; it was as if two different teams had played in each leg, but they are like that, these guys. At Celtic Park they had been rubbish. We were knackered at the end of the 90 minutes – for us it had been just chase, chase, chase – and we really did not want to play the 30 minutes of extra-time. I can remember Jock Stein geeing us up for the extra-time and I thought we would never make it, but we did it and we survived. I don't know how we survived because they absolutely destroyed us. Sometimes that's the way it works.'

The 3–3 aggregate meant that the Dutch referee Louis van Raavens had to produce once again the two-and-a-half guilder piece that he had used at the beginning of the game when the two captains had come together before kick-off. Now, after extra-time, and with the spectators drifting away from the towering terraces of the Stadium of Light, Van Raavens had made his way deep inside the great Lisbon ground, where he brought the two team captains together again and used the same coin to decide which of the two clubs would now proceed into the quarter-finals of the 1969–70 European Cup. As Van Raavens' coin went spinning into the air, the Celtic captain, Billy McNeill, was a nervous man. 'I didn't think we would carry the luck in that toss because it was the second one I had faced. The first thing the referee had asked us to do was to call to see who would spin the coin. I called heads and won that one. When I then span the coin I couldn't believe that I would win again but I did, and it was the greatest relief of my life.'

Eusebio and his teammates had been twice-winners of the European Cup and had lost in the final three times during the 1960s but they knew that their tremendous team could not go on forever and that they might not have too many more tilts at winning the great trophy. Celtic had pipped them in what they saw as the most unsatisfactory manner possible and Benfica's best did not like it one bit. Celtic would now push onwards to the European Cup quarter-finals whilst Benfica would go back to the routine of their domestic league. 'Yogi had a run-in with Eusebio's bouncers that night,' remembers Evan Williams, a goalkeeper who had signed for Celtic shortly before that tie. 'He got the boy, pulled him aside and threw him outside. They didn't take it too well – getting beaten on the toss of a coin – and there was a wee bit of a stramash in the players' foyer. There wasn't a fight or anything; just some pushing and shoving. Big Yogi was a strong, big lad.'

Tommy Gemmell is ambivalent about the means by which Celtic had progressed past Benfica. 'We went through on the toss of the coin,' he says, 'which ain't a way to get through in a European Cup tie. We had a wee bit of luck with us there in as much as that we got through that, although it should never have happened; we were very careless at the back and gave away silly goals. In the second leg in Lisbon Eusebio was carrying an injury and he played with a great big piece of strapping on his thigh. He played for about an hour. He scored a great goal and after about an hour he went off; he was substituted.'

A tough, two-legged tussle with Basle had preceded the tie with Benfica, the first leg of which had featured a thunderous strike from 25 yards from Gemmell. 'It came at the right time as well,' says Gemmell. 'It was only about a minute and a half into the game and we got a free kick about 25 yards out. Bertie just touched it to the side and I knocked it into the postage stamp. I'd been left out of the team after I got sent off playing for Scotland against West Germany in a World Cup qualifier and Benfica was my second game back after big Jock had left me out. I had actually

asked for a transfer in between times because of that. It was bittersweet to
score in that first minute and a half and big Jock would have understood
fully what my actions meant when I made certain signs at the dugout; as
if to say, "Up yours" or "That'll put your gas at a peep."'

Celtic's chain of challenging European Cup matches continued after
the tie with Benfica when they were drawn against Italian opposition in
the quarter-finals for the second successive season. This time Fiorentina
would provide the opposition. Celtic's build-up to that match would be
identical to that for all of the club's major matches in the Stein years.
'For big games he would have his team talk at Seamill,' explains Bobby
Lennox. 'If he had a settled team he would bring us into a room at the
Hydro and say, "Same team as last week." Then we would go to
Glasgow and the team would go into the dressing-room and we would
start getting organised. Jock would keep away from the players a bit. I
think he did not want to keep being in the dressing-room on top of
people. He would come in and make sure everything was all right and
then he would go away out of the dressing-room and then he would
come back in before the kick-off and offer a wee reminder here and a
wee reminder there; a few words here and a few words there. He wasn't
in your face in the dressing-room all the time.'

Evan Williams experienced his first European Cup tie for Celtic
when he played in both legs of the match with Fiorentina in March of
1970. The first leg was at Celtic Park. 'It was quite a cold night that
night and the ground was quite bumpy and hard,' says Williams. 'The
thing I always remember about that time, when playing with Celtic in
the European Cup, is that the players were so confident in their own
ability; not cocky but confident. They gave you confidence with the
way that they played. Everybody wanted the ball and that helped me
out, as a goalkeeper. I think I only had one or two saves on the night of
that first leg against Fiorentina at Celtic Park, but we played very, very
well that night and scored two late goals to make it 3–0. There were
always huge crowds for those European Cup games. In those days you
were talking, say, of a crowd given as 75,000. That was the attendance
that would be revealed officially, but I think there were more than
75,000 people at those games.

'Celtic didn't fear anybody in those days. It was a strange feeling,
whereas when I played with Wolves the players would say, "Oh, we're

playing Manchester City this week and then Everton next week."' The Wolves players would be worrying about those games, filled with fear as to how they were going to cope against those teams, who were among the best in England during the late 1960s and early 1970s. 'With Celtic,' continues Williams, 'you had that feeling that even if you went a goal down, the team would always get one or two back. It was a joy to play in that team – they were all such good guys to get on with; there was no bigheadedness. They worked as a team, they argued as a team, they fought as a team. Everything was done together. We also had a bunch of really competitive guys at the club: we used to play five-a-sides after training and they would be played like the World Cup final. Even those little games were taken seriously. You used to get the yellow jersey if you were the worst player in those games. Teams do that nowadays, but Celtic used to do that way back in the '60s.

'My favourite player was Bobby Murdoch. I think he was unbelievable. He did everything properly. I always said about him that he couldn't run and he couldn't jump but by God he could play football. He must have been the best passer of a ball ever to play in the British Isles. He could pass with either foot too, first time, none of this stopping it and caressing it – when the pass was on he made it right away. Jimmy Johnstone and Bobby Lennox were other great players, Tommy Gemmell was a great left-back, but I think the whole team at that time was great.

'An unsung hero was John Clark. John didn't play much longer at Celtic after I had joined the club but he had been part of all the great teams in the years before I arrived. I don't think people realised how great a player John Clark was; his reading of the game was unbelievable. He just did everything so simply: he never got caught on the ball, he marked up properly and he was very, very skilful. He wasn't as flamboyant as Tommy or Bertie Auld or Bobby Lennox – everything they did was always a wee bit special. John just did his job and did it properly. Willie Wallace was another player whom I don't think was recognised as much as he should have been, but they were all great players. Bobby Lennox was unbelievably quick, with very, very good skill. You wouldn't like to play against him every week; you'd end up with your tongue hanging away down to your ankles. Apart from their ability on the park, they were all characters.

'I signed from Wolves and was accepted within minutes. They made you feel welcome. Jock created a family atmosphere at the club, but he was also the boss. There was no arguing with him; what he said went. With other managers you could give a spiel about what you thought, but big Stein would just say to you, "No, you do it my way" and that was it finished with. I think Stein must have been one of the first ones to be like that. I never heard him shouting or bawling much. He would talk to you quietly about a lot of things rather than shout and bawl. Obviously he had his moments, but not many. He was a very, very astute man.'

This tightly bonded group of players travelled to Florence for the return with Fiorentina desperate not to repeat the mistake of the previous round, when they had seen their three-goal lead over Benfica dissolve in front of their eyes. It was to be a memorable trip, not least for some attempted Fiorentina gamesmanship, pre-match, that Bobby Lennox recalls as being laughably obvious. 'When we were playing in Florence,' he says, 'we went up to the stadium on the night before the game to see the lights. They had four big poles with lights on them and they would switch one light on, then it would start to go off and the next light would go on. Then it would start going off and the next one would go on. So they were showing us the lights but they were not allowing us to see all four of the floodlights on together, the way it would be on the night of the match! The great thing about becoming more experienced in Europe was that things like that didn't bother you.'

Williams was introduced to the mania that surrounded Jimmy Johnstone when the team went for a stroll around the *palazzos* of central Florence during their visit to that historical city. 'When we went abroad,' says Williams, 'we always went out together for a walk and a wander. The banter and the patter were unbelievable and it kept you going when you were on a foreign trip with Celtic. I always remember, from when we were in Italy for the Fiorentina game, going into the town centre to the market. We always got two or three hours free to go and buy presents and so on and all the people in the city were following Jimmy Johnstone about. He was like a god. He was world-famous then and he was so distinctive, being small with the red hair, and people were following him all over the place. It was as if somebody had come down from heaven and had appeared in Florence. That always stuck out in my mind about Jimmy; I will always remember in that market the kids being all round about him. Everywhere he went when he was abroad they always came to him. I think they called him the "Flying Flea".

'Being abroad with Celtic was always very, very low-key, with Stein. He obviously thought out everything in terms of what to do in terms of the training and the rest periods – he always put us to bed in the afternoon. We used to go over to the city where we were playing on a Monday morning and we used to go to bed in the afternoon. Then we would come out from the hotel and have a wee walk or a wee five-a-side, have our tea, another walk, then, at half-nine, bed again. You weren't allowed out much. I don't think the big man ever slept, because every time you went out of your room he would be sitting in the corridor. You couldn't get moving. Obviously, we used to sit and play cards, have a little bit of banter and watch the TV but mostly it would just be blethering and sitting in the gardens of the hotel. It was very low-key but with that crowd it was never boring. With the Lisbon Lions and that crowd of players that came into the team, like Davie Hay, things never became dull because the patter was unbelievable. It was non-stop all the time. If you did anything wrong you got roasted alive, you got hammered.

'Jock Stein was a great man for having us go out on walks; Jock didn't go but Neilly Mochan took us for walks all the time. Also, when we were abroad, everyone used to end up in Jimmy Steele's room for a massage. We would all go there for a massage and because the boss wasn't about you could sit in Jimmy's room and have a bit of patter without Jock being there. You don't say things in front of the boss sometimes. Then big Stein would end up coming along. He would walk along and find 20 players in Jimmy's bedroom for a massage all at the one time. Sometimes we used to fly back after the game and sometimes we stayed overnight, but if we were staying overnight we weren't allowed out late. If you did go out late you were in trouble – there were not any in-betweens with big Stein.'

Celtic were in control for most of the return match with Fiorentina and although they had to sit back and sit on the lead, they never felt under severe pressure. The string of strong opponents that they had faced in the previous four years of European Cup ties had toughened up the team to the point where they were now able to adapt to the circumstances of any given game. At one point late in the match, with Fiorentina 1–0 ahead on the night, the Italian side were awarded an indirect free kick outside the box and outside-left Amarildo curled it into the top corner and ran away roaring in celebration and looking for acclaim from the crowd. His teammate Giancarlo 'Picchio' De Sisti, a magnificent player who would play in the World Cup final later in 1970, looked at Bobby Lennox and said, 'He's a crazy man.'

Celtic goalkeeper Williams remembers that incident well. 'In the away game with Fiorentina I had more to do,' he remembers. 'They had already scored to put them 1–0 up when, later in the match, they got a free kick outside the box and Amarildo took it and bent it round the wall. The ball came straight towards me and I jumped out of the road and it went into the net. Stein came out of the dugout and round towards me and went off his head but the referee had had his hand up to indicate it was an indirect free kick. I could see the ball swirling as it came towards me and I thought that if I touched the ball and it hit me and went into the net it would be a goal. So I got out of the road of it. We were given a goal kick and the referee came over to me and praised me for knowing the rules of the game. It was also OK with Stein when he realised that I had used my head rather than trying to go and save the ball. That will always be my main recollection of the match away to Fiorentina because I think the second half was live on TV over here and the family were saying, "What did you do that for?" And when I told them why I had got myself out of the way of the ball they looked at me as if I was daft to have had the nerve to do that.'

Once again, a European Cup draw proved unbending, dealing the Glasgow side the hardest task possible in the semi-final, with a meeting against Leeds United, champions of England and the dominant club in English football from the late 1960s to the mid-1970s. The Leeds manager Don Revie instilled an arrogance in his players and he himself could be forthright in his opinions. Back in 1965, he had stated unequivocally that Scottish football would be 'dead' in five years' time – Revie was typical of a certain type of Englishman who make themselves feel better by having a random swipe at the standard of football north of the border in comparison to its counterpart in the south. It seemed appropriate that exactly five years after his prognosis he would now have the opportunity to discover the accuracy of his cheap prediction as Celtic travelled to Yorkshire for the first leg.

'Jock Stein talked about the Leeds match for the whole four days before it; how we were going to play,' says Evan Williams. 'We didn't change ourselves much but he explained what they were going to do; how Leeds United played. He had always done his homework on his opponents but I always remember he would say, "We will worry about the way we play; not the way they play. If we're playing well, we'll do well."

'With the Leeds United game, I think it was not so much the result but the way we played in both games that showed how good that Celtic team was. Down at Elland Road, they weren't in the game and we could have won by three or four that night. I don't think they got a kick of the ball. The English press had written us off before we went down there. I think that, even with the Scottish press, Leeds were favourites and I couldn't really understand that. Celtic had won the European Cup three years before and here they were in a semi-final again and had for five or six years frequently been in European semi-finals or quarter-finals. Leeds United had never reached the same pinnacle as Celtic in Europe. They had a lot of great players but the way we played against them opened everybody's eyes down south as to how good we were. I used to go back to Wolverhampton and some of the players came down to Elland Road to watch the game. I had often told them how good Celtic were and when they watched them live they said, "You're right enough, they are some side when they are on song."'

The press in England, determined to put the Scottish upstarts in their place, had been almost hysterical in talking up Leeds' chances of winning the game. This was something Stein used. 'Leeds were being hyped up by the English press to be unbeatable,' says John Hughes. 'There was no messing about with them. It was "Leeds will win 4–0"; there was no 1–0. We were turning up just for the sake of making a game of it and Leeds were going to wipe the floor with us. Jock used all that. He came in on the morning of the game and brought all the papers in, saying, "What about them, eh? What about them?"'

Only one minute had passed at Elland Road before Celtic put together a decisive move. George Connelly shot from the edge of the

Leeds penalty area and the ball nicked off a Leeds defender before spinning into the net. Connelly had a second goal disallowed, questionably, but Celtic, on the night, were the dominant side and 1–0 was a lot less than their efforts deserved. 'The Leeds game was a great thing,' says Evan Williams. 'I always remember that when we came back to Glasgow Central, the station was packed with about 20,000 people to greet us coming off the train. We couldn't believe all these people cheering because we had beaten Leeds. There was a line of police to get us from the train to the team bus. I think we had had an idea that there would be a few people there but I don't think they expected anything like the crowd that actually did turn up to greet us.'

Four days prior to the return with Leeds United, Celtic faced Aberdeen in the Scottish Cup final at Hampden Park. It proved a highly contentious match after three poor decisions by referee Bobby Davidson gave the Dons a massive advantage in the first half of that final. He awarded Aberdeen a penalty for handball even although the ball had clearly not struck supposed offender Bobby Murdoch on his arm. The resultant goal put Aberdeen 1–0 ahead and Celtic were subsequently denied a goal and a penalty by Davidson when they fully deserved to get both. Jock Stein, who would normally keep his own counsel with regard to refereeing decisions, exploded in anger at the end of the match, which Aberdeen went on to win 3–1. Despite the circumstances of the defeat and a lingering feeling of injustice, that reversal did not leave the Celtic players in low spirits as they prepared for their momentous meeting with Leeds in Glasgow.

'The Celtic team then never got down,' explains Evan Williams. 'I always thought they were more determined to do better the next time to prove to people that they were the best. They seemed to have an inbuilt feeling that they had to prove themselves and they always seemed to raise the crowd. They just seemed to keep going and going and going until all of a sudden things started to click – and when they did click with Celtic in those days there weren't many teams in the world that would stay with them when they were right on top of their form.'

A more practical worry for Stein and the team was an injury to Billy McNeill that left the centre-half doubtful for the return with Leeds right up until kick-off. It was vital for McNeill to be fit, as Leeds would have to try to exert sustained pressure on the Celtic defence to attempt to get back into the game. 'I can remember Billy being in and out of the water at Seamill with his ankle in the days before the Leeds match, but he made it OK,' recalls Evan Williams. 'I think you'd have needed to have dragged Billy away for him not to have made it.

'Another one of Jock Stein's things was that, when it came to defending, his teams never defended back in the box: they defended in the middle of the park to stop the opposition coming into the box. That worked against Leeds because they were one of those teams that played diagonal cross-balls up to the two strikers – Jones and Clarke – in the air. Big Billy just ate everything up. Leeds played everything up to those two and on both nights they never got a touch. At Hampden, Leeds were in the game for a short period but as the game went on, Celtic were more and more in control.'

The return with Leeds had been fixed for Hampden Park because Celtic Park was, at the time of that match, undergoing extensive improvements to the east terracing, at a cost of £100,000. Rather than play on their home ground in front of a drastically reduced crowd, the Celtic board decided to move the match to the national stadium. Demand for tickets was such that the public sale at Celtic Park resulted in every available ticket being snaffled up within two hours. The attendance on the night at Hampden was 136,505, which surpassed the previous highest attendance for a match in European competition, the 135,000 crowd that had attended the Bernabeu Stadium, Madrid, for Real Madrid's 1957 European Cup semi-final with Manchester United.

Less than quarter of an hour of the match with Leeds United had been played when Celtic were knocked out of their stride. The Leeds captain, Billy Bremner, a Celtic supporter as a boy in Stirling, picked up the ball in midfield, moved forward and then put everything he had into a shot from 35 yards that went swirling into the top corner of the Celtic net. 'I'm still looking for it,' laughs Evan Williams, as he remembers a goal that he could do little to prevent. 'Big Stein said to me at half-time, "What were you doing there?" I said, "Boss, I never saw it." I literally didn't because it came through quite a few players and it twisted and turned in the wind because there was a bit of a gale blowing in that first half. I never saw the ball. I don't think Billy ever scored another goal like that in his life, God rest him.

'After that goal, I think we went through a flat period. I'm not saying that Leeds were dominating the game but I remember Stein saying at half-time, "Look, we're beginning to play. Keep going and things will happen." I think Leeds had their centre-forwards crossing over and the crosses were coming in from Gray and Lorimer. That was the only consistent threat they had and, again, as I say, that night big Billy had a great game. Eventually we started knocking it about and playing and Bertie Auld started giving wee Bremner a lot of problems whilst Murdoch wasn't giving Johnny Giles a minute. We ended up with Bremner and Giles running after Murdoch and Auld rather than, as the English press had said, their midfield dominating. When Auld and Murdoch played well they were two great, great players.'

Stein's half-time prediction was soon fulfilled. Two minutes after the break, Bertie Auld sent a cute cross curling into the Leeds six-yard box and John Hughes nipped in front of Leeds centre-half Jack Charlton and launched himself, full-length, at the ball to head the equaliser. Five minutes further into the half, Bobby Murdoch drove forward and passed to Jimmy Johnstone on the right wing. The outside-right steadied himself and drew the Leeds defenders Terry Cooper and Norman Hunter to him. That opened up space in front of their goal and when Johnstone returned the ball to Murdoch the opportunity had opened up for him to power a shot on goal. David Harvey, the Leeds substitute goalkeeper, appeared to be unsighted by Jack Charlton as Murdoch hit the ball and the ball was very close to the goalkeeper's body as it flew under him and over the line.

After the match a friend of Evan Williams, a priest, collected him from Hampden to give him a lift home – Williams was one of several Celtic players of the time not to have a car. En route, they dropped in to a chapel house in Shettleston. 'There were a load of priests there and the highlights of the game were on TV,' says Williams. 'The priest who was giving me a lift said, "Come on and we'll watch it on TV before I take you down the road." In those days not everybody had a car – if you had a car in those days you had money. There were a number of priests all sitting in front of this television. They didn't know who I was and the priest I was with said, "What about the goalkeeper tonight?" One or two priests said, "He did all right tonight." Then another one piped up, "I'm not convinced yet." So my friend said to him, "Oh, by the way, I'd like to introduce you to Evan Williams."'

Jimmy Johnstone relished the victory. 'The English press had had Leeds down as the greatest team ever,' he says. 'Of the four semi-finalists Leeds had been the one we didn't want; we thought we could maybe beat them in a one-off game but not over two legs. I tore Terry Cooper apart; his cartilages went that night, I think! I must hand it to Terry that he didn't kick me once; good players don't resort to that. He had actually started off as a left-winger, Terry Cooper. He was a great player and a gentleman. I appreciated that. I said to him afterwards, "Terry, that was great: I gave you a roasting and you never kicked me once!"'

Jock Stein had shown the utmost respect for Leeds United. In his programme notes for the return with the English team at Hampden Park he had described them as 'a club that represents the might of England' and had written that he expected an 'epic struggle' and that 'the better the opposition the higher Celtic can raise their game'. He had then allowed himself a brief look towards the final itself, 'Tonight San Siro is our goal – San Siro and a second European Cup victory for tonight the victors must indeed be favourites for that honour.' Those words certainly suggested strongly that Stein thought that the match between Celtic and Leeds was the final before the final. 'I think when we beat Leeds he thought we had won it,' says John Hughes. 'His whole attitude to the final gave us the impression that we just had to turn up and win. Milan had beaten Ajax 4–1 in the final the previous year and he told us that half of the Ajax team had collapsed with nerves in the dressing-room before the match. He told us that Feyenoord would be the same when we played them in the final.'

Stein and his players may well have felt, during the fortnight after the match with Leeds, that the hardest work in that season's European Cup had been completed, but on arrival in Italy prior to the final at the San Siro stadium, Milan, the manager was keen to try to bring everyone back down to earth. 'Feyenoord are more or less in the same position as we were in 1967,' he said at Celtic's hotel at Varese, close to Lake Como, two days before the final. 'We were the underdogs then, with nothing to lose. If we had not won, no one would have worried too much. While we are confident of winning, I cannot agree with the current impression that Celtic cannot be beaten. As far as I am concerned, it is certainly a problem and not an attitude I fancy at all. The occasion should bring out the best in our team. They won't be professionals if they are caught out by all this talk at this stage and I will be driving the point home to them in our discussions after training tomorrow.'

The Celtic team for the final was: Evan Williams, David Hay, Tommy Gemmell, Bobby Murdoch, Billy McNeill, Jim Brogan, Jimmy Johnstone, Bobby Lennox, Willie Wallace, Bertie Auld and John Hughes. 'I don't think Stein underestimated them,' is the opinion of Evan Williams, 'and we, as players, were keyed up. I never really was the nervous type but I was a bit nervous before the European Cup final. Once you are on the park, though, you have just got to concentrate. In training in the three or four days in Milan before the final, at Lake Como, where we were based, there was a buzz among the players. You could feel the atmosphere building up. When we went on to the bus and had our sing-song going as normal when we were going to finals, you could feel it and the atmosphere among the players going into the stadium had been very good.'

It did not take Feyenoord long to let it be known that they were in Milan on business. Celtic goalkeeper Williams was presented with prima facie evidence that the Dutch were no soft touch. 'I had a save in the first few minutes up in the top right-hand corner from Van Hanegem,' he explains. 'They played it about and he volleyed it from about 25 yards and the ball was going at quite a speed from the moment he hit it. I caught the ball but it had me saying to myself, "By God, this team's not here to mess about." Even the way he hit the shot told you something about them – it took an awkward bounce but he still made sure he hit it properly and he made sure it was on target. They were like that all night.'

The Italian Concetto Lo Bello had been the referee in Celtic's match against Benfica at Celtic Park and he was also given charge of the final in his homeland. As the Celtic and Feyenoord teams had lined up in the tunnel before the 1970 final, Bertie Auld had introduced a light-hearted moment by immediately nicknaming the Italian referee 'Cesar Romero' after the handsome Latin-American who had become a Hollywood matinee idol after a previous existence as a dancer. After half an hour Lo Bello awarded Celtic a free kick a yard outside the

Feyenoord penalty area and almost directly in front of goal. Bobby Murdoch took the kick but instead of moving it forward he used a natty back-heel to nudge the ball into the path of Tommy Gemmell. The left-back came thundering towards the ball like an express train and pounded a shot goalwards. The ball eluded the Feyenoord defensive wall but as it did, Lo Bello went dancing, Romero-like, across the penalty area and directly across the line of vision of Feyenoord goalkeeper Eddy Pieters Graafland. Gemmell's shot went whistling close to the keeper's body and into the net.

'I would say that when we scored they were just about ahead of us on the balance of the play,' states Evan Williams, 'but when Tommy got the goal for us after half an hour I thought, "Here we go; that's us on top." Then, as the game went on, they started to create chances and to open us up a wee bit, which was at that time quite frightening in the sense that Celtic never really had that against them because teams didn't really open them up. It wasn't just in midfield either where they were opening us up; it was all over the park.'

Celtic found it difficult to cope with Feyenoord's typically Dutch style of play. Their players were masters of maintaining possession of the ball but that was not unique to Feyenoord – all of the top-class continental teams whom Celtic had encountered had shared that characteristic. The difference in Feyenoord's style was that the ball was always on the move even when they were holding on to it. Players did not dwell on the ball or hold on to it for several touches. Instead, the ball would be continuously shuttling from one player to another. That meant that the Celtic players had to work extra-hard and do a considerable amount of chasing of the ball to try to regain possession; a tiring task.

The early goal advantage did not last long. Within two minutes, Feyenoord had equalised when a looping header from their centre-half Rinus Israel described an arc across the Celtic six-yard box and landed inside Williams' back post. There was little the goalkeeper could do about it and, as it transpired, Williams would go on to be Celtic's premier performer on the night, making a series of superlative saves to defy Feyenoord as the Dutch team's grip on the game grew ever stronger.

Evan Williams remembers that Feyenoord goal well. 'It was a long cross to the far post, but it went beyond the far post,' he says. 'I have an inbuilt thing about this that I'm not going to blame any players. I know that some people say that certain players did this and that but I have got so much time for those guys that I would never decry anybody or even suggest anything, but one of our players headed it back when it was going out and the Feyenoord guy headed it back across me when I had come over to that far post.

'I think we got caught on the hop that night because people didn't realise how good a side the Dutch were. They were a great side. They had some great players. I don't think we had that much of the ball that night. They held possession of the ball more. They didn't go forward too much to start with; they just probed away. I think they made us work a wee bit and it was normally the other way about. We made other teams work.'

At half-time Stein encouraged his players to keep plugging away and be confident that if they did that, things would soon click into place. Evan Williams explains, 'One of his great things was, "We've not started to play yet; we'll get going now." He would say that because he had a great belief in the players. I think he had a great belief in them because he had brought most of them up and had brought most of them through the ranks and had done things with them. Even we ourselves thought we were going to come through because in most games once we started playing and turned it on for half an hour we would be three or four up. The boys would just destroy teams.

'Once Celtic got on their game, it would be wave after wave of attack, although they weren't a team for just throwing the ball into the box. They worked it about the box and got it back out and they created so many shooting and scoring chances in those years that it was, at times, frightening. I always remember that when teams came to Celtic Park the star man every week was always their goalkeeper. So I think at half-time in the Feyenoord game we still thought we were going to win.'

As the game resumed for the second 45 minutes, Celtic found that, contrary to their expectations at the interval, Feyenoord were still in control. 'In the last 25 minutes they gave us a turning over,' admits Evan Williams. 'I think at one point I had four or five saves within about ten seconds; I think I blocked three or four shots all one after another. I would say that the European Cup final was my best game for

Celtic because of the number of saves I had in the match.' Despite the pressure they were under, the innate confidence of the Celtic team meant that they continued to believe that they were going to prevail. That was even after 90 minutes had finished with them being fortunate to hang on to a 1–1 scoreline. 'Even going into extra-time,' adds Williams, 'we still thought we were going to do it, even though by then Feyenoord had come on to a right good game and had got on top. In extra-time I think they came into it even more.

'In those days there were no penalty shoot-outs. There was a replay scheduled and I think if we had finished extra-time with the score at 1–1 we would possibly have played a lot better in the following game. In fact, I think we missed a chance near the end.' John Hughes takes up that story. 'I think a Feyenoord player tried to play a square ball across the front of the penalty area and I intercepted it. I can't remember what I was thinking at the time but I possibly had too much time to think about what I was going to do. With the likes of the chance at Hampden, when I scored against Leeds, you have no time to think about it. The ball comes to you in an instant and in the next instant you have put it in the net. Sometimes when you go through with the ball at your feet and you are one-on-one with the goalkeeper you get more of a chance to think and I think that's why you miss them. Anyway, I hit the ball against the goalkeeper. It was just one of those things, but I reckon that when I did that, that was me finished at Celtic. That was him, Jock Stein, he was like that; he tended to blame you for things. If I had scored that goal, I think things would have been different for me but within a year of that I was finished at Celtic. It's just my personal opinion that he would hold that kind of thing against you.'

Feyenoord remained unruffled despite having gone so close to conceding what could have been the winning goal for Celtic. They kept probing and pressing the Celtic defence even as the game entered the final minutes of extra-time. With three minutes to go, Feyenoord's speedy Swedish international striker, Ove Kindvall, made a run deep into the Celtic penalty box as yet another long, accurate pass from midfield floated down in his direction. Billy McNeill was the only Celtic defender in any position to deal with the ball but it was behind McNeill and too high for him to reach with his head as it dropped out of the sky. The Celtic captain, stumbling backwards in desperation, instead handled the ball in mid-air but he succeeded only in slowing the ball down and it dropped down in the penalty area to sit up perfectly invitingly for the Swede. Evan Williams raced from his line to try to smother the ball but Kindvall reached it a fraction of a second before the Celtic goalkeeper and, with consummate expertise, Kindvall poked the ball past the Celtic goalkeeper.

'At the second one,' remembers Williams as he pictures those moments in his mind, 'big Billy handled it, the referee didn't give a penalty kick and the guy stuck it away. I just missed getting to it and no more and Kindvall got there just before me. I think that with Billy handling it, it slowed the pace of the ball down – if you look at it, it may have been going out for a goal kick. Kindvall just got his toe to the ball in front of me and toed it over the top of me. I stopped once Billy had gone for the ball and then I had to restart again. To be fair to Kindvall he was very, very quick. All night he was very quick. I stopped for that split second before he scored because I was thinking the referee was going to give a penalty. Then I realised that the whistle had not gone and that he was playing the advantage, which was unusual in those days because they didn't play the advantage rule.'

It is beyond doubt that Feyenoord, due to the overall excellence of their football on the night, deserved to win the game and take the European Cup, but plenty of teams have dominated European Cup finals only to draw or lose to an inferior team on the night. The question that remains unresolved is whether Kindvall's goal should have been allowed to stand. If the Swede had made a mess of his shot and sent it past the post or over the bar or if Williams had reached the ball first and blocked it, the referee, Concetto Lo Bello, would almost certainly have awarded a penalty to Feyenoord because of McNeill's clear handling of the ball inside the penalty area. As Evan Williams points out, in the early 1970s referees tended not to play the advantage rule and that strongly convinces the man who was Celtic's goalkeeper on the night of the 1970 European Cup final that referee Lo Bello should have awarded a penalty instead of a goal to Feyenoord.

'Yes, he should have awarded a penalty,' says Williams, 'because if Kindvall had missed his chance there would have been an outcry if Feyenoord had not been awarded a penalty.' Williams believes that if Kindvall had missed his scoring opportunity, the referee would have brought play back and given Feyenoord a second chance to score. 'If Kindvall had toe-poked it over the bar,' says Williams, 'I think the referee would have given a penalty kick. I think the referee had quite a good game that night but I can always remember that in those days referees didn't play the advantage rule; not unless the guy was tapping the ball into an empty net. I remember that if it was a penalty kick, that was it, it was given; a penalty kick. In fact, I remember a few times that a penalty kick was given even after the ball went into the net. They would bring it back and give a penalty kick.' It is clear that Lo Bello should have done exactly that instead of simply awarding Feyenoord a second goal. He had not played the advantage – the goal had happened so quickly that he had not had time to do so – and, even more crucially, Williams had paused before coming for the ball because he was sure that Lo Bello was going to give a penalty as a result of Billy McNeill's handball. As such, that second, decisive goal was hugely unfair on Celtic. The fact that Stein's team had not been their normal selves on the night is irrelevant; the decision to allow Feyenoord's second goal to stand was incorrect. Celtic should have been facing a penalty kick and with Williams in exemplary form on the night there is every chance that he could have pulled off one final, vital save to keep Celtic's chances of landing their second European Cup alive.

Celtic's outstanding player on the night, Williams, is still magnanimous in praising the Feyenoord team as he looks back on that game. 'I think that they were the better team on the night and that happens in football. Just as Celtic, in 1967, were just becoming a force in European football, so I think that was the start of the Dutch doing the same. They were a very, very good side, with some great players such as Wim Jansen, Ove Kindvall and Wim van Hanegem, whom I always rate as having been one of the best players in the world. Of the players that I have seen and played against I would rate him in the top ten. He could knock the ball about and, even though he wasn't a quick player, he had a great presence on the park. The main thing about them was that they were such a good side. They were the better team on the night. I don't think you can be the best team every night. Even the best teams in the world get beaten. I think the better team on the night did the business.'

Jim Brogan, a utility player brought into the Celtic team to play in central defence, had picked up an injury in the opening minute but Williams does not remember that hampering the team in any particular fashion. Bobby Murdoch and Jimmy Johnstone also suffered injuries during the game. 'I remember wee Jimmy got hurt and Bobby got an injury as well,' says Williams. 'In saying that, it's possible that some of the Feyenoord players maybe picked up injuries too. I think the wee man got a bad one. I think he was on the end of a few harsh tackles early on. I'm not saying that they were dirty – they just caught him early bells. They were a tough side; they didn't take any prisoners, but we were a tough side as well. Celtic in those days were a great footballing side but also a very competitive side. We wouldn't let teams kick us off the park and let them away with it. We would compete against them. If a team was going in heavy we would go in heavy as well. There are not many players in the world ever got the better of Bertie Auld. The wee man was famous for coming out on top. I just think that that night against Feyenoord we didn't get as much possession of the ball as we normally did.

'Feyenoord were simply a good side. I think the press underestimated them possibly more than the Celtic management and players did. All the British guys were telling us that Feyenoord weren't a good side. We found they were a right good side. I don't think it was any one particular player's fault that we lost and I would say that we didn't underestimate them because we were playing in the premier tournament in Europe and whether you've won it once, twice, three or four times you want to win it all the time. That's the way the Celtic players in those days thought. They wanted to win more and more things.

'I enjoyed the European Cup final even though we got beaten – just to play in it was something. I was still sad afterwards – I broke down in tears on the park right after the final whistle and I'm not usually that type of person.' Williams was not consoled in any way by the fact that he had proved himself a top-class goalkeeper with the way in which he had kept Feyenoord at bay on a night when they had been well on top in the game. 'The way I played didn't really matter,' he explains. 'It was more important for the team to win the trophy. I would have preferred to have played badly and won than to have had a great game and been beaten. I think we were all just deflated, shattered, after it. There was just this deadly silence on the bus going back to our hotel. It was as if the whole world had collapsed. We went back to the hotel and you could sense how disappointed all the boys felt. Nobody spoke.

'Jock really didn't say much after the Feyenoord game. The thing I remember about Jock Stein is that if things went against us he didn't say anything after the game. He waited until the next training session at the Park. I think there was good logic in that because he would maybe say some things to some people immediately after a match that he would regret, whereas if you go home and think about it and then come in once everybody has settled down you can talk it over. I think he knew how we all felt after we had been beaten by Feyenoord. So I can't remember him analysing the Feyenoord game in detail afterwards. He always looked to the future. We went to America a few days after that match for four weeks and you could feel how deflated everyone was. It was a sad trip because the guys couldn't get going in the games we played over there. The spark had gone – then again, it might have been a good thing going over there and getting the badness out of your system before coming back for the pre-season and starting all over again.'

It is with more than a tinge of regret that Billy McNeill, Celtic's captain in that match in Milan, looks back on the events of that evening. 'We underestimated Feyenoord,' he says. 'Obviously, it hadn't been recognised that Dutch football was getting better and better all the time and Feyenoord were underestimated; and where the 2–1 victory over Inter Milan flattered Inter, the 2–1 defeat by Feyenoord flattered us. They were a far better side than we were on the night. They were far better, far more ready for the game, far more up for it. We were unlucky in one sense in that our season had basically finished whereas theirs was still going on, so they were much more battle sharpened than we were, but I think our whole preparation for it was far too relaxed, too easy-oasy. There was too much thought given to what should happen after it; whether we should get an open-topped bus to travel through the streets of Glasgow and things like that.

'Don't get me wrong: there was no disgrace in losing to a Dutch team as good as Feyenoord but I would like to go back and to have had the preparations much more realistic and much more to the point than they were. We brought them back to Glasgow a few months later and it was billed as a friendly game but it wasn't a friendly game and we drew 1–1 with them. They were a hard outfit, they would have been hard to beat; they had world-class players and a whole load of players that played in the World Cup finals with Holland. They were a good, good side.

'I think that defeat in the 1970 European Cup final took a lot out of the club and took a lot out of the self-belief and everything else. We never, ever quite got to that level again. It must have affected Jock because obviously he must have wondered about his own judgement. It was after that that the team started to break up quite dramatically. There was every reason for that: if you looked at the squad that you had in the reserves, they looked as though they were going to be world beaters. So you could understand that he maybe said, "Well, this team's gone as far as it could have done." It must have affected him greatly.'

Tommy Gemmell was to learn that few people wish to associate themselves with defeat. 'Nobody ever talks to me about the goal I scored against Feyenoord,' he says. 'If someone says to me, "What about that goal you scored in the European Cup final?" I say to them, "Which final are you talking about?" They are invariably talking about Lisbon and 1967; no one ever mentions the goal I scored against Feyenoord. It just shows you: when you are losers, nobody wants to know. When you are winners, everybody wants to know.'

There had been, for Jimmy Johnstone, uncanny similarities between that defeat and Celtic's great victory in Lisbon three years previously. 'It was Inter Milan and us in reverse,' he recalls. 'We thought we were the bee's knees. Of the three other teams in the semi-finals we had wanted to play Feyenoord. Everybody wanted Feyenoord. Nothing had even been heard about Dutch football! We had won the European Cup and had beaten Leeds United in the semi-final. We got off the bus at the San Siro in Milan and we were walking down through this big, open, wide corridor to the dressing-room. Feyenoord's dressing-room was next door to us and they were all out watching us coming in; they looked as if they were kind of in awe of us. Nobody had rated them and our game against Leeds had been beamed all over Europe. We had also already won the European Cup and we were the Celtic. I think our heads went a wee bit and we became over-confident. I definitely think we underestimated them. We honestly thought that we were just going to go out and lift that trophy again, hands down.'

Eddy Pieters Graafland, the Feyenoord goalkeeper that night, concurs with much of Johnstone's assessment. 'We had a lot of self-confidence that we would win the European Cup final,' says Pieters Graafland. 'Celtic was a top club, especially after winning the Cup in 1967, and automatically we were the underdogs, which was a welcome bonus. Of course, it was fantastic for our team to achieve a place in the final and it would not have been too dramatic if we had lost the match. In my opinion, this was the reason why, from the kick-off, we gave a good performance.

'The day before the game, Ernst Happel, our coach, had already completed his preparations. He knew everything about our opponents and discussed with several players their strong and weak points. I got the impression that the Celtic players had a bit of arrogance at the beginning, especially when they were taking their places in the tunnel, and that is why they were overwhelmed by the tremendous efforts of the Feyenoord players. Every player reached the top that night, there was no weak point in our team. It was not right that Celtic got their free-kick from Lo Bello. Moreover, he stood in the wrong place when the free-kick was taken, so that my view was totally blocked.

'Especially after we made it 1–1, the Celtic players looked unsteady. They had no luck any more and with a bit of luck on our side we could have made it 3–1. Only the goal-post and crossbar stood in the way. However, in extra-time Feyenoord won deservedly through Ove Kindvall's goal. The Celtic players were totally disappointed because they had been convinced of scoring a victory.

'What will stick in my mind forever is that after the game the Celtic players were extremely good sportsmen and, together with their supporters, they gave us a standing ovation when we were receiving the Cup. By the time our bus was departing, there were many Celtic supporters around us, who congratulated us on our play and wished us good luck.'

It had been the most disappointing and surprising defeat in Celtic's history but Stein's team possessed special powers of recovery. It would not be long before they would once again be rubbing shoulders with Europe's elite and homing in on another European Cup final.

SEVEN

Paying for Penalties
INTERNAZIONALE 1972

The Internazionale players that Celtic had faced in the 1967 European Cup final were portrayed at the time as the most dour and defensive team of all time. Five years later, Celtic faced Internazionale once again in the European Cup and the Inter of 1967 could be portrayed as the epitome of devil-may-care, footballing cavaliers in comparison to the team that took the field to face Celtic in 1972. They showed that defensive football had not been killed in Lisbon – its head had been lopped off but its roots were deep and it had grown back and flourished in an even more virulent form. Celtic's famous final victory over Internazionale had been hailed widely as the victory of attacking football over Italy's cautious *catenaccio* but it had merely banished *catenaccio* to the shadows. The Italians, conservative to the core, were too committed to that tactical style to give it up as long as it could win them matches.

Celtic had recovered steadily after the disappointment of defeat to Feyenoord in the 1970 European Cup final. Their next tilt at the tournament, in the 1970–71 competition, had again brought them face to face with Dutch opposition, this time in the quarter-finals, and there was no possibility of Celtic underestimating Ajax of Amsterdam when the two clubs met in March 1971. Jock Stein sent his team out in the Olympic Stadium, Amsterdam, to play cautiously and contain Ajax, most especially their most creative player, Johan Cruyff, rapidly developing into a figure of world-class stature. David Hay was assigned man-marking duties on the 24-year-old Dutchman, already three times Dutch Footballer of the Year, who had the individual spark that could single-handedly start his team playing at their best.

The phrase 'total football', in association with the progressive Dutch teams of the early 1970s, would not begin to be coined until 1972, but Ajax already had honed to perfection the capability of playing in that style, an even more refined style than the one that Feyenoord had shown to great effect in Milan back in the spring of 1970. Total football would see the ball whipped around from player to player at speed and, crucially, every player had to be able, at any time, to fill in for a teammate who was out of position. Full-backs had to have the capability of fitting into any role in the team when required, even at centre-forward or on the wing. Forwards had to be able to flit back into defence without giving it a second thought. That was the tactical explanation for total football; to carry it out, every player in the team had to have exceptional ball-playing skills. There was no room for a centre-half who could not use the ball or a wide player who could not tackle and such multi-skilled personnel made teams such as Ajax and Feyenoord extremely difficult to combat.

Celtic players would cover for each other to a considerable degree; an overlapping Tommy Gemmell would know that John Clark would shift sideways into his left-back position to compensate for his absence. Ajax, though, were taking things several steps further and there was even a striking contrast between the two sets of players as they milled around on the pitch before the match in the Olympic Stadium. Celtic, for the early 1970s, looked staid in their blazers, club ties, short hair and slacks. The long-haired Dutch players came out looking casually confident in jeans, joshing with each other and happy to chat in a relaxed manner, in English, with the Celtic players. The Dutch were even accompanied by their girlfriends and wives, a concept that would have been entirely unimaginable for Jock Stein.

'We were comfortable for an hour over there,' is how Bobby Lennox remembers the events in the earlier stages of Celtic's visit to Amsterdam for the first leg. 'Then Cruyff weaved his wee bit of magic.' With 62 minutes gone in the Olympic Stadium, Johan Neeskens spotted Cruyff making a run, picked him out with a quick flick, and Cruyff guided the ball past Williams to put Ajax 1–0 ahead. 'Then they scored with a free kick,' adds Lennox. 'It was a terrible goal to lose – we didn't get organised; we didn't get set up properly.' Barry Hulshoff took advantage to slip the ball through a slack defensive wall and Ajax were 2–0 up with 20 minutes remaining. Celtic held out until the final minute before conceding a devastating third goal, as Bobby Lennox explains. 'Big Piet Keizer scored in the last minute of the game with his right foot and his right foot was just a standie-uppie foot. An hour into the game you would have thought, "We'll not get beaten here tonight." That was even though we hadn't played particularly well. Davie Hay was great against Cruyff that night but Cruyff got a wee break one time and smacked it into the net and the game then turned. A flash of genius turned the whole tie because we were chasing our tails after that.'

Evan Williams also remembers Cruyff having a major bearing on that game. 'I remember Davie Hay went out and marked him and Davie did a good job. Up until half an hour to go it was 0–0 and then they scored. At one point in that match, Cruyff went away back into the left-back position for a period of the game. He started to play very deep. And then he made three runs and we were 3–0 down. He was a genius, a great player. They were a great side too. They had great players, such as the big outside-left, a big, tall fellow, broad-built, called Piet Keizer, and the defender Ruud Krol; what a team they had!

'We were still capable of giving those teams a right good run for their money but just near the end Ajax got on top of us. We had played quite well up till then. We had held them, we had contained them and we had had one or two chances ourselves, but then Cruyff turned on that little bit of extra magic, the way Jimmy Johnstone could do, and the whole thing turned upside down. That happened with Celtic for years; the wee man would be quiet and then suddenly he would do two or three things and we would be two or three up and the other team were just shattered. I think Cruyff did that to us that night. He was a great player.'

The second leg was scheduled for Hampden. The Celtic board, encouraged by the huge turnout for the Leeds United match at that venue one year previously, had opted to bring another big game to the same venue in the hope of another triumphant take at the turnstiles.

Two days before the game, as Ajax flew into Glasgow, Stein and his team received a bit of a boost when it was revealed that Cruyff had become the victim of a heavy cold. 'When Cruyff has a cold, all of Ajax has a cold,' said the Dutch team's manager Rinus Michels. On the night, the inspirational Dutchman proved fit enough to play, but it was a slightly subdued Cruyff who took to the field at Hampden in front of a crowd of 84,000. Half an hour had passed when Celtic midfielder Tommy Callaghan nodded the ball into Jimmy Johnstone's path and the winger nudged the ball into the net. That offered Celtic a glimmer of hope, but within minutes Gerry Muhren had cracked a shot off the Celtic post. For the rest of the match, Ajax were content to contain Celtic and although it was the Glasgow side who had most of the ball for most of the game, they were unable to add to their single goal. 'Ajax came to Hampden and it was just one of those games where they played well enough not to let us back into the game,' is how Bobby Lennox sums up that evening.

'At Hampden,' says Evan Williams, 'we played quite well but they were so good at keeping possession of the ball. They were one of the first teams that could hold the ball even in their own half without giving it away and they would prod away all the time, whereas the football in those days used to be about going at people. They held possession, but Ajax weren't boring with it. A lot of teams would be dour and could play the ball across the back without doing anything interesting but Ajax played it up and back, in and back and back out again. They were all good players. They were all comfortable on the ball but I think Celtic matched them at Hampden. We had a good result, but just didn't do enough to get through.'

John Hughes had been struck by the immense fitness and stamina of the Dutch players. 'We thought they were on something!' he says. He recalls running flat out to try to win possession, straining to get to the ball before Ajax opponents who looked almost serene and who would be cruising gently in the direction of the ball. 'Maybe it was just their demeanour, but we seemed to be really struggling and they were coasting.' Celtic's scorer Johnstone admits that the team had met their match in Ajax. 'I couldn't have seen us beating them at that time,' he says, 'because they were superb. Cruyff was running the show and every time he got the ball it was absolute mayhem. His pace was electric and it was very, very hard for a defender to cope with him. He just loped, with big strides. The boys were saying after the first game that they would think they had the ball and he would just nick it away with the turn of pace he had. He was a terrific player – 60 fags a day he smoked as well!'

All football clubs are constantly in a state of flux: players get older, lose form, pick up injuries, lose confidence. Younger men, merciless in their desire to find their feet in the first team, jostle to take the places of their predecessors. Celtic Park in the early 1970s was no different, and that was reflected in the Celtic team that was named by Jock Stein to face Ujpest Dozsa of Hungary in another European Cup quarter-final the following year. Only three of the Lisbon Lions would play in that game: Bobby Murdoch, Billy McNeill and Bobby Lennox. Five years had passed since their great triumph in the European Cup final, but in 1972 Celtic did not look much like a team in decline. Outstanding young players such as Danny McGrain, George Connelly, David Hay, Kenny Dalglish and Lou Macari had filtered through to the team and were of a suitable calibre to convince all who saw them that Celtic's place as leading lights in Europe was assured for some time to come. Those young players still required guidance and, before the game against Ujpest Dozsa in Budapest, Jock Stein had stressed to Bobby Lennox that he was the elder statesman of the team and that the manager would be relying on him to help the youngsters through a tough game against accomplished opponents. Ujpest Dozsa, in common with Vojvodina in 1967, were midway through the golden period in their history, with a team that were in the process of winning seven Hungarian league titles in a row.

The game in Budapest was played with thunder and lightning as its backdrop but the young Celts proved to be the epitome of calm during the storm. With five minutes remaining, Dalglish prodded the ball into the penalty area where Macari, showing great presence of mind in a tight situation, controlled it on his chest before spinning quickly to slide the ball home and give Celtic an impressive 2–1 victory.

Evan Williams had excelled against Ujpest. 'I made some good saves that night,' he says. 'I had one that was right up in the top right-hand corner that I held with one hand. I don't know how I got near it. That

night, every time I went for the ball it stuck to me. If I had got my
pinkie to it, it would have stuck to me. Even big Stein said to me
afterwards, "That was some game you had tonight." And he wasn't one
for going up to goalkeepers and saying, "You did well."' Jock Stein had
been overwhelmed by the quality of his team's display on the day. 'At
this level and when you consider the age of this team of ours,' he
commented, 'it is probably Celtic's best European Cup display since
Lisbon.'

Williams adds, 'Ujpest were a good side. I always remember the
crowd at Ujpest Dozsa – they were so solemn, quiet; it was an eerie
feeling. It was a communist country at the time and when you walked
down the road in Budapest they never smiled. Nobody seemed happy.
That was until their team scored a goal and then it was a different ball
game. They would go bananas – and then they would go quiet again.'

It was a pleased party of Celtic players who returned home that
evening – the match in Hungary had been played during the afternoon.
On their arrival in Scotland, Stein had arranged an unorthodox
welcome back. 'We came back from Hungary,' says Evan Williams, 'and
he trained us at Celtic Park at 11 o'clock at night so that we didn't have
to come in for training in the morning.'

European evenings at Celtic Park in the early 1970s were still distinctly
different. The stadium would be packed tightly, unlike for most League
games other than that with Rangers. The ground would be filled with
Celtic supporters – away fans at European matches in the 1970s were
rare – and there would be a crisp sense of expectation and anticipation
among the support about what might unfold on the evening. Small
details helped add to the feeling that Celtic were now a team that
belonged firmly in the top strata of European competition: in the early
1970s, the Celtic Park goalposts had been redesigned. The traditional
square posts, with stanchions reaching back behind the goals, had been
replaced by ultra-modern, continental-type posts, streamlined and
stanchion-free, from which the goal nets hung loosely. A new, space-age
stand – with unimpeded views and angular architecture – had been
erected in the summer of 1971. This advanced structure, which
contained 10,000 plastic seats, even had a futuristic press box
suspended in mid-air over the heads of the spectators. Nothing like it

had been seen previously at any ground in Scotland, appearing to emphasise how much Celtic were forging forward as a leading club on the European scene. Profits from Celtic's European runs had helped, in large measure, to finance those improvements at Celtic Park.

The football was also still of the highest quality. On European evenings at Celtic Park in the early 1970s, there would be an electrifying speed about the football on display from Celtic. Pace was everything to Jock Stein and his plan was almost always for his team's opponents to be pressed and harried and harassed all evening when they came to Glasgow. The return against Ujpest, though, presented an unusual dilemma for the Celtic manager. The usual all-out tactics would not apply in this instance. Stein was well aware that the Hungarians had the ability to win in Glasgow, so his side would have to strike a difficult balance between defensive caution, to hold on to their 2–1 lead, and attacking enterprise. The quandary deepened after only five minutes when Anton Dunai slipped in to score for the Hungarians. With the score at 2–2 on aggregate, Celtic had the advantage of being ahead on away goals, but even when Macari equalised midway through the second half, the Celtic players were nervously treading a tightrope that could have snapped with tension; one more goal from Ujpest would have meant extra-time. The final whistle offered blessed relief, a place for Celtic in the semi-final and a rematch with Internazionale for the first time since Lisbon.

The Celtic team that filed on to the pitch at the San Siro Stadium, Milan, for the first leg of that semi was: Evan Williams, Jim Craig, Jim Brogan, Bobby Murdoch, Billy McNeill, George Connelly, Jimmy Johnstone, Kenny Dalglish, Lou Macari, Tommy Callaghan and Bobby Lennox. They soon found that their Italian opponents were unwilling to push too many men forward for fear of being caught upfield and punished by Celtic scoring a vital away goal. Celtic were content to hit on the break, playing a 4–5–1 formation with Lennox and Johnstone withdrawn into midfield but prepared to dash forward whenever the counter-attack was on for Celtic. Scots-Italian Lou Macari – of whom there had been a huge fuss made on his arrival in his ancestral land – was the team's sole attacker. Consequently, neither side created too many chances. Celtic were even able to throw 19-year-old left-back Pat McCluskey into the fray as a replacement for Brogan with half an hour of the match remaining. It was only McCluskey's third appearance in the first team but he played in a composed, controlled fashion.

'I remember the game in the San Siro,' says Evan Williams, 'where we played very, very well, defensive-wise. Jock Stein never ever played six at the back and all that carry-on. We played, basically, in much the same way as we would do usually. Obviously, the midfield players played a little bit deeper but we had players like Bobby Lennox, which meant that if teams did come on top of us and the ball broke, Bobby was gone. You wouldn't catch him. There would be a big gap from the halfway line up to their goal-line and if you put a ball through Bobby would zip on to it right away. He was so quick. He used to go across the back four of other teams and then, when the ball would be played, he would shoot away. He would look offside sometimes, but in reality he wouldn't be offside because he would not have been in an offside position at the time when the pass was put through to him. He was pulled up quite a few times for offside in Milan in that very way. I remember that.

'We played well that night. They didn't really create many chances, as such. I think I had just two or three saves. We played well and I think we thought we were through when it ended up 0–0. We brought Pat McCluskey in at left-back – Pat was only 19 – and he had a great game. It was Pat's first European tie and you'd have thought he had played there all the days of his life. What other manager in those days would stick a young boy like that in the team for a European Cup semi-final? But Jock Stein had so much faith in the boy as a player. I think he was up against an outside-right who was an international player.' That was Jair Da Costa, the Brazilian who had missed the 1967 final through injury, and who was McCluskey's direct opponent in the San Siro. Inter had also fielded Roberto Boninsegna, the Italian international who had scored in the 1970 World Cup final, at centre-forward and the number 10 was the tall, thin, Sandro Mazzola, the man who looked like a Mexican bandit and who had been the scorer of Inter's goal in Lisbon in 1967. The great Giacinto Facchetti was also still with Inter and still the captain of the Italian national team.

It was questionable whether Inter ought even to have been in the semi-finals at all. There was a suspicion of corruption over the means by which they had emerged as winners after their second-round tie with

Borussia Moenchengladbach and also over Inter's quarter-final with Standard Liege, just as there had been when Inter had defeated CSKA Sofia in their 1967 European Cup semi-final.

Pat McCluskey retained his place in the Celtic defence for the second leg against Inter, with Brogan missing out. Otherwise, the team that had finished the match in Milan was the same one that met Inter in the return at Celtic Park. Inter's stellar striker Roberto Boninsegna had suffered an injured ankle in his team's Italian League match against Fiorentina the previous Sunday and had not travelled to Scotland. It left Sandro Mazzola as the Italian side's sole striker. The loss of such an important attacker as Boninsegna meant that Inter would now place even more emphasis on defence.

Jock Stein was still sure that Celtic could take the tie. 'He was always positive about the way the game should go,' says Evan Williams. 'He believed that if we played we would beat anybody. That was always one of the things he said. He discussed in depth the way they would play and they played in exactly the way he said. He knew them inside out and he kept saying that they would slow us down and stop us playing and stop the flow of the game and that was exactly what they did.'

Bobby Lennox says of that match with Inter: 'Within 20 minutes in Glasgow the game should have been wrapped up. We got our chances early on and then it developed into a stalemate. They were after a draw and we tried to get the goal we needed to make the breakthrough. We made three or four good chances early on but couldn't get the ball in the net.' Evan Williams watched in growing frustration as the Italians snuffed out the match as a spectacle. 'The harder we tried that night, I think the worse it got. Again, you've got 80,000 fans all willing you to win and I think they were even more disappointed than us that we were struggling to break down the Italians.

'The crowd was one of Jock Stein's big things. He always used to say to us, "If you go out there and win tonight, all those thousands of Celtic supporters will go to work tomorrow happy." The fans today are not as vocal as they were in those days. I think they were more passionate in those days, when football was the working man's outlet. They had a team that had won the European Cup and that got to quarter-finals and semi-finals. Celtic fans in those days could boast about how they had four or five world-class players in the team; the Lions. They made all the Celtic fans happy, the way they played. They entertained them.'

As the Celtic goalkeeper on a night when Inter Milan proved themselves the ultimate stultifying side, Evan Williams had plenty of opportunity to assess the match from his prime position at the end of the field where the action wasn't taking place. 'They were a very good side, Italian-wise,' he says, 'but when they came to Parkhead they were so boring. I don't think they had a shot on our goal all night! They had great players, the Italians, but their football wasn't so good to watch in those days. That night, the Italians were on top of their game and sometimes the harder you try the worse it gets. We were expected to go through because you could sense from the fans and the press beforehand that they were saying we were through. I don't think we were great the way we played that night but I think we were the better team of the two. We just didn't prise them open. I think we only had one or two chances the whole game.

'The Italians in those days were very cynical, especially in the way they would deal with players like Johnstone and Lennox. They didn't think twice about whacking a player. Once Lennox or Johnstone had gone past a player they were just brought down. Referees were not as strict in those days, whereas nowadays players would get away with it once or twice, then they would get the yellow card and then they would be off. I don't think in those days they sent players off as easily as they do nowadays or I think every left-back that played against Jimmy Johnstone would have been sent off every week!

'There was a good atmosphere that night and we attacked them, but they seemed to win everything. I don't think they lost a ball in the air that night from our crosses into the box. The Italians in those days could defend all night and day and not lose anything. They just set their stall out and were very hard to break down. The Italians stopped us playing. They never let the game flow. Once Celtic got a few passes together and got the thing flowing the Inter players stopped it by giving away a free kick and they just slowed everything down. I don't think Celtic really got into their stride that night but that's the way the Italian teams played in those days.'

Long before the end, the Celtic support had grown resigned to a 0–0 draw. Throughout the game, all 11 Inter players had withdrawn to within the confines of their 18-yard box, killing the game, and there was simply no way through for Celtic. The 1970s was the golden age for time-wasting teams such as Inter Milan. Players in that era were allowed to pass the ball back to the goalkeeper, who could then hold on to the ball for as long as he wished, drop it to the ground, make as though he was about to pass it, then pick it up again. The goalkeeper could then throw the ball out to a defender who would immediately play it back to him and the entire process would begin again. It all helped to disrupt the rhythm of the opposition and the Italians were masters of that dull game. It would be the 1990s before this method of time wasting through the repeated use of the pass-back would be eliminated from the game. The offside law at the time also mitigated against the attacking team. An attacker had to have two players between him and the opposition's goal to remain onside; in the 1990s this was changed so that the attacker now only had to be level with the second-last man. Only one ball would be in use in the 1970s, so, again, the rhythm of the game could be disrupted by a team taking their time to retrieve the ball when it went dead. At Lisbon, in the European Cup final, Inter's 1967 team had been cautious and careful but by 1972 they had developed into fully fledged wasters of football. This was not even *catenaccio*; there was no desire to break forward at all. It was clear that the Italians wished only to claw their way slowly to the end of the game without either themselves or Celtic having scored.

There would be no toss of a coin to decide at random the winner of this tie, as there had been at the conclusion of Celtic's match with Benfica back in 1969. There was now a new ruling in place to obtain a winner in European ties where the two teams had drawn on aggregate but could not be separated on away goals. At a meeting of UEFA in Como, northern Italy, on the day of the 1970 European Cup final, it had been agreed that penalty kicks would be introduced to European competition from the 1970–71 season onwards. Celtic, when their tie with Inter ended 0–0 on aggregate, were about to participate in the spectacle of the penalty shoot-out for the first time. That meeting in Como had put into a coma Celtic's meeting with Inter but it meant that now, at the end of 120 minutes at Celtic Park, there would be a sudden switch from tedium to high drama. The Italians had dulled down the game because they were convinced that after obtaining a 0–0 draw they could win on penalties: now they would have the opportunity to put that theory to the test. The spectacle resembled a shoot-out in a western, with goalkeeper and penalty taker facing each other across a 12-yard-long strip of land to see whose nerve and aim held best. It was like nothing the Celtic Park crowd had seen before and the fans, having anticipated at the beginning of the evening that Celtic would overwhelm the Italian side, watched in bemused fashion as the unexpected mini-drama unfolded.

Prior to the penalty shoot-out, the Inter players, coaching staff and management formed a circle, linked arms and, watched by intrigued Celtic players, including a bemused Jimmy Johnstone, chanted and bounced up and down in a slowly revolving circle as a way of building up their morale for the shoot-out. 'I always remember one thing about the penalty kicks,' says Evan Williams. 'Big Jock put a coat round about me while we were waiting for the penalty kicks to start but what I actually wanted was to be given a ball because I had had nothing to do all night. I wanted a wee, quick warm-up. I was actually cold even though I had kept running up and down to keep myself active during the game. I remember saying, "Boss, can I get a ball and do a wee bit of diving around?" He said, "No, no, wait here until we tell you who is going to do what." He actually said where the penalty kicks were going to go, to be fair to him – and he was right!

'I didn't feel as confident as I would normally do,' adds Williams, 'because I had had nothing to do all night and it was a really cold evening. The importance of it all was going through my mind and I was saying to myself, "If I save one or two of these we're in a European Cup final." So it was focused in my mind to save something, which is more of a positive thought than going the other way.' Williams was thinking not so much of the pressure on him if he was to fail to save the kicks but was instead thinking positively of the benefits for Celtic if he could find a means of saving a penalty or two and winning the tie for his club.

It would be Sandro Mazzola, the penalty taker in the 1967 final, who would step up to place the ball on the spot and take the first penalty. Again, as in 1967, Mazzola approached the ball steadily, deliberately, before brushing the ball to his left, relying on precision rather than power to try to make his kick count. Ronnie Simpson had been wrongfooted in 1967 but now Evan Williams anticipated the direction of Mazzola's kick correctly and dived low to his right. The Celtic goalkeeper had been helped by Stein's advice in telling him that Mazzola would put his penalty there. Williams almost got a hand to Mazzola's kick but, as in 1967, the Italian's low, accurate strike ensured that the ball rolled smoothly over the line to nestle low in the corner of the Celtic net. Inter, through Mazzola, had seized the initiative.

Dixie Deans then stepped up to take Celtic's kick. His strike from the spot began to gain height from the moment boot struck ball. It looked as though it might be heading for the top right-hand corner of the Inter net but instead it veered over the bar, leaving the net unruffled as it sailed into the black night sky. Williams now had to do his best to retrieve a place in the European Cup final for Celtic.

'Years ago,' says Williams, 'they used to come up with the theory that a goalkeeper picks his way to dive – and years ago you used to see goalkeepers going long before the player kicked the ball – but the clever player just waits and sticks the ball in the other corner. I used to try and stay up as long as I could because if the penalty taker didn't hit it well it wouldn't be too far away from me. I would then have a chance of saving. It's a strange feeling being involved in a penalty shoot-out, especially in a big tie like that, because, obviously, apart from the players' bonuses, there is the chance of getting into the final again with all the publicity and the money that that generates for the club and then you know what it means for the supporters. So with all that there is a lot of pressure on you.'

Inter's second kick was taken by Giacinto Facchetti, another survivor of 1967, but the defender's strike contrasted sharply with the one that had been taken by his long-time teammate Mazzola. This time the ball flew close to Williams. 'Their penalties were so well placed,' recalls the goalkeeper, 'although I managed to hit one – the second one – on to the bar. It hit the bar, then went behind the line and bounced out. I dived and just put my hand up and I actually thought I had saved it, but it bounced over the line.

'With three of their penalty-takers,' continues Williams, 'Jock Stein had said that they would go to my right-hand side and they did – but their penalties were stuck away in the corner so well that I just couldn't get to them.' When Jair, who had missed out on the final in 1967, hit the fifth for Inter, Celtic were beaten. It is an indicator of the novelty of penalty shoot-outs in the early 1970s that the formalities were completed by Bobby Murdoch stepping up to take, and score from, Celtic's fifth penalty even though that was by then a mere formality. Inter had squeezed through 5–4 on spot-kicks. 'I was unlucky with a couple of their kicks,' says Williams.

'The Italians had the knack of playing for a draw and then looking to win on penalties,' adds Williams. 'What other team would go and play for penalty kicks? It was just unreal but I think they did that because they were quite afraid of Celtic. Again, in saying that, they contained us so well that night. We didn't open them up the way we generally could open teams up at Celtic Park, which we had done from '66 up until '72 in European ties. It didn't matter who came to Celtic Park; they got opened up. Even Ajax got opened up when they came to Glasgow and they were on their way to becoming European champions three times, but we just couldn't prise Inter Milan open that night.'

Bobby Lennox says, 'Dixie Deans scored hundreds of goals in his career: great goals, important goals, wonderful goals, but people always say, "Oh, Dixie missed the penalty." The thing that should be remembered is that Dixie put his hand up and said, "I'll take a penalty kick," which was great. Also, at the time Dixie didn't take penalty kicks but he volunteered to take one in that game. When he went to take the kick, he changed his mind at the last minute, wee Dixie says, but it saddens me when people remember Dixie only for that. He scored two hat-tricks in Cup finals for Celtic, after all.

'I took the penalty kicks at one stage in my career at the Park and it's not a job that you like. I never liked being the penalty taker. Big Jock told me to take penalties but if somebody else had been taking them I would not have thought, "I'm missing a chance to score a goal here." I think penalty takers are more relieved than anything else when they score. Even good strikers of the ball will sometimes say, "I'm not interested in this." It's a strange situation. I wish they would devise another way of winning games rather than that. Although it's exciting for people watching it on television, I always like to see a team getting beaten in a shoot-out by about three penalties so that there is not one lad sitting in the dressing-room feeling responsible for the defeat and there are instead two or three of them sharing that responsibility.

'Inter just concentrated on putting every one of their penalties in the net. They were good, good technical players, but for the game to end like that made it so frustrating. To me, that was like getting put out on a technicality. When a team wins on penalties they have not proved themselves to be a better team than you. It was a hard way not to get into the final of the European Cup.'

Evan Williams points to one missing link on that night of frustration, when Celtic struggled all night to find the right combination to unlock the Italians' defence: the absence of the pinpoint passing of Bertie Auld, who had moved on to Hibernian at the age of 33 in the spring of 1971. 'We had brought a few other new players into the team – such as Dixie, Harry Hood, Tommy Callaghan – they were good players, great players some of them, but wee Bertie was away and I think we were missing a little bit of magic in the middle of the park at that time because Bertie could do things to open games up. He was a cheeky little bandit! He would go back to his own six-yard line and collect the ball and start things. You can't keep that level of class football that the Lisbon Lions could play all the time. Obviously, good players came in, like Kenny Dalglish and Danny McGrain, but they were young players then, in 1972.'

Billy McNeill accepts that Celtic were competing with top-class opponents but suggests that if there had been more ambition on the directorial side of the club during that era, then Celtic might have been able to do even better than they did in the years after the victory at Lisbon. 'They were good sides!' he says firstly of Inter and AC Milan and the other top clubs that Celtic faced in the late 1960s and early 1970s. 'This is the whole thing. They were top-quality sides and when you get to quarter-final and semi-final stages you expect to meet good sides – and we did. The Italians were really difficult to beat. They were never, ever going to slaughter you, that was one thing, but they were helluva hard to break down. With us, it may be just that the edge had started to go. At the time when we won the European Cup, that was the time when the club should have been more forward thinking and, having beaten the big Italian squad in the final, we should therefore have been competing with them to sign the better players, not necessarily foreign players, I don't think that would have particularly suited us, but what they could have done and I think should have done is look round the Scottish market and the British market and buy players who were better than those we had and who would have complemented the squad.

'Had they done that at the time, I honestly think we would have had much more success in Europe than we had. After Lisbon we never improved in European terms. We got to a final but we never won it again. It looked for a long period, with the players who were coming through – such as Danny McGrain, George Connelly, David Hay, Lou Macari, Paul Wilson, and Kenny Dalglish – as though we had the chance to progress and maybe, when you think about it, perhaps we should have done; whether we started to get careless I don't know. Those lads looked as though they had the potential to go on to great things, and many of them did have great careers in the game, but maybe the spectre of the Lisbon Lions was too much for a lot of them to handle when it came to the big occasions with Celtic; I don't know.'

Glasgow hosted two European semi-finals on that same night in April 1972, with a combined official attendance of 152,000. Celtic went out on penalties to Inter while Rangers were getting past Bayern Munich in the semi-final of the European Cup-Winners' Cup, a tournament that Rangers had entered after losing the 1971 Scottish Cup final 2–1 to Celtic. Strangely, BBC Scotland decided to televise the Rangers match live, in the less prestigious tournament. It would be interesting to discover the mental mechanics that went into justifying that decision; or perhaps not.

Jock Stein, taking stock, commented, 'I don't think there's any country could say that they would dare put on two European ties on the one night, as Glasgow did. You wouldn't find this in Rome, Milan, Barcelona, Madrid or any of the top German cities.'

The defeat to Inter was only the second time a European Cup tie had been settled on penalties, and Stein's description of the penalty shoot-out as 'a circus act' seemed wholly appropriate. 'They beat us on a technicality,' he stated. All connected with Celtic were of the opinion in that spring of 1972 that it was the cruellest possible manner in which to be denied a place in a European Cup final. It would not be long before they would discover just how wrong they were.

EIGHT

The Mean Machine
ATLETICO MADRID 1974

The shrill ring of a telephone shattered the night-time tranquillity of a Madrid hotel room and Jimmy Johnstone reached out to take hold of the receiver. 'I was in my bed at one o'clock in the morning,' he says. 'I was half-sleeping. The voice on the other end said, "You're dead." Then they put the phone down. I thought it was some crank.' He would soon discover he was wrong. Celtic were in Spain, under protest, for the second leg of their high-tension 1974 European Cup semi-final with Atletico Madrid and Johnstone was quickly made aware that the telephone threat was to be taken seriously. 'On the morning after I got that call,' says Johnstone, 'big Jock took me aside and said, "Look, we've had a death threat. They're going to shoot me and you." I said, "What? I'm going home!" He said to me, "Listen, what chance have they got of hitting you when you get out there and you start jinking and jiving? I can't move; I'm sitting in that dugout."' It was typical of Stein to use his quick wits to make light of such a serious incident and also to think of a way in which he could turn the threat on its head as a means of persuading his star player to take the field and show off the best of his twisting, turning runs.

The Scottish club's reluctance to visit Madrid had been induced by the Spanish side's approach to the first leg – Atletico had made that match so much of a farce that Celtic fully expected to be awarded the tie and given free passage into the final. UEFA had failed the club and had instead insisted that Celtic should face Atletico in Madrid for the scheduled second leg. Atletico's conduct on the field of play at Celtic Park had been openly appalling. Now, more covert means were being used to intimidate the Celtic players.

Jock Stein had required all of his renowned expertise to guide Celtic through some difficult times for the club in European football from the early 1970s onwards. The defeat to Internazionale on penalty kicks was still fresh in the minds of all connected with the club when, in the autumn of 1972, Celtic had suffered a 3–0 mauling at the hands of Ujpest Dozsa in Budapest that knocked them out of that season's European Cup at the uncomfortably early stage of the second round. Stein had never had a great deal of time for the art of goalkeeping so when he made special mention of his goalkeeper the occasion had to be quite special and on that night Evan Williams had done much to prevent the defeat becoming one of unacceptable proportions. Williams had been pleased with his own performance in the match, even though the Hungarians had scored all three of their goals inside the first half of the first half and Stein stated afterwards that only the excellence of Williams had stopped Ujpest from handing out a hiding.

'I think they brought wee Jimmy back for the 3–0 game,' says Williams, 'the second game; and the wee man wasn't fully fit.' Bobby Lennox had also been carrying an injury in late 1972 when Celtic had faced Ujpest for the second time that year – the Celtic captain Billy McNeill, acting as go-between, had, before the game, approached Lennox and asked him if he was fit to play and had stressed that Stein desperately wanted to field the forward. Lennox did play, even though he was feeling the injury, but he had to be replaced during the game by Harry Hood. Stein had also employed his tried and tested method, in an away tie, of playing with three players who could fill up the central defence: McNeill, Pat McCluskey and George Connelly, the latter of whom could flit back and forth between central midfield and centre-back as and when required. It was of no use: with experienced wingers Johnstone and Lennox less than fully fit, the Hungarians had taken advantage of Celtic being lamed in attack to exert non-stop pressure on the Celtic defence and had cracked it open with the ease of breaking an eggshell.

That defeat reflected how the heat of competition in Europe was becoming more and more intense for Celtic. Teams from less recognised nations were now becoming more and more resilient and that was underlined when Celtic faced Basle in a quarter-final of the European Cup in 1974. A decade earlier, Celtic had beaten the Swiss on a 10–1 aggregate, scoring five goals in each leg. Five years previously, in 1969, the aggregate in a European Cup tie against Basle had been a much less comfortable 2–0 in Celtic's favour. Now, in the spring of 1974, Celtic found themselves 2–1 down at half-time in Basle. Evan Williams, who by then had become out of favour with Stein, had been brought into the side for the first time that 1973–74 season. He had made several good saves against the Swiss, but had lost one bad goal, Basle's second. 'One of their boys hit a shot,' recalls Williams, 'I dived to my right and the ball bobbled over the top of me. I had thought I had it covered and I maybe took it too easy.' That first leg ended in a 3–2 defeat for Celtic.

On the aeroplane home the further perils of an away trip in Europe were revealed to Williams when he unknowingly spoke to a reporter from *The Sun* newspaper, whom he believed to be a friendly fan, and said that he believed he ought to be given another chance in the team. Next day a huge spread appeared in *The Sun*, based around Williams' comments, and a ballistic Stein stressed to Williams that he had to be wary of sneak reporters at all times. It was to take extra-time in Glasgow before Celtic finally were able to dismiss the Swiss by winning 4–2 at Celtic Park and 6–5 on aggregate.

This pushed Celtic into a semi-final with Atletico Madrid in the spring of 1974 and those who crammed into Celtic Park for the first leg anticipated seeing opponents in the mould of Real Madrid, Valencia or Barcelona, Spanish sides who had provided rich entertainment in Celtic's previous encounters with clubs from that country. Instead, from the first minute to the final minute, the Atletico players hacked and whacked, nipped at and spat on the Celtic players at every opportunity, making no attempt to play the ball. It was murderous stuff as they went about their task of killing the game. 'Teams at that time were scared of coming to Glasgow,' says Bobby Lennox. 'I have since often met players that I played against in those years and they say how much they were worried by coming to Glasgow. So Atletico's coach decided to counter that by putting a team of hatchet men on the park.'

The Atletico coach was Juan Carlos Lorenzo, who had also had that role for Argentina at the 1966 World Cup in England. Lorenzo's team, in that tournament, had received a warning from FIFA for their conduct in a group match with a talented German side at Villa Park in which one of Lorenzo's players had been dismissed and the others had kicked and gouged their way to a 0–0 draw. The warning from FIFA bothered Lorenzo and his men as much as a parking ticket on a getwaway car's windscreen might bother a bank robber. The Argentinians had achieved their objective in reaching the latter stages of the tournament and the only punishment that would really have registered with them would have been expulsion from the World Cup. Lorenzo's team had then moved on to a notorious quarter-final with England after which Alf Ramsey, the England manager, described them as a team that had not come out to play football but one that had, instead, opted to 'act as animals'. Jock Stein, a keen student of world football, had been aware of all this and knew what to expect from Atletico at Celtic Park. He had consequently warned his players not to react to any provocation but even he was shocked at the extreme viciousness of the Atletico players. Stein's team for that first leg with Atletico was: Denis Connaghan, David Hay, Jim Brogan, Pat McCluskey, Billy McNeill, Stevie Murray, Jimmy Johnstone, Harry Hood, Dixie Deans, Kenny Dalglish and Tommy Callaghan.

'It was a non-game,' is the opinion of David Hay, who featured in midfield for Celtic against Atletico. 'Big Jock said, "Whatever you do, don't get involved." And in a strange way, looking back, we probably were too controlled, although maybe in terms of the history of the club it's better that you don't get involved. We maybe accepted too much until we blew up at the end in the tunnel. There was no flow to the game. We all got kicked that night, even me, and I was normally associated with kicking other people! They were just doing everybody. It became farcical. Their goalkeeper would get the ball and just kick it up the park and they wouldn't come out of their box. That was just the way they wanted to play it. They wanted a result at all costs and were prepared to go to those lengths.'

Evan Williams was an interested spectator at that match and was horrified at the mauling handed out to the Celtic players by their opponents, and in particular to Jimmy Johnstone. 'As the game went on,' he says, 'even though they had nine men with half an hour to go, you couldn't see Celtic scoring. It was a strange feeling. They were like animals. When you look back at that game, nowadays they would have ended up with about six men on the park; the wee man got some doing that night and the wee man was around 30 then, so he wasn't a spring chicken as such.'

Atletico ended the match with only eight men – three of their number had been dismissed by Turkish referee Dogan Babacan – but also with a goalless draw. UEFA's observer, sitting high in the new, stanchion-free stand at Celtic Park, had enjoyed an unimpeded view of the mayhem and Celtic fully expected that his report to European football's governing body would recommend that the tie be awarded to Celtic, or that it would at least be switched from Madrid, where the Atletico fans were being worked into a frenzy by the Spanish media. Instead, UEFA administered a mere smack on the wrist to Lorenzo – another caution from officialdom for the Atletico manager to place in his souvenir album – and Celtic had no option but to face Atletico again in Madrid.

It was suggested then, and in the years since, that Celtic should simply have scratched from the tournament and walked away, but that was never a realistic option. They did not have to look far into the past to see the severity with which UEFA might punish a club that threatened to pull out of a fixture. Benfica, prior to their 1965 European Cup final with Internazionale, had threatened not to take part in the match unless it was switched away from the San Siro stadium in Milan, the home ground of their opponents. The promise of retribution from UEFA was swift and sharp. In the event that Benfica did not turn up, stated UEFA, they would fine the Portuguese club a sum approximating to £40,000; a figure composed of a fine plus compensation for lost gate receipts, a substantial chunk of which were due to find their way into the Swiss vaults of European football's self-satisfied governing body. UEFA clearly viewed the merest hint of dissent against them, or any threat to their projected income, to be of far greater import than a club tarnishing the game itself, as had been the case with Atletico Madrid at Celtic Park. In 1974, a decade after that threat against Benfica, a projected estimate of the financial punishment Celtic might expect from UEFA was in the region of £100,000; a sum of considerable magnitude and one greater by far than any transfer fee the club had paid out up until that time. UEFA might also have imposed a ban from European football. Celtic had only to look as far as Glasgow Rangers for an example of that: just two years earlier Rangers had been banned from defending the European Cup-Winners' Cup after their fans had invaded the pitch at the final in Barcelona.

It had been in the gift of UEFA to take action against Atletico and they had failed in their duty to act for the good of the game. It is also no exaggeration to state that UEFA's insistence on Celtic travelling to Madrid for the second leg of that European Cup semi-final placed the lives of the Celtic players in serious danger. 'It was a nightmare in Madrid from when we got off the plane until we left,' comments Jimmy Johnstone. 'It was just hatred. At the airport we had the police and the army to protect us and they escorted us back and forward to and from training sessions. We had the army behind us and the army in front of us going to training. At the hotel, there were plain-clothes policemen walking about, gunned up. We were told beforehand that they were there for our own protection.'

The Celtic team arrived at Atletico's stadium on the banks of the Manzanares river for the second leg to find that it was ringed by 1,000 police officers with a mounted division in operation to keep at bay the Atletico supporters, whose inferiority complex at living constantly in the shadow of Real Madrid had been inflamed to hellish proportions by the propaganda of their newspapers, which had written up the events in Glasgow in such a way as to make Atletico appear victims of harsh treatment on Celtic's part. Spain, in 1974, was a country that had for four decades been in the grip of a fascist dictatorship, headed by General Francisco Franco, and newspapers were tightly controlled to report stories along strict nationalistic lines.

Water cannon and tear gas were part of the armoury deployed by the police to help keep the crowd at bay, and Jimmy Johnstone remembers distinctly the moments when the frothing Spanish crowd were finally given the chance to release their pent-up emotions on sight of the Celtic players. 'When we got to the ground, it was a cauldron,' he says. 'We went out before the game to kick the ball about and you should have heard them! I had never seen as much hatred in my life.' After just three minutes of a warm-up, the Celtic players had to evacuate the playing field for their own safety. It was already clear that, regardless of the various pompous statements that had been issued by UEFA, this was never going to be a game played under normal sporting conditions. UEFA had warned Atletico as to their future conduct but the hostile atmosphere generated by that second leg meant that Celtic had next to no chance of winning the tie. The Celtic team that took the field in Madrid under the most adverse conditions was: Denis Connaghan, Danny McGrain, Jim Brogan, Pat McCluskey, Billy McNeill, David Hay, Jimmy Johnstone, Stevie Murray, Harry Hood, Kenny Dalglish and Bobby Lennox.

The threat of being shot had, unsurprisingly, a severe effect on Johnstone's game and, once the match got underway, he and his teammates discovered that the referee too had been affected by the atmosphere of intimidation. 'The Atletico players were just at it all night,' Johnstone explains. 'Any opportunity they got, they were just nipping you and spitting on you and the referee was just turning a blind eye. He was looking at the crowd and must have been thinking, "I'm not getting into any bother here." They were nutters. That wasn't football. That was the sadder side of football. Football is a great game, a lovely game; it's great to play in matches where there is a great atmosphere and you meet lovely people. UEFA should have given us the tie, without a shadow of a doubt; it was ridiculous that we had to go and play over there.

'There were a number of Argentinians in that team and big Jock met the Argentinian manager at the World Cup later that year and he said that if there had been dope testing done on that team there would have been about five of them who would have tested positive for using stimulants in that game. They were just mad. That wasn't football at all. They were just animals really.'

Bobby Lennox also remembers well that visit to Atletico, and playing in front of their 65,000 supporters, stirred into a state of dementia. 'That's the noisiest away crowd I've ever heard,' he says. 'They were really screaming and bawling. They hated us. The team that beat us in Madrid should never have still been in the tournament. Had they come and played football against us in Glasgow we would have beaten them.'

The match in Madrid ended in a sour 2–0 victory for Atletico. Against Bayern Munich in the final in Brussels, Atletico were winning 1–0 until a long-range, last-minute effort from Georg Schwarzenbeck saved the game, levelled the match and forced a replay that Bayern won 4–0, bringing justice down on Atletico's heads at last. 'I was really glad Atletico got beaten in the final – and they were a minute away from winning it,' says Bobby Lennox.

That spring of 1974 Celtic supporters could look back over a decade of enterprising, attacking football from their club that had seen them reach the latter stages of European competition eight times. The European Cup semi-finals of 1972 and 1974 could, with some justification, be dismissed as aberrations, particularly in the case of the match with Atletico, where the eventual outcome was taken out of Celtic's hands. As all connected with Celtic looked forward to their ninth successive crack at the European Cup in the 1974–75 season, there was no reason to believe that the club's successes in reaching semi-finals and finals of European tournaments could not continue indefinitely.

NINE

Turf Luck
REAL MADRID 1980

Real Madrid have every reason to regard Glasgow as the second city of their sprawling footballing empire. The Spanish club have left their imprint on all corners of the world but it is in Glasgow that they have enjoyed their most sublime moments in European competition. It was at Hampden Park in 1960 that Real won a record fifth successive European Cup with a 7–3 defeat of Eintracht Frankfurt that lays claim to be the greatest club match of all. Four decades later, in May 2002, watched by several of the Lisbon Lions, the Real of Raul, Roberto Carlos and Luis Figo crowned their club's centenary by winning the trophy for the ninth time, consolidating their reputation as the greatest club side Europe has known over five decades of continental competition. Zinedine Zidane's scintillating volley on the night of that match against Leverkusen made for one of the great European Cup-winning goals.

Three meetings between Celtic and Real Madrid took place in between those two momentous European Cup finals, and each one would be of serious significance to the two clubs. Max Benjamin, a Glasgow businessman, organised the first meeting between Celtic and Real Madrid, in 1962; a friendly from which the proceeds would go to the Jewish Blue-and-White charity to benefit orphaned children. Real were paid a £10,000 fee for this match, their second visit to Glasgow, and they nobly decided to donate the money to the charity. The match, on 10 September 1962, took place just a fortnight before Celtic were to meet Valencia in their first-ever European tie but it was the game with Real Madrid that proved to be, by far, the most eagerly anticipated of the two encounters.

Real had already begun their policy of bulking out their team by buying big international names and for the match at Celtic Park they included some of the greatest names to have graced the game of football, including Argentinian forward Alfredo Di Stefano and his side-kick, the Hungarian Ferenc 'Pancho' Puskas, Uruguayan centre-half José Santamaria and the Spanish winger Francisco 'Paco' Gento. For Real, it was a pre-season friendly and their final warm-up before the Spanish league fixtures began; for Celtic it was billed by the less excitable press as 'the match of the season' and by their more sensationalistic counterparts as 'the most glamorous occasion in Celtic's history'. The Real players were on a hefty bonus of £100 a man to win – such games may have been friendlies but the club still had a reputation to maintain and Real's reputation in the early 1960s had snowballed through their players strutting their stuff in friendly matches at various venues across Europe and leaving the locals goggle-eyed in admiration. The Glaswegian football supporters who turned out for Celtic's friendly with Real would, as always, prove even more exceptional than those elsewhere on the continent in the way in which they would show their appreciation of Real.

A 76,000 all-ticket crowd was drawn to the match at Celtic Park that Wednesday evening; the biggest crowd that had been seen at a midweek game at the ground up until that point. Bobby Carroll, who did well against Real when he took to the field that evening, comments, 'For us, even to think about being on the park with these guys was a thrill.'

The two clubs agreed to allow four substitutes; Celtic were not keen on this and acceded, slightly unwillingly, only because it was the wish of Real to have such an arrangement. Substitutes were still taboo in the Scottish game in the early 1960s and Celtic chairman Robert Kelly was among those most opposed to the introduction of such a new-fangled idea. On the night, the use of substitutes worked in Celtic's favour in that the replacements freshened up the team and pepped up its performance. The starting line-up had been: Frank Haffey, Dunky

MacKay, Jim Kennedy, Pat Crerand, Billy McNeill, Billy Price, Bobby Lennox, Charlie Gallagher, John Hughes, Mike Jackson and Frank Brogan. The forwards misfired in the first half, so at half-time Stevie Chalmers, Bobby Carroll and Alec Byrne replaced Lennox, Hughes and Brogan. The change of personnel enlivened the team and Chalmers whipped in a fine goal for Celtic even though they went down 3–1.

A frenzied Celtic Park crowd remained rooted to their individual spots on the terracing from beginning to end that night, mesmerised by the football on show and at the conclusion of the match they demanded that the players return to run a lap of honour. It was still not enough for the fanatics: 10,000 of them marched from the stadium to the Central Hotel at Glasgow Central station to pay further tribute to the teams as they enjoyed the post-match banquet. Inside, Real manager Miguel Munoz and star man Di Stefano were enthusing about Pat Crerand, whom they picked out as the player of note in the Celtic team. Crerand and his Celtic teammates were later presented with gifts of souvenir tartan travel rugs by Real Madrid.

'That was brilliant that night!' says Bobby Carroll. 'The fans went wild! We went back for a reception at the Central Hotel that night and there were 10,000 at the Central Station; it was mobbed. That game gave us a bit of confidence because we had a bit of success against them that night. We never won but we weren't disgraced. It was 3–1 but we did give them a game and we were a young team. I didn't know I was coming on at half-time and it was quite a thrill to get on against the great Real Madrid.

'I played centre-forward against Santamaria – I felt I did all right when I came on, although I never won anything in the air! He was a brilliant centre-half, a giant of a man. I remember that he towered above me. Real Madrid tended to let you play up until their penalty box and then they won it and Di Stefano would break out and set up an attack again. I think they were prepared to let you get the ball and then they would win it at the 18-yard box when it was getting cluttered up and break away. It looked as if we were playing some good football that night, passing it about, but once you got to that box it was more difficult.

'We didn't get swapping our jerseys in those days; I think we only had two sets of jerseys – one set would be getting cleaned and we would be wearing the other set. We were told not to swap our jerseys that night. If we had been allowed to do so, I might have got Puskas's too; when the whistle blew I was a couple of feet away from him and he was the first one to shake my hand.'

Five years later, in June 1967, the two clubs met for a second time and the atmosphere surrounding the clubs' second friendly was much less amicable. Celtic had become European champions just a fortnight earlier and at the final Alfredo Di Stefano had approached Jock Stein to ask if Celtic would supply the opposition for his testimonial in Madrid. It was a request that Stein simply could not refuse and so, rather than allow his players to go on holiday after the European Cup final in Lisbon, they gathered together for one last push in that momentous season. It was a huge honour for Celtic to be involved in such a game: Di Stefano was, by 1967, 40 years of age and he had proved himself the greatest player in the world game during the post-war years, before reluctantly leaving Real in the summer of 1964; 'Don Alfredo' was at that time 37 and the team was being rebuilt, but to sweeten the blow the Real president, Santiago Bernabeu, had promised him the biggest testimonial match in the history of the Spanish club, and in the summer of 1967 that came to fruition with the match against Celtic.

The Real players were in a less than friendly mood as they approached the game: they had won their sixth European Cup in 1966 and felt that they were still the best side in Europe. Di Stefano had been in Lisbon determined to bring the European Cup winners to the Bernabeu Stadium – whichever of Celtic or Internazionale were to win the 1967 final – for his testimonial. Not only would the winning team prove the best draw for Di Stefano's match but Real would, they hoped, prove emphatically by beating the European Cup-winners that it was they, the Spanish side, who were still the real European champions. It was great box office for Di Stefano and while the world may have been limbering up for the 'Summer of Love', it appeared to have bypassed Madrid that June of 1967.

Bobby Lennox recalls with clarity that early summer visit to Madrid. 'Real kept telling everybody how wonderful they were and that they were the real champions and that they would beat us. It was a hate game. Bertie and Amancio got sent off for fighting. There were battles all over the field that night. The headline in one Spanish paper was, "We will prove we are the real champions" and another headline was "We will prove Celtic are false". Oh, it was hatred that night. That was a real European Cup tie over there.'

Amancio Amarro, a fast, skilled forward who relished the physical side of the game, was Real's great hope as the torchbearer of the inimitable Real style now that Di Stefano and Puskas had moved on. Jock Stein was well aware of that, as Bobby Lennox explains. 'Before the game big Jock said to Bertie, "Look, Amancio's the man. If he plays, they'll play. So get close to him. Work him hard." So Bertie said, "I solved the problem. We had a fight 20 minutes into the game. The two of us were put off – problem solved." There were a good few bust-ups that night. Real Madrid might have had great players but they could all handle themselves. It was still as good a game of football as you could play in, with two teams really going at each other, desperate to win.

'It was supposed to be a friendly and there were 135,000 there for Di Stefano. He played for the first quarter of an hour and he was flicking the ball this way and that. The boys were glad to see him going off the park. Willie O'Neill had come into the team that played in the European Cup final in place of Stevie and John Fallon came in for Ronnie, and Di Stefano continually nutmegged Willie. Wee Jimmy and I were giving him some amount of stick during the game!' After those opening 15 minutes, the players watched Di Stefano leave the pitch and walk up a red carpet that had been rolled out for him from pitch to president's box, where, on receiving a mini-replica of the European Cup, he could not hold back his tears.

Jock Stein had been among the crowd at Hampden Park when Real had won the European Cup in 1960 and he was an enormous admirer of the way in which they played football but, by 1967, his own team had surpassed Real for style and their skills made the highly rated hombres of Real look ordinary. The match finished in a 1–0 victory for Celtic and Jimmy Johnstone produced what he considers to be his finest performance as a footballer. The Celtic goal exemplified his individual brilliance on the night: Johnstone picked the ball up from Tommy Gemmell, deep inside the Celtic half, and took it for a stroll past two hefty Real Madrid challenges, opening up numerous options for himself before splitting the Real Madrid defence with a crafted, crafty pass into the penalty area for Bobby Lennox to slide home an angled shot. 'Without a shadow of a doubt,' says Johnstone, 'that was my best game for Celtic.' During the closing stages of the match, the Spanish team's defenders were turning their backs on the Celtic winger rather than trying to stop him; they had done that too often and too unsuccessfully on the evening. 'None of them would come near me with about a quarter of an hour to go!' he says. The ball was drawn to Johnstone so much that it arrived at his feet simultaneously with the final whistle. He lifted the ball above his head and the crowd rewarded him with a standing ovation.

'Our boys were thrilled they won that night,' says Lennox, 'because we had won the European Cup a fortnight before it and we proved to Europe that we truly were the European champions because we went to Madrid, to the Bernabeu, and won 1–0. Everybody was exhausted at the end of it – it was a really tough, bruising game. Their right-back scudded me one right on the back of the nut – I hope he broke his hand.

'It is interesting to remember that we had played Madrid in a friendly in 1962 when I played a half and we got beaten 3–1 and got the greatest reception ever at Celtic Park. We went into a coach to go back into the centre of Glasgow and all along the road there were people cheering us. We got into town and there were people all over the town cheering us. That was after we had been beaten at home 3–1! At that time, we thought those teams were streets ahead of us. Then, within five or six years, we had won the European Cup and had gone to Real Madrid and had beaten them 1–0.'

The Celtic players had found that circumstances had conspired to deny them a big celebration of their European Cup win in Lisbon. It was in Madrid, after that great victory over Real in the Bernabeu on 7 June 1967, that a happy Stein let his team off the leash to toast in style their achievements of the 1966–67 season. 'I would say we celebrated winning the European Cup better after we beat Madrid a few days later,' says Bobby Lennox. 'The boys had a good night out; we enjoyed ourselves.' Real had set the standard for excellence in the European Cup when, spearheaded by Alfredo Di Stefano, they had won the first five consecutive tournaments in magnificent style, with fast, free-flowing football. Celtic's win over Inter had made them European champions, but for Stein and his players that win over Real, friendly or not, had almost been a test to verify that they were winners of the highest pedigree and that night in Madrid they proved to the aristocrats of European football that they could live with, and beat, the very best on a consistent basis. All connected with Celtic had known that Lisbon had been no fluke and now the Madrilenos had received proof positive that Celtic bore the mark of champions of the highest class.

Thirteen years were to pass before Celtic and Real Madrid would contest a match again, and this time it would be a European Cup tie in the spring of 1980 that would provide the excuse for the two clubs to renew their acquaintance. The 1970s had not been particularly kind to either side; both Real and Celtic had struggled to adapt during a period when the European game was being strangled by negative tactics. Safety-first football had resulted in a series of desperately dull European Cup finals from the mid-1970s onwards, and a number of very ordinary sides had become European champions. Neither Celtic nor Real Madrid, whose positive reputations were both founded on enterprising, attacking play, had found it easy to adjust in that era of functional football.

The match with Real in 1980 was particularly special to Celtic in that it was the first time since the mid-1970s that they would be facing a club of genuine stature in a European tie. It was an evening that promised to provoke recollections of the great nights of the Jock Stein era when Europe's finest would pay regular visits to the East End of Glasgow. Celtic's seamless run of success in Europe from the mid-1960s to the mid-1970s had lulled the support into taking it for granted that their team would have a permanent place among the upper echelons of European football. They had been rudely awoken from that presumption during the second half of the 1970s when Celtic had gone into a steep decline. Suddenly, Celtic had started struggling to live with the most ordinary opposition in Europe.

Celtic's ninth successive Scottish League title in the club's glowing sequence under Jock Stein had been won in 1974 and their subsequent entry into the European Cup had seen Celtic pitted against Olympiakos of Greece in the first round of the 1974–75 tournament. After a 1–1 draw in Glasgow, two Olympiakos goals in the opening 25 minutes had left Celtic floundering in front of a frenzied 45,000 inside the Karaiskakis Stadium in Piraeus. Bobby Lennox was pitched into the fray as a substitute for Jimmy Johnstone during that match, with Jock Stein hoping that Lennox might be able to help retrieve something for the team on a desperate evening. 'I remember the pitch was a cowp on the Monday night,' recalls Lennox of that trip to Greece, 'but by the Wednesday the pitch was really quite good. It was also really noisy inside the ground.

'They scored a goal after four minutes and then we went 2–0 down. I was on the bench and I came on with 15–20 minutes to go. I had only been on the park for a few minutes when they got a free kick. So I was standing in front of the ball at the free kick while a substitution was being made; their inside-left and I were standing smiling at each other as he was preparing to take the kick. Then the referee came from the far side of the park and booked me. He said I hadn't retreated far enough at the free kick. I pointed out to him that a substitution was being made so the ball wasn't in play. "I decide the substitutes," he said. Two minutes later, their right-back went to cross the ball, I blocked it, it went over my shoulder and the referee came across the park and put me off. Big Jock at the time actually got on to me for the first booking and I said, "They were making a substitution." I didn't feel I was doing anything wrong and if I had seen the referee coming I would have stepped out of the road but both myself and the Greek player were looking to the side of the pitch where the linesman had his flag up for their player to come on.' Lennox and Celtic had been reminded once again of the inevitable, hidden dangers of European competition, including incomprehensible refereeing decisions. The Celt is, however, willing to accept that Celtic's first-round European Cup exit that autumn of 1974 was not entirely down to misfortune. 'At that stage we weren't going too well,' he admits. 'That team wasn't just as good a team as the one we had had.'

That Celtic team of the 1970s was in the process of being stripped of its assets piece by piece as if it was some stately home that the owners simply could no longer afford to maintain. Lou Macari had left for Manchester United in early 1973, having become disillusioned by Celtic's system of paying only a modest basic wage, supplemented by big bonuses for wins in Europe. He was followed 18 months later by

David Hay, who moved on to Chelsea in summer 1974 after a lengthy dispute with Stein over pay. George Connelly, an outstanding prospect as a cultured midfielder, was absent from the team that faced Olympiakos. He was finding it difficult to cope with the pressures of professional football and he was soon simply to walk away from Celtic and stardom to quit the game. Billy McNeill had appeared in his 72nd match in European competition against Olympiakos in Greece: Jimmy Johnstone in his 67th. That away match in Piraeus was to be the final match in Europe for both of those great Celts: at the end of the 1974–75 season both left the club. They were the two Celts who had made most appearances in European football by the mid-1970s. It all meant that Celtic were being simultaneously deprived of their best young talent and their most experienced players; not a formula for success. It also made the club a less attractive environment for those young, ambitious players who did remain at Celtic Park.

The departure of so many top-quality players punched several holes in the Celtic team and that was compounded in the summer of 1975 when Jock Stein suffered life-threatening injuries in a car crash on his way home from a holiday in Spain. The manager pulled through, but he would require one year of rest and recuperation and for those twelve months he handed over control of the running of the team to his assistant, Sean Fallon. It was the Irishman who was at the helm as Celtic entered the European Cup-Winners' Cup in 1975, Celtic having failed to win the Scottish League and gain entry to the European Cup for the first time in a decade.

Jock Stein was a member of the travelling party that made the journey to Oporto in Portugal in the autumn of 1975 for Celtic's second-round Cup-Winners' Cup tie with Boavista, but Stein took no active part in the team's preparations for the match, which took on an unconventional hue when Fallon led his players to a nearby beach and used the sand as a temporary tactics board to show how Boavista would play. His talk was suddenly interrupted when a wave rolled up the beach and washed away his illustration. Bobby Lennox, the only Lisbon Lion still at the club, was made captain by Fallon for that second-round trip to play Boavista in the autumn of 1975. 'I remember that we stayed in a hotel quite near the beach,' says Lennox, 'and went for a couple of walks along the beach. We walked for a bit and then, all of a sudden, we found ourselves in an area of real poverty. It was amazing to go from this really palatial hotel into an area of poverty.'

Portugal had undergone a revolution in the previous year and there were thousands of soldiers milling in and around the ground on the day of the game, with a considerable number of those stationed directly behind the Celtic goal. The Celtic of the mid-1970s had a new goalkeeper, Englishman Peter Latchford, and whenever he went to take a goal kick, soldiers would prod him with their rifle butts to encourage him to speed things up. Latchford and his teammates had suffered an even nastier jolt to the senses in the minutes before the match. They had left their dressing-room and had been standing in the players' tunnel awaiting the arrival of the Boavista team when they were overwhelmed by the most putrid stench. They had no idea why the tunnel should smell so badly, but were soon enlightened when the Boavista players arrived and began their pre-match ritual of relieving themselves against the tunnel wall.

'I was captain in the first leg,' says Bobby Lennox. 'It was the only time I was ever captain in Europe. I also remember that it was an afternoon kick-off because the game finished in daylight. Big Peter Latchford saved a penalty with a couple of minutes to go and that meant we kept the score at 0–0. Sean Fallon had seen Boavista a couple of times and told Peter that if the boy Alves, who wore gloves, took a penalty kick, he would put it to the right and he told Peter to dive to his right if they got a penalty kick. Peter dived to his right and saved it.' Their surroundings at that match with Boavista seemed to be a reminder to the Celtic players that they had stepped down a level in Europe after nine successive seasons in the European Cup. 'The stadium wasn't the most intimidating stadium we had been in,' says Lennox, 'although it was a wee bit like Lisbon in that it had dressing-rooms, then a courtyard and you walked across the courtyard where people couldn't see you, and then into a small tunnel and out on to the field. I remember it not being a big and intimidating ground.'

One of the most distinguished things about Boavista was their black and white checked shirts, which resembled a chess board. Celtic's shirts also looked somewhat unusual as they took to the field for the second leg against the Portuguese side: that match at Celtic Park, on Guy Fawkes Night 1975, was the first time ever that Celtic had worn

numbers on their hooped shirts. A first-minute goal from Kenny
Dalglish sent Celtic on their way to a smooth 3–1 win and a place in
the Cup-Winners' Cup quarter-finals. There they would face
Sachsenring Zwickau, one of a host of clubs from the communist state
of East Germany to have been founded in the post-war years. It was
Zwickau's first bite at the big time and although they were a little-
known club, they had already knocked Panathinaikos and Fiorentina
out of the 1975–76 Cup-Winners' Cup. They also featured the
excellent goalkeeper Jurgen Croy, capped 67 times by East Germany.

The quarter-final first leg at Celtic Park drew a crowd of 50,000 to
the ground and Celtic looked sure to seize a secure lead from the first
leg as they launched attack after attack on the East German goal. By
half-time, though, having been repelled repeatedly by Croy and the
Zwickau defence, all Celtic had to show for their efforts was a solitary
goal from Kenny Dalglish. Celtic were lacking creativity in midfield,
but the opportunity to create an even greater lead was passed up when
Bobby Lennox misplaced a penalty midway through the first half. 'I
had been practising taking penalties up at my own wee local park,' he
recalls. 'I would take two canes up and put them down a yard inside of
a goalpost and I had three or four balls and I would just keep pushing
them in, pushing them in. I would then run behind the goal and come
from the other side and push them in again. Against Zwickau I changed
my mind at the last second and the goalie saved it.' It would prove a
costly miss. With Celtic 1–0 ahead with only two minutes remaining,
and every Celtic player except Peter Latchford planted in the German
half in search of a second goal, the ball fell to Zwickau forward Ludwig
Blank on the halfway line. He shuttled it swiftly away from Roy Aitken,
the last man before Latchford, and Blank kept his nerve to stride
forward at speed before slotting the ball past the Celtic goalkeeper to
provide the Germans with a precious equaliser. A fortnight later, in
Zwickau, Celtic conceded a goal after only five minutes when Blank
sent a stunning shot past Latchford, and although Celtic subsequently
created a number of scoring chances, they missed them all and the East
Germans advanced into the semi-finals of the 1976 Cup-Winners' Cup.

An embarrassingly early exit from Europe in the following season saw
Celtic lose in the first round of the 1976–77 UEFA Cup to Wisla

Krakow of Poland. 'We went to all the duff places,' says Peter Latchford as he thinks back to that trip to a communist Poland that was beginning to creak under pressure from a population that had been repressed for too long and where extreme measures were taken to keep this Western football team away from the locals. 'I remember getting beaten in Poland,' adds Latchford. 'I remember that, because my first daughter was born while I was away and I didn't know for a day or so because we were locked up in an embassy somewhere under armed guard. It was an embassy outside the city and we even had to train in the orchard of the embassy, watched by armed guards with rifles and alsatians. We went for a run around the orchard one morning to loosen up because we were only allowed one training session at the ground. It was only the following day, the day of the game, that a journalist phoned me up to tell me that my wife had given birth 24 hours previously. We went to East Germany, Poland, Romania, when you're looking for the Spains and the Italys. We always tended to get the Eastern European destinations. Happy days!'

Krakow 1976 was followed by Innsbruck 1977, where Celtic toppled out of the 1977–78 European Cup to the Austrian champions at the second-round stage. Jock Stein was still the Celtic manager for those ties, but he was a changed man from the driven winner who had pushed his Celtic teams to their limits in European matches during the 1960s and early 1970s. 'He was towards the end of his career at Celtic and he had also had his bad accident,' remembers Peter Latchford. 'He came back from that but he was a changed man, a different guy; much more mellow. He took things much more easily and didn't let things hassle him so much. He was still as thorough then as he could be for the time as far as preparation was concerned. He would tell you how the other team was going to play and usually he was spot-on. He was meticulous and would have checked every detail relating to the match.

'As a player you don't worry about details when you go on a European trip, but you get a different perspective on things when you move on to the coaching side. As a player you get to the airport, drop your bag down and say, "Where's the coffee?" Somebody hands you your passport, you go to the gate, you hand back your passport, sit and wait for the flight, get on the plane and the only moans you have are if you don't get fed quickly enough. Then you get on a bus, go to a hotel, go to sleep. Everything is done for you, but you take absolutely no notice of it. It's only if you go into coaching and management that you then see the preparation and planning that goes into it. Everything has to be done so that these guys, the players, have no hassle. As a player, the only time you question things is when things aren't going properly. You are concentrating on the game, on keeping fit, eating the right food, sleeping, getting as much rest as you can and trying to relieve the boredom. The background to all that is the planning that the coaching staff have to do to make sure everything goes OK.

'You never really got any hassle when you went abroad with Celtic because the coaching staff and the manager smoothed it all out. While you were lying in bed resting they were actually buzzing about trying to organise your food properly, organising the bus to make sure it was there on time and to make sure there was somebody at the stadium to open it up when you got there and that they would put all the lights on when you did get there. Now it's all much more organised because they have people from UEFA supervising all this, but at that time they relied on the hospitality of each club to make sure that they got to train with the right balls, the type that would be used in the match, that the lights were on, that the water in the showers was hot. Everything was organised behind the scenes in the days leading up to the match so that in the hour before it began the players would be in the right frame of mind for the game.

'Everybody abroad held Jock Stein in such high esteem. Everybody knew him – it didn't matter where he went. So if he asked for something he tended to get it. I don't ever remember any problems as such; he knew what he was doing. He had had nine or ten years of a very settled team, when he was bringing in quality players and he had broken up that great team and had spent most of the time after that trying to rebuild. The club was in a bit of turmoil: he had his accident; Sean took over; players left and players came in who were not of the right calibre. There was all sorts of movement.'

Things became even worse for Stein and Celtic when the club missed out on qualifying for European competition entirely for season 1978–79; it would be the first season in which the club had been absent from European competition since 1962 and it was a symptom of that

turbulent time for Celtic, a time when the club was struggling to find
equilibrium and a way forward after the exceptional era of the Lisbon
Lions. Kenny Dalglish, the multi-skilled forward who was the jewel in
Celtic's crown during the 1970s, had been swiped by Liverpool in the
summer of 1977 and a dismal domestic showing in the season after his
£440,000 British-record transfer had meant that Celtic had failed to
win a place in any of the three European competitions for the final full
season of the 1970s.

Celtic supporters could only look on wistfully as Dalglish scored the
only goal of the game for Liverpool against Bruges in the 1978
European Cup final; the player had departed for a club at which he
hoped to have the chance to win medals in Europe and that meant,
conversely, that Celtic in the late 1970s was no longer such a club.
Dalglish's exit from Celtic Park had weakened the club even further and
helped lead to the departure of Jock Stein as manager in summer 1978.
He was replaced by Billy McNeill, whose young, reconstructed Celtic
side surprisingly took the Scottish League title in spring 1979, winning
entry into the European Cup in season 1979–80. 'Billy came in,' adds
Latchford, 'and had to start from scratch again. So there was a bit of a
search for stability inside the club.'

No one was sure how far McNeill's youthful bunch of players could
travel in European competition, but their adventures in the 1979–80
European Cup would prove to be almost as extraordinary as anything
the club had ever experienced in Europe. Those adventures would take
them on a journey into the land that time had forgotten, take them
close to the biggest disaster in the club's European history and then
provide them with the opportunity to obtain one of the club's greatest-
ever results.

The first-round draw offered a new dimension to Celtic's European
experiences when they were paired with Partizani Tirana of Albania.
Celtic had visited communist countries many times before but a visit to
Albania in 1979 was like stepping out of reality and onto the set of a
science-fiction movie. Under Enver Hoxha, the 72-year-old first-
secretary of the Albanian communist party, the country had adopted a
strict Marxist-Leninist regime but one that was even more eccentric
than those of the other Eastern European communist states. It made

countries such as Hungary and Czechoslovakia look sleepily suburban and middle class in comparison. Among Hoxha's dictats were the strict banning of private motor cars and a decree that males were forbidden to have facial hair. The Celtic right-back of the time, Danny McGrain, sported a full beard and debate raged long and hard prior to the tie as to whether he would have to shave it off in order to be allowed to enter the communist enclave of Albania. He was eventually granted leave to enter without taking that most drastic of measures but the Albanian authorities proved unbending in insisting that no representatives of the Scottish press or Celtic supporters would be permitted visas to travel to Albania.

Bobby Lennox remembers distinctly the few days the Celtic party spent among a clean-shaven, bicycling population who were absolutely fanatical about football and who, deprived of Western free-market goods, were desperate to obtain the denims that some of the Celtic players were wearing. 'That was the strangest country we ever went to, out of all the countries we visited,' says Lennox. 'That was a weird place. When we got there they kept us waiting at the airport for ages, looking at our passports and our faces.'

The culture shock of arriving in Albania is also etched clearly on the mind of Peter Latchford. 'Strange, strange things went on on that trip,' he says. 'I remember the reports that Danny would have to shave his beard off and it was similarly comical stuff from the moment that the plane landed in Albania. We were looking out of the window and there was a tiny, little tank-like thing with a gun turret on top of it and the gun turret followed the plane until the plane came to a stop. We then unloaded all the baggage and had to go through three sets of customs checks at the same place. The second time we began to wonder what was going on, so we walked round and looked behind the guy who was supposed to be checking the baggage and he was just sitting there looking into a machine that had no screen in it. It was just a box with a hole in it and he was watching through the hole as the bags went through. We had to go through that three times. They kept us there, checking this and checking that. They were very friendly people but for some unknown reason they wanted to check everything.

'Tirana was just . . . you could write a book about our trip there on its own,' continues Latchford. 'That was a weird city. There were about

10,000 folk watching us train and we caused a riot after training because someone gave one of those little pin badges to an Albanian and we got into trouble for that. They were clamouring for anything, anything you could give them as souvenirs; they were desperate for anything so they surged round the bus and the police were battering lumps out of them. Those people didn't have anything. It was a strange place anyway, because there were two sets of police, we discovered through watching things, and the ones that everybody feared were the ones with the big sticks. The bus we travelled in when we were in Albania wouldn't even have got an MOT certificate over here. The country was just diabolical, to say the least.

'The bus that we used was a charabanc and if you look that up you will find that that is an old-fashioned word for an old-fashioned bus but it was the only bus we ever saw. I also think we only saw about three cars the whole time we were there, if that. I remember a big, long boulevard in the city centre that was massively wide, with these imposing buildings and roads off it and big traffic islands every couple of yards. It was lined with men walking up and down; no women. I think we saw three women the whole time we were there; it was all guys. If you looked up the side streets there were police, with rifles and guns. Nobody went up that way! Again, you got this weird impression that they got people into this boulevard and let them walk up and down to make sure we thought the place was alive. Albania will live in my memory for lots of reasons; it was so funny. It was just a strange, strange country.

'The place was so tightly controlled. The hotel we were in felt as though somebody had just dusted it down. You went into a room – and the rooms were furnished 1950s-style – and you just had the impression that somebody had been in dusting the cobwebs out of it especially for you. There was a Dutch guy there who was building a sewer plant for them and he was virtually suicidal; when we all trooped in he couldn't believe his luck because he hadn't been able to speak English to anybody. I think we left him every book and magazine that we had brought because he had about another six months to go. He was telling us, "I'll hang myself." There was also the obligatory guy in the lounge behind a big paper. He had been reading the same paper for three days.'

Bobby Lennox comments, 'We went to train at the ground on the day before the game and there were 10,000 there. We got into the coach to leave the ground and there was a guy with a blue uniform and a blue hat on – he was from their security or the police – and he kept them all back from the bus. We were in the bus pointing at him and all the Albanians started laughing and he would then turn round and the boys would all be looking away as if they hadn't done anything – but I'll tell you what, that one guy kept everybody away from the bus just by threatening people. At night we stayed in this big hotel and hundreds and hundreds of people walked up the street and then back down again and then up again. I don't know whether it was because they didn't have any televisions or radios. They were just walking up and down constantly.'

The oddness of this outpost of extremities continued into the match itself. The Celtic players made the short journey from their city-centre Dajti Hotel to the match venue, which was within walking distance. A crowd of 30,000 was jammed into the Qemal Stafa Stadium on the afternoon but, as with all else in Albania, their behaviour was unpredictable. 'The crowd at the match were fanatical,' says Peter Latchford, 'but it was odd because they would go deathly quiet and then if something happened they would all go mental. That was if their team did anything. If we did anything there was total silence.

'It was a fairly hard game actually; their players were hugely enthusiastic and I think they had been playing very well. We lost the game over there 1–0 and I got some awful stick off Billy for that one; how we lost that goal. One of their guys made for our byline and crossed the ball and it went about two yards behind the goal. Now I was in the middle of the goal and I saw the ball go behind the goal, over our net, but then come back in, and the linesman was in the right place to see it. So I shouted at the linesman that the ball was out but he kept his flag down and as I turned around their guy had got in at the back post; he then nodded it down and they had scored. The referee gave the goal and Billy gave me pelters but I said, "Billy, I couldn't get to it; it was behind the bar, it was over the net, it was out." Our full-back Alan Sneddon told him, "Gaffer, it was miles out." You couldn't do anything about it. I had followed the ball all the way round.'

That goal had been awarded late in the first half and in the second 45 minutes Celtic exerted extreme pressure on the Albanians. 'In the last 20 minutes over there it was shootie-in,' says Bobby Lennox. 'They just couldn't get out of their box.' Despite Celtic's siege of the Albanian goal, the final score at the end of that first leg remained 1–0 in Partizani's favour thanks to that Agim Murati goal.

In Glasgow a fortnight later, quarter of an hour had passed when a high, hopeful, long ball, deep into the Celtic half, was met by the Celtic full-back Alan Sneddon, who, in attempting a headed back-pass to Peter Latchford, instead sent the ball on a bizarre trajectory high into the night sky from where it looped down over Latchford and into the Celtic net to put Partizani 1–0 ahead. It was the Albanians' second freak goal in a freak tie and it meant that Celtic would now need at least three goals if they were to avoid the ignominy of making a sharp exit from the 1979–80 European Cup. Two headers at the other end, from centre-back Roddie MacDonald and central midfielder Roy Aitken, put Celtic 2–1 ahead on the night. A simple tap-in from Vic Davidson had Celtic 3–1 ahead on the half-hour and another Aitken header a minute before half-time put the tie beyond the resistance of Partizani. It remained 4–1 and Celtic were through. So ended one of the most bizarre episodes in the history of Celtic.

The European Cup's first round had taken Celtic into the most unfamiliar territory possible, but the draw for the next round would provide them with reassuringly recognisable opposition: Dundalk of the Irish League. Celtic's Irish roots meant that they would often visit Ireland for the friendliest of pre-season friendlies; Celtic even flew with Aer Lingus, the Irish national airline, on trips to away matches in Europe. After Albania, this tie was welcomed as one that would present few logistical problems. Dundalk were also expected to be easy opposition – teams from the part-time-professional Irish League had made little impact on European competition. It looked a simple assignment for Celtic and even more so when Roddie MacDonald and George McCluskey put them 2–0 up after half an hour of the tie at Celtic Park. Then Dundalk scored, unexpectedly, and although Tommy Burns made it 3–1, another Dundalk goal meant that Celtic ended the match hanging on nervously to a 3–2 advantage. It was suggested that the Dundalk players had sat up drinking Guinness well into the night before the match – a claim that angered Celtic manager Billy McNeill and one that he dismissed as disrespectful rubbish.

That result put a whole new complexion on the tie. Dundalk's two precious goals meant that a 1–0 or 2–1 victory would put the Irish team through on the away-goals rule and the surprising strength of the Irish team's organisation and ability meant that it was an apprehensive Celtic party that made the journey to the little town on Dundalk Bay on the east coast of Ireland, where the local team's freshly laundered strips would be hung out to dry on their ground's perimeter fence after each match. 'I remember Billy was nervous before the game and that they pounded us,' says Peter Latchford. 'These are the games you don't like. They did everything to upset us; anything they could possibly do to try and get at us, and it was a really nervous performance by us. You name it, they tried it. They knew they were in with the best chance of their lives, and in their club's entire history, of causing a major upset if they could beat Celtic.'

The score remained at 0–0 as the final seconds of the 90 minutes began ticking away. Celtic had proved unable to grind out of first gear during the match and the threat of a Dundalk goal remained as real as ever as the match rolled towards its conclusion. It was at that point, in those final seconds, that the ball came flying into the Celtic goalmouth for one last time and Celtic were staring in the face their most ignominious exit ever from Europe. 'That was panic stations,' recalls Peter Latchford. 'I remember in the last minute of the away game there was a stramash and the ball broke to one of their players and he took a runner at it and he could have blown it in; if he had blown his nose the ball would have gone into the net. I came diving out towards him and he was about two feet away from me, with the ball coming in, and he took a swipe at the ball. It turned out to be a fresh-air swipe – and he missed it completely. I think big Roy then got a tackle in against him and cleared it from two yards out. If they had scored that goal in the last minute we would have been out. I tell you what: you have never seen so many relieved faces in all your life. If he had put the ball in the net he would still be a hero now. The Dundalk boys would still be living off that now if that goal had gone in and they had won the tie. The boy who missed that goal is forever the dumpling: if he had scored it he would have been the hero. That's football.

'I think it's easier to go and play at the Bernabeu in Madrid, with 110,000 against you, than to play in Dundalk. I think so, anyway. We went to Dundalk knowing that if we lost one goal and couldn't score one we were in trouble and were in for the most embarrassing time of our lives. It was a nervy, nervy game and we just couldn't score. It was one of those games, but you get through it.'

There could hardly have been a greater contrast between opponents in successive rounds when Celtic found themselves drawn against Real Madrid in the quarter-final; at last, after negotiating the jagged hazards of Partizani Tirana and Dundalk, this was the perfect prospect; the Real thing. Peter Latchford has fond recollections of the evening in March 1980 when Celtic entertained Real Madrid in the European Cup. 'The game when we played them over here was fantastic,' he says, 'because that was the biggest crowd I think I ever played in front of at Celtic Park. One of the talking points, besides us playing so well and beating them, was the size of the crowd; in fact, you couldn't see a bit of concrete anywhere when you looked around the stadium and I, more than most, had the chance to let my eyes wander a little bit at times, whenever the game went dead or play was away down at the other end of the park. That is what you normally do when you are a goalkeeper, and when I looked around I could not see a bit of concrete on the terracing or any part of the stand anywhere because every spare available space was filled with bodies.'

The official crowd figure released by Celtic was 67,000, which was the recognised capacity of the ground at that time, but Celtic's attendance figures during that era were notoriously unreliable and Glaswegian fans have always been adept at finding ways and means to get inside a football ground. 'I bet you there must have been between 80,000 and 90,000 inside the ground that night,' says Latchford. 'Neilly Mochan, the trainer that was at Celtic at the time, reckoned that that was the crowd and he was never far wrong. That game fired everybody's imagination. The supporters were sitting on the track. They were spilling out from the terraces over on to the trackside. I can remember them moving folk down the track to try to get them on to the terracing and they were squeezing them in. As players, we would look out of the window of the dressing-room half an hour before kick-off and at that game there was just a sea of bodies. As the kick-off got nearer, there seemed to be as many folk outside as there were inside. People in those days just queued to get in; there was none of this queuing early for hospitality. Hospitality then was a pie and a Bovril if you were lucky, and if you were extra lucky the pie was warm! So you could really judge the size of the crowd by looking at the queues outside the ground and they were still squeezing them in at kick-off time. I remember that more than anything else, the crowd, and that was never, ever reported properly at the time of the match.'

The Real team of 1980 followed the Madrid club's tradition of blending top Spanish talents with highly coveted players from other nations. The 1980 vintage saw Spanish internationals such as José Pirri, José Camacho, Juanito and Santillana playing alongside the German international sweeper Uli Stielike, whose steely demeanour matched his name, and Laurie Cunningham, an English international striker. The match lived up to the expectations of the supporters, who had dug deep for highly priced tickets and had, as a result, generated record Celtic Park gate receipts of £250,000. A youthful Celtic team lined up: Peter Latchford, Alan Sneddon, Danny McGrain, Roy Aitken, Tom McAdam, Roddie MacDonald, Davie Provan, Murdo MacLeod, George McCluskey, Johnny Doyle and Bobby Lennox. Celtic's approach was to go for the jugular, to attack Real with speed and precision, and to allow Real's quality players as little time on the ball as possible.

'We knew what we wanted to do,' says Latchford. 'You have got to be fair to Billy McNeill; he knew what he was doing. He'd played in enough European games himself over the years to know exactly what he was about. It's all about motivation, but in a game like that you shouldn't really need too much motivation. In actual fact, with a bunch of young pups like that, you would rein them back a little bit and then let them out. Team-wise, Billy knew how Real were going to play, he knew what their strengths were – they were very strong in midfield – remember, Del Bosque, who went on to become their manager in later years, was in there kicking lumps out of everybody: he was a hard, hard player. Overall, they were a good team.'

Real lived up to their reputation in the first half, moving the ball around assuredly and arrogantly, but at half-time the score was 0–0 and as the game resumed after the interval, Celtic's young players went at Real in a whirl of movement. It did not take long for cracks in the fissure of the Real defence to appear. Early in the second half, Murdo MacLeod pushed the ball wide to Alan Sneddon on the right. His low shot ripped into the penalty area, where it was spilled by goalkeeper Garcia Ramon and George McCluskey came bowling in to send the loose ball spinning into the net. The occasion now inspired the Celtic players, pushing them to display previously unseen dimensions to their game. Full-back Alan Sneddon was revealing a propensity for dynamic, incisive attacking play and 15 minutes from time he again flighted a tempting cross into the penalty area where diminutive winger Johnny Doyle climbed like a centre-forward to flash a header past Garcia Ramon. Bobby Lennox remembers well the closing stages against a Real team that wore all-blue as opposed to their traditional all-white at Celtic Park. 'At 2–0,' he says, 'you were thinking to yourself, "Two–nil is a good result. Do we push for a third and take the chance we will lose one?"'

Goalkeeper Latchford had to remain alert even in that second half, as Celtic chased goals and put Real on the back foot. 'It was a good game,' he says. 'I can remember Laurie Cunningham was playing. He had been at West Brom just after I had left and he had done very, very well for himself. He was a very good player. Again, in relation to him, little things stick out in my mind. We were 2–0 up and he was coming up the left, in the inside-left position, and he played a one-two with one of his teammates just outside the box and he went to get the return. He was in; he had only me to beat, but I had read it. It is funny how these things happen; it is like slow motion in your mind. I had seen he would play the one-two and get past the defence and I had thought to myself, "The ball's just going to end up in that spot." So I told myself that if I could just go and get myself there, to that spot, which was about 12 to 14 yards out on the angle, I could just stop him. All of that thinking to yourself happens in a couple of seconds. I remember sliding out and taking the ball off his toes. I just slid out, using my body, and took the ball. It was quite pleasing to do that because as he was playing the one-two he was watching the ball and was thinking about what he was going to do with it next. So it was quite satisfying for me to have intercepted him and stopped him carrying out what he had planned.

'At that point it was 2–0 and it was late on in the game. If they had got one back, a goal away from home, you would have been thinking it did not look very good for us when we went to Madrid for the second leg. I didn't think much of it at the time – I was too busy concentrating on the match – but when you look back on it, you think, "That wasn't too bad. I got something right there." Generally, I thought I had a pretty good game, did everything right and didn't let any in. So there were no problems and I was delighted that we had scored a couple of times because we actually took the game to them and dominated them. I don't think they were too happy about that. They didn't play too well because we didn't allow them to play well. It was very enjoyable.'

Pie crusts had been aimed at Cunningham from some of the more boisterous inhabitants of the 'Jungle' terracing on a couple of occasions when the Englishman had ventured close to the touch-line on that side of the stadium and he may still have been simmering with resentment at that when, in the days after the game at Celtic Park, he stated how shocked he had been to have finished on the losing side in Glasgow and how he was still puzzled that a side that, in his opinion, was as limited as Celtic had beaten the mighty Real. Celtic, he stated, had enjoyed their moment of glory and would be put firmly in their place in Madrid.

'Players say things just to wind you up,' comments Latchford. 'He probably couldn't believe that Real had been beaten because we were actually quite an inexperienced team. We weren't a good team. You would not have said, "This Celtic side is a great side." We had a lot of young players coming into the side and we were playing well but you wouldn't say it was a great team that Billy had at that point because he was still trying to put a team together. We just happened to be on a good little run. It wouldn't surprise me that Laurie Cunningham had said that. We played above ourselves on the night and they were a good team. As I say, I don't think we allowed them to play and we took our chances. Of course, by keeping those players together and making progress the thing goes on from there and then you can get to be a very good team. I think Real were very surprised at the performance that we put on. We did them on the night. It is a pity it wasn't just one leg!'

The visit to Madrid for the return match was a little bit special, as Peter

Latchford remembers. 'Whenever you travelled on any European trip you would always enjoy going to somewhere you had never been, but when we went to Madrid there was a little bit of extra anticipation because we were looking forward to going and playing in *that* stadium. Again, that is the biggest crowd in front of which I've ever played; they reckoned there were about 110,000 in the Bernabeu for our game with Real Madrid. That was before they put the roof on it. Looking forward to that was great. On European trips, you tended to go away for a few days. You would leave on the Monday and maybe not come back until the Thursday morning in those days, depending on where you were going. So you would have a day or two days of training there, in their weather, to get a little bit more acclimatised.'

An essential part of the preparations for any away match in Europe is to visit the stadium on the day before the game to get a feel for it. Prior to the match with Real, the Celtic party had been allowed their customary visit to the ground and goalkeeper Latchford had spotted a development that would prove to have a major bearing on the match. 'I remember when we went into the stadium to have a look at it, the remarkable thing was that they had dug the goalmouth up,' he recalls. 'They had dug the six-yard box up and they were returfing it for the game. They were packing it in so that it was nice and tight, but it created a ridge and it was a different bounce. I wanted to get on to it to train on it and test it and, when I did, I found that it was dead. The six-yard box was dead because it was brand-new turf.

'On the rest of the park, you were getting a nice, even bounce, but when it hit that stuff . . . That was the first time I had ever seen anybody renewing turf in the middle of the season. It wasn't even heard of at that time and they were digging about a foot deep and were packing in the turf like cubes, really tightly. I have seen six-yard boxes done since, but not as deeply as that. It was strange. Who knows why? It was done to both goals. The rest of the park was in magnificent condition, but when you went into the six-yard boxes you could see the change; not the whole six-yard box but an area just past either side of the goals and out to the edge of the front of the six-yard boxes, which is the area that gets most wear and tear. That was that.'

There were 110,000 bodies tightly packed into the multi-tiered Bernabeu Stadium at Chamartin, northern Madrid, on the day of the return match, and that had generated a record take for Real of £500,000. The elegant stadium, with its bleached-white stonework, and its many layers of terracing, looked like nothing so much as a giant, high-society wedding cake: there could hardly have been a greater contrast for the young Celtic players to experience than the one between the Bernabeu and the venues at which they had played on their previous trips that season: the Qemal Stafa Stadium in Albania and Oriel Park, Dundalk. For young players such as Davie Provan, Murdo MacLeod and George McCluskey, this was an initiation into what it was like to play at the highest level in Europe; for the experienced Bobby Lennox, appearing in his 66th European match, at the age of 36, it was merely the latest in a long list of famous stadiums at which he had performed. 'This'll maybe sound blasé,' says Lennox, who relished the opportunity to perform at the Bernabeu with Celtic for a second time, 'but you get used to things like that. You don't even notice the size of the crowd, really. I think you'd notice more if there was hardly anybody there. If there were loads of empty seats you would notice that. The build-up and getting to the ground is the exciting part of it. Once you have walked out of the tunnel the game takes over.' This Celtic team strolled out at the Bernabeu: Peter Latchford, Alan Sneddon, Danny McGrain, Roy Aitken, Tom McAdam, Roddie MacDonald, Davie Provan, Murdo MacLeod, George McCluskey, Johnny Doyle and Bobby Lennox.

It would be a formidable task for this largely inexperienced team to hold on to their 2–0 advantage in such a tension-filled arena but after only five minutes of the match Celtic had a wonderful chance to double their advantage, as an away goal would have meant Real would need to score four, not two, to remain in the tie. Murdo MacLeod took hold of the ball in the centre of the park, pushed it forward to Johnny Doyle and the Celtic winger set up George McCluskey, who was carrying an ankle injury, with an excellent scoring chance. Only goalkeeper Garcia Ramon stood between the striker and a goal, but the 22-year-old's shot slid past the post. 'George was right through with just the keeper to beat,' says Latchford, 'and through inexperience, he was just a young lad, he blasted it wide. If we had got that goal, it would have been a whole different ball game.

'We were under pressure most of the time in that game. At one point, the ball came into the box around the penalty spot and I came out, shouted for it and, with players coming in towards me, I went right over the top of them and walloped it with my fist – I got a great fist to it – and in doing so my momentum took me more or less to the edge of the box because I had fisted it into the centre circle in our half. It was a big, looping punch but I could see Del Bosque coming on to it right away and doesn't he just hit it on the half volley, straight back towards the goals. By this time, I was racing back, back, back with two defenders coming in and I just managed to get up in the air in time to tip the ball over the bar.' The player who hit that shot, the heavy-set midfielder Vicente del Bosque, would two decades later become Real Madrid manager and would lead the club to two European Cup triumphs, in 2000 and 2002. 'I can remember him just looking at me, stroking his chin, and growling at me,' says Latchford. 'He was very much like he is now, dour-looking, with the moustache and the dark hair. That would have been a spectacular goal from his point of view – and it was a hell of a scramble back for me to get to that one. I had to move a little bit quickly to get back. It was still 0–0 at the time, still in the first half.'

Bobby Lennox had been happy with the way he and his teammates had held Real at bay during that first half at the Bernabeu. 'Over there the boys did fine,' he states, 'then we lost a goal right on the half-time whistle. I remember I volleyed the ball up into the third tier and it went for a corner. I thought, "By the time that comes back the referee will blow for half-time." Instead, the ball came in and Santillana just got a toe on it to prod it over the line; it was a real scrambled goal from a corner kick. You could see the change in our team at half-time. It was a youngish team and you could see the boys thinking, "They're back in the game." With your Aulds, your Murdochs and people like that they might have been saying, "Come on, we're still in front." Lennox could see from the body language of the young players, as they sat, deflated, in that Bernabeu dressing-room during the interval, that doubt had entered into their minds.

Goalkeeper Peter Latchford spent the ten-minute break at the Bernabeu fulminating about the weak refereeing from the Hungarian Karoly Palotai that had allowed Real's opening goal to stand. 'Their first goal was a foul,' says Latchford. 'It should have been given as a foul.' The goalkeeper believes that the goal was an illegal one and that Celtic were dealt with unkindly by the referee both at the goal and during the build-up to the goal. 'In the '80s,' he explains, 'they had in place the four-step rule for goalkeepers, which meant you had to get rid of the ball in four steps. We were only a couple of minutes away from half-time and we had done well. I was having a great game, flying about all over the place, making saves, coming for everything, catching balls and really enjoying it. There was a great atmosphere, with 110,000 fans screaming, going bonkers. It was fantastic to play in and the adrenaline was going. Then at one stage I picked up the ball on the edge of the box, took one, two, three steps and banged the ball up the field but the referee blew his whistle and pandemonium broke out. He had given a free kick. He said I had taken more than four steps but I hadn't. I knew the four-step rule, so I had taken one, two, three steps and had then kicked it. Anyway, I got back into the area, set up the wall and got everything right. They took the free kick and it came off one of our players and went out for a corner. That was right on half-time.

'I lined up the corner exactly the same as I had always done and they hit a long ball over, one that came in on top of me but that went towards the back post. I went back to jump for it and had one Real Madrid player in front of me, one beside me and one behind me, along with two of our defenders. Everyone was crowding in to get to the ball. So I went to jump up and felt a hand in the small of my back and my shirt being tugged down. I caught the ball but, after having had my shirt tugged and having been pulled down, I dropped the ball behind me. There was an almighty stramash and the ball went into the net and we were 1–0 down.

'When you've got four or five guys round you and one of them is going up but pulling you down as well, it is just enough to make sure that you don't catch the ball where you intended to do so. Instead, you catch it a little bit less strongly and less firmly and when you are just falling away. I should have punched it away, I suppose, but then again, the thing I was thinking was that if I caught it they couldn't score. I would have just folded up on to the ground with the ball tucked underneath me and the whistle would have gone for half-time. It would have been great and we would have gone in with the game goalless. It was such a psychological barrier for them to have overcome; to get one before half-time, to get one back. If they had not, we would have come out still at 0–0 with only 45 minutes to go. I think that was what made it so important for them to get that goal before half-time, I really do. We went mental at the referee and chased him all over the place but he was having none of it. You can think and say what you like about that, but they needed something and he gave them something before half-time – and that was vitally important for them, especially as it was right on the stroke of half-time. That's football for you when you are in Europe.'

Ten minutes after half-time, the 'dead turf' effect paid off for Real. Both sides had been aware before the game that it would be Real, 2–0 down from the first leg and in front of their own fans, who would do most of the attacking, and that the lack of bounce from the turf in the two goalmouths would be likely to favour the attacking team and disorientate the opposing goalkeeper. With Latchford the busier of the two goalkeepers, the lack of bounce in the turf in the goalmouth would bother him more than it would Garcia Ramon, his opposite number. As Latchford says, 'That didn't help with the second goal because the ball hit that turf and didn't come up again. It changed the direction of the ball at the second goal. At that second goal, one of their players headed it down on to the turf but it didn't come up and I could only parry it. Again there was a stramash and – bang – the ball was in the net. By this time we were chasing the game and then we gave away a third goal.'

The resurgence of Real reminded Bobby Lennox of a previous encounter with one of the great names of European football. 'We lost a couple of goals in the second half to make it 3–0,' says Lennox. 'It was like the Ajax game back in 1971, where we were comfortable for an hour and then Cruyff scored a goal and all of a sudden we were under pressure. Santillana's goal just lifted Real's whole game.' Yet even at 3–0 down, as the match entered its latter stages, Celtic were still very much in with a chance of going through if they could only pierce the Real defence just once. An away goal in a 3–1 defeat would put the Glasgow side into a European Cup semi-final and with just minutes to go the Celts were presented with the type of opening that they had desired. 'Late on in the game,' recalls Lennox, 'Billy switched me from wide left to through the middle and I got played in with my back to goal. I flicked it and the big boy Stielike took it away with his hand. To me, it was a stonewall penalty kick but the referee played on. There were only three or four minutes to go and if we had made it 3–1 that would have taken us through to the semi-finals of the European Cup.

'The only thing was,' continues Lennox with a laugh, 'I was the person who was taking the penalties for Celtic at the time so I was the only person that shouted for the referee to play on! That would have been a good penalty kick to take in the Bernabeu, wouldn't it? One to knock them out of the European Cup with 110,000 in the ground! Seriously, although we got beaten 3–0, it was really disappointing to get beaten in Madrid because I felt we could have got through that night. We missed a couple of chances early on too. George missed a chance and big Tom McAdam had a great volley from which the goalie made a terrific save. If we had gone 2–0 up away from home we would have had a good chance of getting through.'

Peter Latchford was equally frustrated at how close Celtic had come to obtaining a famous result. 'If George had scored that one goal early on, the whole thing would have changed,' he comments. 'Then if we had been given the foul, as we should have done, and they hadn't got the goal on half-time, then who knows? We could have hung on and gone through. At the end of the day, we were inexperienced. We had too many players who did not have enough experience to go into that atmosphere. It was red-hot – the atmosphere was electric – but it had been an enormously enjoyable event.'

TEN

High Fliers
AJAX AMSTERDAM 1982

A solo supporter went weaving down one of the steep terraces inside Amsterdam's Olympic Stadium with his arms outstretched as if in preparation for flight. Celtic were also ready for take-off after a clever Charlie Nicholas goal that had put them 1–0 ahead against Ajax Amsterdam in the second leg of the club's landmark 1982 European Cup tie. As the ball curved into the net, Nicholas darted towards the terraces to point at the celebrating Celt; one exuberant entertainer acknowledging another.

That goal put Celtic ahead in the tie on a 3–2 aggregate but Nicholas acknowledges that Celtic had been lucky to have had something still to play for when they travelled across the North Sea to Amsterdam for the second leg. 'I don't know how we got out with a 2–2 draw,' he says of the first leg at Celtic Park. 'They really were a footballing machine, superb to watch. It was probably the best game I ever played in.'

Ajax were under the guidance of Johan Cruyff, now 35 and back at the club he had inspired to three European Cups in his youth, prior to his move to Barcelona in 1973. The Dutchman, in the early 1980s, was enjoying his final years as a footballer whilst at the same time cajoling the best out of a group of youngsters that he was successfully encouraging to play in the traditionally fluid, attractive Ajax style.

Celtic were progressing nicely too, with a team built around Billy

McNeill's core group of young players, especially Davie Provan, Roy Aitken, goalkeeper Pat Bonner and Murdo MacLeod, who were gradually becoming the talismanic figures for Celtic during the 1980s. The memory of Madrid in 1980 had helped them hold their own against Juventus in a European Cup first-round tie in 1981, a 2–1 aggregate defeat for Celtic, and McNeill's team grew stronger through learning well from such experiences. It meant when they travelled to Amsterdam in autumn 1982 the players were not fazed by the prospect of facing a hostile 65,000 crowd, especially as two of the team's home-produced players, Paul McStay and Charlie Nicholas, were showing signs of possessing special qualities. The Celtic team in Amsterdam was: Pat Bonner, Danny McGrain, Mark Reid, Graeme Sinclair, Roy Aitken, Tom McAdam, Davie Provan, Paul McStay, Frank McGarvey, Charlie Nicholas and Murdo MacLeod. The only change from the team that had drawn in Glasgow was the introduction of defender Sinclair for midfielder Tommy Burns.

Celtic had more than held their own as the second leg entered its final stages at 1–1: Gerald Vanenburg had equalised for Ajax in the second half. With two minutes remaining, and Ajax looking good to head into the second round on away goals, George McCluskey cut into the Ajax penalty area and sent the ball past goalkeeper Piet Schrijvers for a dramatic winner. It was the first time for a decade that Celtic had beaten a major European club and it had been done in style, with Ajax starved of time to fight back. That was of major importance in Celtic's victory, as that side was never at its best when it had to focus fully on defence. If there had been any longer than two minutes remaining, Celtic might have begun to creak. McNeill's team was geared to go forward.

Charlie Nicholas, scorer of Celtic's first goal that night, recalls how the manager motivated his players for the game in Amsterdam. 'Billy McNeill's words before we went out in the second leg were, "You are out of this competition. So you might as well go for it." He was spot on because we were. It was kidology, but at the same time it was fact. To win was tremendous. I think Ajax would have won that competition that year if it hadn't been for us. It was such a high to beat a club like Ajax, with Cruyff and all their stars. We had got Celtic's respectability back.'

The following round proved less exhilarating. Another tough draw took Celtic to north-west Spain to play Real Sociedad of San Sebastian. Two late goals, both deflections off Celtic players, gave Real Sociedad a flattering 2–0 home victory and an early away goal from the Spaniards at Celtic Park killed the tie stone dead.

Billy McNeill moved on to Manchester City in the summer of 1983 after the latest in a succession of disputes with the Celtic board. His successor, David Hay, maintained the momentum established by McNeill of a dynamic team that blended skill with aggression and Hay made few changes to the personnel he had inherited. One signing, striker Brian McClair, had been lined up by McNeill, prior to the manager's departure, as a replacement for Arsenal-bound Charlie Nicholas, and McClair was part of the party that travelled to Lisbon for a memorable UEFA Cup tie with Sporting in the autumn of 1983. 'We got hammered away 2–0,' he remembers. 'They gave us a bit of a doing and I was quite impressed by them. The atmosphere in their stadium was wonderful.' Celtic had been fortunate to leave Portugal only two goals down and still in the tie, but that first leg was to herald one of the great Parkhead nights.

'The home game with Sporting Lisbon was my first European start,' remembers McClair. 'On the drive up to the ground on the bus from Seamill there was quite a positive attitude among the players. The official crowd was 42,000 but if you could have got anybody else in the stadium I would have been surprised. As a player you feel the desire of the crowd and the European nights in which I was involved with Celtic were always really memorable.' Celtic pulled Sporting apart to go 3–0 up by half-time, taking the overall lead in a tie against a team that had threatened to overwhelm the Celts in their own José Alvalade Stadium.

'Everybody played very well against Sporting Lisbon,' says McClair. 'You just occasionally get games where everybody is focused. There just seemed to be quite a focused and humorous atmosphere on the bus and no particular nervousness. I think a lot of that would have stemmed from Davie Hay, who just told us to go out and play our normal game. The problem they had was that we started so quickly and so well. We were 3–0 up at half-time and when we scored again in the 47th minute that was it all over.'

All-out attack enabled Celtic to push on for a 5–0 victory. It had helped them that Sporting had been a team geared to going forward and, with both sides being stronger at home, the tie had turned on which team would capitalise on their opportunities in their home leg. The Glasgow side would encounter a very different beast, in the shape of Nottingham Forest, in the next round. Forest had been European champions in 1979 and 1980, but they were a largely unattractive side, one that relied on hitting teams hard on the counter-attack and, as such, were not keen on taking the initiative. It meant that the first leg, at the City Ground in Nottingham, would witness Celtic playing most of the football in a 0–0 draw.

'The pitch was frozen at the City Ground,' says McClair, 'and I remember Celtic supporters in T-shirts climbing up the floodlight pylons that night. Forest had more experience than us in Europe and we were happy with the draw down there but, under Clough, Forest always played on the break so they were probably quite happy with the result at the City Ground because it was not their style to force the pace of a game. I don't think Celtic were ever noted as a defensive team at that time: the idea was to score as many goals as you could, especially at home. You have just got to play in the style that suits the players you have got, but we didn't play at all at Celtic Park.'

Two quick counter-attacks knocked the stuffing out of Celtic as Forest went 2–0 up before Murdo MacLeod snatched Celtic's only goal late in the match. The 2–1 victory was classic Clough and Celtic had lacked the resources to cope with the tactical sophistication of the English side. It had, though, been a night when the ground had been packed yet again, with the majority of the 67,000 supporters squeezed in tightly on the vast, old terraces. Those early-1980s matches against Forest, Sporting, Real Sociedad, Ajax, Juventus and Real Madrid had rebuilt the club's confidence as competitors in Europe and those great occasions had been redolent with all that is good about European football. A very different experience was now around the corner for Celtic.

ELEVEN

Bottle Merchants
RAPID VIENNA 1984

Visitors to Vienna in the 1980s could enjoy the city's Baroque architecture and classical culture but the more perceptive could not fail to miss a certain atmosphere in the air. Prissy, prim-faced locals presented the frostiest of welcomes to outsiders, and the Viennese seemed to harbour a pent-up resentment that hinted at another side to the city's character: it was almost as if there was a frustration all around at some stifled identity, some unfinished business for which foreigners were held responsible. Vienna, after all, is the city that housed the young Adolf Hitler in his formative years, the city that played host to one of the most repressive fascist governments of the 1930s and whose streets later on in that decade rang out with the enthusiastic applause of Viennese citizens as they greeted the Nazi soldiers who had arrived to begin their 'occupation' of Vienna after the Germans had annexed Austria.

Only the Austrians could, post-war, have supplied someone such as Kurt Waldheim as secretary-general to the United Nations. He was in that post until the 1980s, when it was revealed that he had had a most questionable history in the German Army during the Second World War. He was not the only Austrian to have been living an outwardly respectable life in the Vienna of the 1980s and to have harboured a secret Nazi past. The city was teeming with such individuals. It says a

175

lot about the Austrians that, despite the revelations about Waldheim's personal history, he would, in the mid-1980s, win their presidential election as the People's Party candidate, regardless of allegations that he had lied about his actions in the German Army during the war. The vote reflected the ambiguous attitude of many Austrians towards their country's Nazi past.

It was into this city, this seething maelstrom of duplicity, discontent and resentment, that Celtic flew in the autumn of 1984, innocently expecting a fair football match in their European Cup-Winners' Cup tie with Rapid Vienna. Eighty years previously, Celtic had been the first Scottish club to tour on the continent of Europe and in 1904, at Vienna, 'they got a wonderful reception' according to Celtic's then manager Willie Maley. This time, the Celtic players found themselves being dragged into the midst of a vicious vendetta.

'It was quite strange,' says Peter Grant, who was in midfield for Celtic on the night of the first leg with Rapid. 'Their fans were crazy. You think when you are travelling to Austria that you are going to a nice, clean, civilised country but my father and my sister were in the stand that night and they said the Rapid fans were pulling their hair and spitting on them; that was Rapid's Nazi squad. Frank McGarvey nearly had his leg broken and Alan McInally was sent off.' The dismissal of McInally looked entirely unjustified, following, as it did, the Celtic substitute's first serious foul of the match. McInally had only taken the field as a replacement for McGarvey after the first-choice striker had been the victim of a wild challenge from the Rapid midfield player Reinhard Keinast.

The match in Vienna ended in a 3–1 win for Rapid but, having scored an away goal through Brian McClair, Celtic were confident that they could turn the tie in their favour at Celtic Park. 'Rapid played very well in Vienna,' says McClair. 'I scored the goal against the run of play, which gave us an opportunity. We got one chance and we scored so we went back to Celtic Park 3–1 down and thinking that if we got a goal in each half without them scoring then we were through.' The Celtic team in Vienna had been: Pat Bonner, Danny McGrain, Mark Reid, Roy Aitken, Willie McStay, Peter Grant, Davie Provan, Paul McStay, Brian McClair, Frank McGarvey and Murdo MacLeod.

Rapid were a highly skilled side and one that featured two of the greatest of all central European players in the persons of the Czech Antonin Panenka and the Austrian Hans Krankl. Panenka, 35 at the time of Rapid's tie with Celtic, was a hugely inventive midfielder who had won the 1976 European Championship final for Czechoslovakia with a daring penalty kick that swerved out then in and entirely deceived the German goalkeeper Sepp Maier. Krankl, 31, had proved himself one of the greatest strikers in Austrian football history. Peter Grant, then participating in only his second European tie for Celtic, was initially awestruck at being on the same pitch as those two players. 'Hans Krankl and Panenka I remember because we kept giving free kicks away in Vienna and Panenka was nicking them past the post and against the post. Panenka had scored the winning penalty in the European Championship against Maier and Krankl had scored goals in big World Cup matches, such as the one against West Germany in the 1978 World Cup, and here you were on the field along with them. It was quite incredible!'

Peter Grant may have been an inexperienced player at first-team level but he had not been wholly surprised when Rapid had started using some underhand tactics in their compact Gerhard Hanappi Stadium. He had encountered plenty of bad sportsmanship whilst playing for Celtic in European tournaments at youth level. 'As British players we just thought people got on with the game,' he says.

'You didn't know about that sort of gamesmanship but it is part of the game in Europe, and I realised soon that it was used by the opposition so that you would retaliate, get sent off and then your team would be a man short. I found that, in most games, British players don't do what European players do. Europeans are a lot more cynical. You had to be wary not to kick out.'

The first leg, on Rapid's home turf, had been tricky, but nothing had prepared Grant and his teammates for the antics of the second leg. He believes Rapid Vienna turned the return match in Glasgow into 'a débâcle'. The Celtic line-up for this match was: Pat Bonner, Willie McStay, Murdo MacLeod, Roy Aitken, Tom McAdam, Peter Grant, Davie Provan, Paul McStay, Brian McClair, Frank McGarvey and Tommy Burns.

Grant recalls the intensity of being in the midst of a match during which Rapid were concocting an explosive cocktail of violence, deception, deviousness and mock outrage to rile their opponents. 'I remember there was a little fellow playing for them in the middle of the park,' he says, 'and I jumped over him and my foot brushed the top of his head. They said I had stamped on his head, but I had not. I felt like stamping on him because two minutes earlier he had caught me with an elbow and almost broken my jaw. I had nicked the ball by him, but I didn't stand on his head. We always felt we had a chance against Rapid and we played very, very well and deservedly won the game. They knew they were getting a doing and that's why they started all their gamesmanship.'

Brian McClair was pivotal to Celtic's high-tempo performance that night, scoring the opening goal after half an hour's play. 'There was a fantastic atmosphere,' he remembers. 'A cross came in from Davie Provan and I scored.' McClair's goal had been supplemented by a superb second for Celtic on half-time when Murdo MacLeod slipped a low shot into the Rapid net. That had put Celtic ahead on the away goals rule but, roared on by the crowd, they continued to drive forward with a performance of controlled aggression. Midway through the second half a loose ball bobbled between Tommy Burns and the Rapid Vienna goalkeeper and, although Burns was further away from the ball, the Celtic midfielder, a skilled and determined competitor, slid in with enough applied aggression to knock it away from the goalkeeper. In one instant the ball had appeared to belong to the goalkeeper and then, in the next, the supporters stacked high on the terracing at the Celtic end were watching Burns force it over the line for Celtic's third goal. 'We were playing some good football,' says McClair, 'and winning the tie and then all hell broke loose.'

The Rapid players were furious that the Swedish referee, Kjell Johansson, had allowed the goal – they thought Burns had fouled their goalkeeper – and they pursued Johansson furiously to express their anger that he had deemed Burns' challenge on the goalkeeper to have been a legal one. Team captain Krankl was cautioned by Johansson for leading the protests too enthusiastically. The red-haired, easily identifiable Burns now became a target for Rapid's simmering discontent and two minutes after his goal he was punched on the back of the head by the Rapid midfielder Reinhard Keinast. The Austrian had attempted to disguise his moment of violent retribution but had not been fly enough and he was instantly dismissed by Johansson. His sending-off inflamed the already heated Austrians even more and they now appeared close to losing control of themselves completely. Within minutes, Burns had been assaulted once again, this time through a kick from the Rapid goalkeeper inside the penalty area. Referee Johansson pointed to the penalty spot and Peter Grant prepared to take the kick.

Again the Rapid players surrounded the referee to protest at his decision and Johansson, under duress, went to his linesman, stationed on the touch-line that ran in front of the Jungle terracing on the Janefield Street side of the ground. The Jungle, a narrow strip of covered terracing that ran the length of the pitch opposite the main stand at Celtic Park, was the section of the ground from which the most boisterous of the Celtic supporters would watch a match and as Johansson conferred with his colleague, still surrounded by revolting Rapid players, a bottle and some coins flew out of the Jungle and on to the pitch. It was a stupid, pointless action on the part of those who launched their missiles from terracing to playing field and in that moment they conjured up a sea of troubles for Celtic.

Rudi Weinhofer, one of the Rapid players, tumbled to the turf, stricken, it would later be claimed by those associated with Rapid, by one of the missiles that had been thrown in the general direction of the Austrians. Now the Rapid players found a different focus for their frustrations, as they milled around Weinhofer whilst he lay prone and received treatment from ambulance staff. This further delay to the match lasted for ten minutes as the Rapid players did their best to string out the situation.

Weinhofer had been the second of Rapid's two permitted substitutes and if he was to leave the field then the Austrians would be down to nine men. At one point, as Weinhofer lay receiving treatment, and to the astonishment of those watching, the Rapid captain Krankl began to march his players off the field. He beckoned his teammates with a raised arm and pointed to the players' tunnel. Around half of the Rapid players began to follow him in the direction of the dressing-room. The others remained at Weinhofer's side. 'I was skipper,' Krankl says, 'and I said to the referee that we had a problem with blood on Rudi Weinhofer's head and I was going off the field, but when I got to the side of the pitch our vice-president said, "We must stay on the field and finish the match." I had wanted to take the players off but we continued to the end and played under protest until the finish of the game.'

As the players hovered around on the field, awaiting the outcome of the incident, Celtic's young midfielder Paul McStay, a most fair and sporting player, finally lost patience with the behaviour of the Rapid players. 'I remember Paul McStay speaking to Hans Krankl in the middle of the park while the game was being held up,' says Peter Grant, 'and Paul saying, in very clear English so that Krankl would understand loud and clear, "You are a cheat." The bottle had landed 20 yards away from their player.'

It was strange to find a player of Krankl's class mixed up in all of this, although the Austrian cannot select from his memory any recollection of that moment with McStay. 'I remember Paul McStay was one of the best technical players in Scottish football at the time,' says Krankl, 'but I do not remember him saying this to me. I was not a cheat. I did not throw the whisky bottle on to the head of a Rapid Vienna player.

'It had been a good match in Vienna,' adds Krankl. 'We won 3–1 and I scored the third goal three minutes from the finish. It was a good result and we were strong and we won this game. There were no problems in this game – yes, it was a tough and hard match, a real football match, but that was what we expected. When we went to play at Celtic Park we thought it would be a very hard game: when we were at home we were very strong and when Celtic were at home they were very strong too, and the game was a very hard game and the referee had very many problems with the players from Celtic and with our players and he had to use a lot of yellow cards. The ref, a Swedish ref, was the bad guy that night; he was not strong, not correct.

'We had a penalty given against us,' continues Krankl, 'and then in the finish the worst moment possible. A Celtic supporter threw on a whisky bottle and one of our players, Rudi Weinhofer, was hit on the head and had blood on his head. I remember the penalty. It was 3–0 and then on came this whisky bottle; it went on to the head of our player and the player had blood on his head; there was no question about that.

'I was captain of Rapid Vienna for more than ten years and I also played in Barcelona for some years and I had never seen anything like this happen. It was not normal for a football game; it was very, very bad.

I always have sympathy for the Scots, the Highlanders, and I like Celtic. They wear the same colours as Rapid Vienna, my team ever since I was a boy, so I always had sympathy for them, but I have no sympathy for the supporter who did this. It's so dangerous and the players of Celtic can't forgive this supporter, this one idiot who threw this bottle. We had never come across this situation before and I said to the referee, "Stop the game!" When I said that to him he became very, very angry with me.'

After the prolonged delay over the supposed injury to the Rapid player and Krankl's return from the brink after threatening to take his men off the park, the game resumed in the most dramatic way possible, with the taking of the penalty for Celtic, a task that fell to Peter Grant, even though he was then only 19 years old and just a few months into his first full season in Celtic's first team. 'I became the penalty taker after we played a match at Dundee,' he says. 'That day Celtic got a penalty and Mark Reid, who was our penalty taker, missed it. Then we got another penalty and I got the ball and picked it up and scored and from then on I started to take the team's penalties.'

Despite his youthfulness, Grant was not fazed by the responsibility of taking a penalty kick in such an important tie as the one with Rapid Vienna. 'I sent the goalkeeper the wrong way with my kick,' he says, 'but I put it wide. That was all; it was nothing to do with nerves. You have no fear when you are young. I didn't think twice about it. If I'd been more experienced I probably wouldn't have taken it. I picked my corner and put it the wrong side of the post. Afterwards, I was unconcerned that I had missed it because I was so delighted that we were through to the next round.'

Brian McClair, now a youth coach at Manchester United, also believed that he and his teammates had earned the right to be in the quarter-finals with their 3–0 win. 'We'd attacked really hard,' he says, 'and had beaten them fairly and had given a good performance. You think that they should accept defeat because we beat them fair and square. I think in this country, in Britain, we are brought up to be humble and accept defeat, but that is not the case in every country. They do not share that attitude but that's not better or worse. As I tell my young players, it's just different. We say it's cheating but it's not cheating to them. They saw an opportunity to remain in the competition and they made the most of it.'

The feeling in the Rapid dressing-room was quite different to that of their Celtic opponents. 'I was absolutely sure after the game,' says Krankl, 'that we were not out of the Cup-Winners' Cup. I think the situation was not normal and we had made a protest and my club made a protest after the game. It was not possible we should go out this way. The next day we went to Switzerland and to all the people of UEFA.'

Rapid Vienna, on their return to Austria on the day after the match at Celtic Park, sent a telex to UEFA to complain that Celtic had been responsible for the behaviour of their supporters and that, on those grounds, the match should be replayed. The Rapid communication claimed that the bottle that had been thrown on to the pitch had incapacitated their player and that the Rapid team had been severely handicapped by playing the final quarter of an hour with nine men. The Austrians also, suspiciously readily and handily, cited as a precedent a case from 1971 when Internazionale of Milan had lost a European Cup tie 7–1 at Borussia Moenchengladbach and, on appeal, had persuaded UEFA to replay the match at a neutral venue. Inter's case, back in 1971, had rested on the allegation that one of their players, Roberto Boninsegna, had been struck on the head by a full Coca-Cola can, thrown by a Borussia supporter. Years later, Sandro Mazzola, a teammate of Boninsegna, admitted that he had switched a full can of Coca-Cola for the empty one that had landed in the vicinity of Boninsegna. Rapid's plea also neglected to mention that Inter had also exerted undue influence on UEFA committee members to persuade them to deliver the verdict the Italian club had required in that episode 13 years previously.

Rapid may also have consulted their own club history for inspiration. The biggest match in their club's history, their 1961 home European Cup semi-final second leg with Benfica – a match that any Rapid Vienna administrator who was middle-aged in 1984 would remember well – had famously been abandoned before the end of the 90 minutes after the Rapid supporters, infuriated that their team was losing 4–1 on aggregate, had invaded the pitch. The burghers of Vienna had been whipped into a frenzy by their club on the night of that match; Rapid had played the Austrian national anthem prior to the match to draw on extreme nationalist feeling among their supporters and the Benfica players had been besieged in their dressing-room in Vienna for hours after the game before an angry mob of Rapid supporters had finally been cleared. The crowd trouble had resulted in the tie being awarded to Benfica and Rapid Vienna had subsequently suffered a three-year ban from playing European matches at home. Two decades later, this may have been at the forefront of the minds of the Rapid officials as they pursued their appeal to UEFA on the grounds that the actions of a few rowdy Celtic supporters had, they claimed, had a drastically adverse effect on the prospect of the match being completed in fair circumstances.

The case against Rapid seemed to be strengthened when UEFA's official observer at the match, Doctor Hubert Claesen of West Germany, commented that although he had indeed seen a bottle thrown from the terracing, it had not struck any of the players on the field. His evidence made it seem an open-and-shut case and nine days after the second leg, which had taken place on 7 November 1984, a UEFA disciplinary committee met to consider the evidence that had been put in front of its members. They looked at television evidence and concluded that Rudi Weinhofer's claim to have been struck by a bottle was completely unfounded and censured him and Rapid Vienna for making such a claim. They then considered the sending-off of Reinhard Keinast and suspended him for Rapid's next four matches in European competition. Otto Baric, the Rapid Vienna coach, who had at one point provocatively thrown another bottle on to the pitch, was punished by being banned from the touch-line for Rapid's next three matches in European competition. Celtic were fined £4,000 for the behaviour of their supporters; Rapid Vienna were fined £5,000 for the conduct of their players and coaching staff. The result of the second leg would stand and Celtic would be allowed to take their place in the quarter-finals. It seemed, from Celtic's point of view, a fair judgement all round.

Rapid appealed against that ruling. Not only did they appeal but they now changed their story. Weinhofer's claim to have been struck by a bottle having been discredited by the television evidence and UEFA, Rapid now stated that he had actually been struck by a coin. Another UEFA committee now met to consider their second set of claims and doubled the fine that had originally been levied on Rapid to £10,000. That seemed to confirm that Rapid were the guilty parties but the committee then, perversely, upheld Rapid's appeal and ordered that the second leg at Celtic Park was to be declared void as it had been an 'irregular' match. They ruled that it would have to be replayed at a venue of Celtic's choice but one that was at least 100 kilometres from Glasgow. The gate receipts from this tie were to be split between the two clubs – those receipts would be more than enough to cover the fine that had been assigned to Rapid Vienna for their misbehaviour at Celtic Park.

Krankl, who is opinionated and animated when discussing most aspects of the tie with Celtic, suddenly proves to be non-committal on the question of why Rapid Vienna changed their story from Weinhofer being hit on the head by a bottle to him being hit on the head by a coin. 'I'm not the club,' says Krankl. 'I was only a football player of the club. I was the skipper. So it was not of interest to me. UEFA said there should be a third game and that was the beginning and end of it for me.'

Brian McClair, in common with most of his teammates, had had his doubts as to what exactly had happened on the Jungle-side touch-line. 'It is easy now to look back and say it was an experience,' he says. 'There were definitely objects thrown on to the pitch, but whether the guy got struck or not . . . They played it very well and eventually UEFA decided there should be a one-off game, which it was decided was to take place at Old Trafford.'

There were five weeks between the final whistle in the match at Celtic Park and the replay of that match, which the Celtic directors took to the home ground of Manchester United. With each passing day before the match in Manchester, frustration became ever more bitter among the Celtic players that their hard-earned place in the quarter-finals of the Cup-Winners' Cup was under threat because the Austrians had refused to accept that Celtic's 3–0 second-leg victory should stand. 'It dragged on for so long,' says Brian McClair, 'and everybody was saying, "We're going to go down and stick it right up these Austrians!"'

That feeling of frustration backfired badly on Celtic, as did the decision of the Celtic board to play the match at Old Trafford. That venue guaranteed Celtic sizeable gate receipts and full-blooded backing from a 40,000-strong travelling support, but it created a cauldron that would overheat and scald, then scar, all connected with Celtic. The match at Old Trafford was one that called for cool heads; a night when it would be best if all of the extraneous detail surrounding the tie were to be set aside so that the players could focus fully on the football. That was an easier task for the Rapid Vienna players than for those of Celtic. Rapid were grateful to have won a second chance to win the tie and they could consequently view the matter clinically. They had lost their collective cool at Celtic Park and it had almost cost them their place in the Cup-Winners' Cup; they knew they would have to adopt a different approach in Manchester. The Celtic players, in contrast, now nursed a collective grudge: they had won the game and now they felt simmering resentment that they were being forced to try to do it all over again. It is a tall order for any team to regain the type of momentum that Celtic had harnessed for their performance of power at Celtic Park, and it was an order the players could not meet. 'Rapid went out and just played,' says Brian McClair. 'Davie Hay tried to play the whole thing down but outside the ground, when we came into contact with our fans, everybody was battering the bus and the supporters were so aggressive. Everybody had felt hard done by.' Tommy Burns was also struck by the pent-up emotion displayed by the team's followers prior to the game. 'The Celtic supporters were so psyched up,' he says. 'You could see the venom on their faces when you were driving into Old Trafford. It backfired on us.'

The Celtic team at Old Trafford was: Pat Bonner, Danny McGrain, Murdo MacLeod, Roy Aitken, Tom McAdam, Peter Grant, Davie Provan, Paul McStay, Brian McClair, Frank McGarvey and Tommy Burns. Celtic had expended too much emotional energy on the entire affair and that handicapped their chances of being a fully functioning footballing unit; the Viennese stayed calm. Slightly more than a quarter of an hour had passed when Celtic mounted a furious attack on the Rapid goal that involved all ten outfield Celtic players surging forward. Celtic were unlucky when Roy Aitken's shot spun off the foot of a post, but when a defending Rapid player gathered the ball and began a counter-attack, it meant that the entire Celtic team, other than goalkeeper Pat Bonner, was stranded upfield in crazy pursuit of a goal to punish the Viennese. The ball was whisked forward at speed to the pacy Peter Pacult, Rapid's centre-forward, and he duly despatched it into the Celtic net for what would prove to be the only goal of the game. 'Rapid were excellent at Old Trafford,' says Peter Grant. 'After beating them at home we were sure we could do the same in

Manchester but Rapid deservedly beat us at Old Trafford. They hardly gave us a kick.' Brian McClair remembers that third game well. He states, 'There was a lot of emotion attached to that game and the pitch was poor – it was still poor when I came down to Old Trafford – and we just couldn't play. There was probably too much emotion involved. We were probably all too emotionally involved. We were on the attack when they broke away and scored a scrappy goal.'

Krankl has powerful recollections of Rapid's return to Britain. 'The third game at Old Trafford was very hard,' he says, 'and for me the worst situation in my career as a football player. The supporters were very, very bad that night. It was not correct. When we went to Old Trafford the Celtic supporters shouted, "Cheats, Cheats, Cheats, Cheats, Cheats!" I understand the reaction of the supporters but my players were not cheats. I understand, it's not a problem for me, but we were the better team at Old Trafford. We had more luck at Old Trafford; we made a goal and Celtic in 90 minutes did not make a goal. At Old Trafford another Celtic supporter went to our goalkeeper and hit him. It's not normal for a supporter to go on to the field like that but on the night we were fortunate to have a referee, Luigi Agnolin, the Italian, who was one of the best in the world, and we won this game and the Italian referee did a good job in a very, very hard game. For me, it was a very hard game for us to play, very difficult, particularly as Manchester is so near Glasgow. For me, the third game should have been in Spain or Italy, not 200 kilometres from Glasgow, which meant that the third game was a home game for Celtic. I would have preferred Italy or Spain.

'The Celtic players were very good. Celtic players played very hard, yesterday and today! They are a team with good players and I had no problems with any Celtic players; I have always liked Celtic and Scottish football. I had respect for them. I did not like this situation, though. Football is a hard game and should be about 11 against 11 on the field, not about rulings off it. The real football supporters from Celtic or Rangers say that Rapid were a great football team. Also, Celtic are a really good football team and club and I like such clubs as they are like my club, Rapid Vienna. Glasgow has two clubs with a great name in European football history. That's more important than stories about us being cheats or not cheats.'

It had been the longest-drawn-out European tie in which Celtic had participated and one that would produce entrenched points of view on both sides. Those connected with Celtic would remain adamant, years afterwards, that Weinhofer, possibly under instruction from coach Baric, had feigned his injury to try to rescue the tie for an ailing Rapid. Krankl is adamant that his teammate Weinhofer was genuinely hurt. Lost in all the outrage, emotion, anger and confusion was the simple fact that it was those irresponsible individuals who had launched their missiles on to the pitch at Celtic Park who had provided Rapid with the key to unlock the door to the quarter-finals.

Wolfgang Amadeus Mozart gave his best years to Vienna and was rewarded with duplicity, maltreatment, premature death and burial in a pauper's grave. Celtic's brush with the Viennese had had less tragic consequences but the Rapid reaction had buried Celtic's best chance of winning a European trophy in the 1980s. The hangover caused to Celtic by that empty bottle of spirits would rage for years afterwards.

TWELVE

An Alpine Avalanche
NEUCHATEL XAMAX 1991

Swiss clubs have rarely made more than a modest impact on European cup competition but by the early 1990s football in Switzerland had reached its nadir. The people of that rich, ordered land at that time believed their clubs were no longer capable of even the most average of achievements in European football. They lacked confidence in their players and Swiss teams were regarded, inside their own country, as amateurish, likely to impress briefly but to lose their nerve if confronted by a vital penalty kick or a clear goalscoring opportunity. So when Neuchatel Xamax were drawn against the famous Celtic of Glasgow in the second round of the UEFA Cup in the autumn of 1991, few inside Switzerland thought their team had any chance of negotiating a safe passage through the tie.

The football followers among the 30,000 inhabitants of the little town on the northern shore of Lake Neuchatel were also aware that all was not as well as it could be inside their own football club. At the Stade de la Maladiere, Neuchatel Xamax's English coach Roy Hodgson was finding that his job was under threat. There was enormous friction between him and club president Gilbert Facchinetti, who held a grudge against Hodgson for the manager having recently wished to leave Neuchatel to join Grasshoppers Zurich. Hodgson, who had previously enjoyed success in Sweden with Halmstads and Malmo FF, was finding

Swiss football a more difficult proposition, with its blend of foreign players and difficult internal politics.

Celtic had a new manager, Liam Brady, who had been appointed in the summer of 1991, and he, like Hodgson, was finding himself becoming tangled up in internal politics inside his club. He had, however, found that European competition had offered him some respite from internal bickering and difficult domestic results. Brady's Celtic had comfortably overcome Germinal Ekeren of Belgium 3–1 on aggregate in the opening round of the UEFA Cup. On hearing of the draw, Brady had candidly admitted that he had never previously heard of the Belgian club but after Celtic's aggregate victory, the Irishman had suggested that it was something of which Celtic could be pretty proud.

'We had gone to Ekeren,' says Brady, 'and I had said something in the Scottish papers that Scottish people, and particularly the Scottish media, jumped on, which was that for a Scottish club to knock a Belgian club out of a European competition was, at one time, expected but that now they're on a level playing field, and to beat Ekeren as we did, 2–0 at home, was a good result. There were a few things in the papers saying that we didn't really play well and that they had a couple of chances, but the days of wiping the floor with a Belgian club were well and truly over and I said that publicly. Then we went to Ekeren for the away leg and got a good performance and a good draw and I thought, "Well, we might have a chance of going some distance in this competition."'

Brady was on the verge of a minor breakthrough as he contemplated Celtic's second-round tie with Neuchatel Xamax that autumn of 1991. Celtic, between the mid-1980s and early 1990s, had never gone more than two rounds in Europe in any one season, a sluggish run that owed its origins to the lengthy shadow that had been cast over the club by the Rapid Vienna affair in 1984. UEFA had punished Celtic severely for the actions of two supposed Celtic supporters who had attacked Rapid players at Old Trafford – one had assaulted the goalkeeper during the match; the other had attacked the goalscorer Peter Pacult at its conclusion. The reaction from UEFA to that was to force the Glasgow club to play their next home European tie without spectators present. That might have been manageable if Celtic had been drawn against one of Europe's minnows but the opening round of the 1985–86 European Cup-Winners' Cup paired them with Atletico Madrid. It seemed ironic that Atletico's second appearance at Celtic Park should be as freakish as their first at the stadium, back in 1974, even if, this time, it was through no fault on the Spanish club's part. The second leg of that 1985 Cup-Winners' Cup tie would be played in the afternoon, at an eerily empty Celtic Park, with the players' shouts echoing from the terracing and with only a handful of journalists, policemen and club officials to witness the match.

'We went to Madrid in the year after the Rapid game,' comments Peter Grant, 'got a 1–1 draw and should have won the game in the return match. We had players such as Derek Whyte acting as ball-boys at the game at Celtic Park because that was the only way they could see the game! It was a strange one. If Atletico had come back to Glasgow there is no way they could have beaten us in front of a full house at Celtic Park. Over there against Atletico it was excellent because it was a great experience to play against a quality side but coming back to the Park was bizarre. It was a massively strange experience even for the older players.

'We had a great chance at Celtic Park when Murdo hit the bar from under the bar. Atletico took the goal kick and went up the park and scored. They scored with two breaks up the park: in Europe if the opposition get a chance they punish you. We thought we had better sides than both Atletico and Rapid and there's no doubt that there's not a hope that Atletico would have beaten us at Celtic Park if we had had a full house behind us. We would always expect to win the game at home in front of our own fans.'

Brian McClair, Celtic's striker in both games, says, 'Atletico were by far the better team. We had a good result away from home, so you are looking for that great European night at Celtic Park but it's behind closed doors with just a few stewards looking on. They just played better, but I think at night in front of a capacity crowd it might have been different. It was no hassle for them, just a stroll, whereas at the Vicente Calderon we had had to cope with their crowd.'

The return to normality the following year had provided the overture for some exciting European nights in the late 1980s and Celtic had won some credit in the European Cup, especially after a 4–2 aggregate defeat to Dynamo Kiev in the autumn of 1986 when the Kiev manager Valeri Lobanovski described Celtic's performance in the City Stadium before 100,000 Ukrainians as the best by any foreign team there in 21 years of European competition. Peter Grant comments, 'People remember that Kiev scored a bad goal when the ball was headed out by Derek Whyte, when he didn't get a shout, but overall we were excellent over there. We had gone 1–0 up in the game, I think, and they had 14 of the national team in their squad, so they were very, very good. Over in Kiev we did really well and deserved to get more out of the game than we did. The experience of playing against the type of players they had was great.'

Brian McClair enjoyed the experience of meeting a team that were more than a match for Celtic. 'Dynamo were an excellent team,' he says, 'with top, top players. They had the benefit of having all the better players from the Soviet Union at the time and they should have beaten us at Celtic Park. It wasn't long after Chernobyl and a lot of players had doubts about going to Kiev. Everybody did travel, after assurances, and I remember that it was a really cold night in Kiev, that it was a big pitch and a sell-out crowd. They played much, much better football than us, even though we did quite well on the night. European football was the best thing; all those European games at Celtic Park and then travelling away to unusual places. Kiev, for example, was at the time under communist rule so it was interesting to look around a place like that.'

Another bash at the European Cup, in 1988, resulted in a narrow 1–0 aggregate defeat to German champions Werder Bremen when, again, Celtic gave a good account of themselves but the team always seemed to fall just short of the standard required to make real headway in Europe. They seemed unable to adjust tactically to the way in which the top European sides could speed up and slow down a match through holding possession patiently for long stretches of a match. The European Cup still held to its original knockout format in the late 1980s; some years were still to pass before the Champion Clubs' Cup would metamorphose into the Champions League. That mini-league-based format, introduced in the 1990s, would allow for a greater margin of error in contrast to the more cut-and-dried two-legged knockout ties, in which razor-sharp concentration was required throughout each and every minute.

'The only thing I regret,' say Peter Grant, 'is that when we were champions we didn't get six games in the Champions League. The Champions League has its critics, and I have at times looked at it and questioned it, but for Celtic it looks, to me, more suitable than the old knockout system because it was very difficult to play against Scottish teams in the Scottish style and then change to play the way you have to do against the continentals. There wasn't enough time for us to prepare for European ties. Sometimes you thought you were playing against three extra players in European ties. I think we'd have had more success if we'd played six games; if we had qualified for the group section of the Champions League. You can't buy that type of experience in Europe. We had the players of quality to do it, but Europe is a completely different game. You don't have enough time from Saturday to Tuesday to change your ways.'

Celtic also enjoyed a rip-roaring 5–4 UEFA Cup victory over Partizan Belgrade in 1989, but that match was typical of the Celtic of the time. They had been 5–3 up in that second leg at Celtic Park, and seemingly ready for the next round as the game entered its dying stages, but had then been undone by continuing to push forward and losing a goal through a piece of slack defending and had made their exit on away goals through a 6–6 aggregate score that said everything necessary about the defensive capabilities of the two teams.

Celtic had simply lost the knack of winning consistently in Europe. The team appeared stuck in a strange rut in terms of European competition: they would play valiantly against strong opposition, but lose, get knocked out of the competition, and leave their supporters believing that that augured well for the following season, when they would surely have learnt from the narrow defeat that had caused their elimination. Then, the following season, there would be a repeat performance; a narrow, sometimes unlucky defeat in Europe, but defeat all the same. 'We suffered because we couldn't get a run in Europe,' says Grant. The Rapid Vienna fiasco had exerted a profound effect on the club: instead of potentially reaching the Cup-Winners' Cup final in 1985 and growing in confidence and experience in Europe, UEFA's ruling in autumn 1984 had brought about Celtic's exit from that tournament. A consequent UEFA ruling had had a powerful bearing on the first-round defeat to Atletico at a deserted Celtic Park the following

season and, as a consequence, the Celtic players had scant experience of
European football to draw upon when they were pitched in against the
better European teams. That inexperience led to early European exits
and that, in turn, meant that Celtic were less and less prepared for
Europe with every passing year.

Fresh hope would still infuse the club and its ever-optimistic supporters
every time Celtic embarked on a new European journey, and the
1991–92 season was no different. So when Celtic were drawn against
Neuchatel Xamax, rather than a club of greater pedigree, optimism
coursed through Celtic Park. Liam Brady's belief that the tie was an
eminently winnable one was given support when he went to watch
Neuchatel in action. 'I had watched them play and didn't think they
were better than us in any shape or form,' says Brady of the Swiss side.
Brady believed that Neuchatel were vulnerable, that Celtic had to take
advantage of the Swiss side and seal the tie by gaining an away victory
emphatic enough to make the return a formality. Prior to the game, the
manager believed that if Celtic were to score, Neuchatel would 'go
under', especially if Celtic played in a traditionally British way to deny
the Swiss the type of space to which they were accustomed in their own
league. The Irishman fielded the following team for the first leg in the
Stade de la Maladiere: Pat Bonner, Mark McNally, Derek Whyte,
Dariusz Wdowcyck, Peter Grant, Brian O'Neil, Stevie Fulton, Paul
McStay, Tony Cascarino, Tommy Coyne and Charlie Nicholas. Brady
fielded the team in a new 3–5–2 attacking formation.

A light snowfall had dusted the shoulders of the players when they had
taken a walk on the day before the match, but that would provide little
warning of the Alpine avalanche that would hit Celtic during the match
itself, which was played in front of 11,300 spectators inside a half-full
Stade de la Maladiere. Nine minutes had passed when the tiny striker
Hossam Hassan, one of three Egyptian internationals in the Neuchatel
side, was allowed to score with a simple header in front of goal from
Christophe Bonvin's corner kick. Ten minutes later, Celtic's lack of
central defensive cover was exposed yet again when Hassan scored his
second, brushing Derek Whyte aside to head a Bonvin cross past
Bonner. The rudimentary 3–5–2 system being employed by Celtic had

afforded the Swiss plenty of space on the wings and in front of goal. Shortly before half-time, Hani Ramzy, another of Neuchatel's Egyptians, crossed for Bonvin to leap and head past Bonner to make it 3–0. Two further simple second-half goals by Hassan gave Neuchatel a tally of five. A single second-half counter from Celtic, a header from Brian O'Neil, did not even merit the description of 'consolation goal' that is traditionally awarded to teams on the end of a sizeable defeat: there could be no consolation for anyone associated with Celtic at being involved in the most calamitous result the club has ever suffered in European competition.

'We went out and really showed the frailties of a poor playing staff, I'd say,' is Brady's opinion of the Neuchatel Xamax game. 'On the night, the players let the club down badly. They went under and I told them in no uncertain terms that that wasn't acceptable. They went under and they didn't fight. They accepted defeat. There was not really anything I could have done about it on the night. I think I made as many substitutions as I could! The team went out there and performed abysmally. I wouldn't put that down to me. Neuchatel were a team that were no great shakes but Packie dropped one in the first five minutes; there was a header from a corner kick inside the six-yard box. Managers can't legislate for things like that.'

Peter Grant, who was part of the Celtic midfield that night in Neuchatel, remains as upset by the events of that evening as he was at the time. His view as to how and why things went wrong differs considerably from that of Liam Brady. 'That's still a bugbear for me,' says Grant. 'You have to use your players in a system they understand. You don't give your players a new system the day before they are to put it into use. I thought that some people underrated Neuchatel Xamax. We always played 4–4–2 and we had never played any other system, but in Neuchatel we played three at the back for the first time ever. We never had enough time to prepare for it and we were ripped apart.

'At that level you are a bit wet behind the ears if you think you can beat anybody in Europe doing that, especially with a coach like Roy Hodgson in charge of the opposition. We played three at the back with a right-back, a left-back and a centre-back, not like Martin O'Neill with two markers and a spare man. We hadn't played with this system before but when the manager tells you to play that way you go into the game and think, "Liam must be confident in this game if we are going this way defensively."

'On that night it was five and I couldn't wait for the final whistle. Every time they went up the pitch they looked like they would get a goal. Hassan must have thought it was his birthday because he got so much room. They had a very big advantage and they did exploit it.

'I think I understand what Liam is saying when he says the playing staff was not the best. We weren't a top-quality side by any manner of means, but if you've not got top-quality players, you hide it by going solid defensively. Instead, we were exploited. We didn't have European quality: he's 100 per cent right. That's a fair argument. He is probably right – we weren't good enough – but you should still pick a team that is solid and in which the players know their jobs.

'The thing that disappointed me was that Liam had played in a top-quality side such as Arsenal when they reached the Cup-Winners' Cup final, and he had also played for Juventus, but we never had a Liam or anything like him so we had to make the most of our resources and that did not happen on the night. There's no doubt in my mind that man for man we were a better side than Neuchatel, so you've got to take the view that on the night Hodgson tactically ripped us apart. He didn't have quality players either, but he used the players that he had properly.'

A team showing three changes to the one that had lost so heavily in Switzerland took to the park for the return match with Neuchatel Xamax in Glasgow. The Celtic line-up, back in a 4-4-2 formation, was: Pat Bonner, Mark McNally, Brian O'Neil, Derek Whyte, Dariusz Wdowcyk, Mike Galloway, Joe Miller, Paul McStay, Tommy Coyne, Charlie Nicholas and John Collins. The fallout from the Neuchatel match had seen both Stevie Fulton and Tony Cascarino dropped immediately, although the expensive Cascarino – a £1.1 million signing from Aston Villa in the summer of 1991 – would be on the bench for the return with Neuchatel.

Brady, for one, believed that the tie could be retrieved at Celtic Park and promised to 'throw caution to the wind' because of the unusual situation and the hefty deficit that Celtic had to try to retrieve. Four minutes into the match, Celtic were awarded a penalty, but that opportunity was immediately discarded when Charlie Nicholas stepped up and floated the ball over the bar. Both sides missed a number of good chances before, early in the second half, Joe Miller scored a simple goal that would, eventually, prove to be the only one of the game. 'We thought if we scored early at Celtic Park we could turn the tie around,' says Peter Grant, 'but it wasn't to be. I think we didn't have the quality of a top European side, and on top of that we missed the penalty and the opportunity to get the crowd going. I think at Parkhead they were waiting to see what happened and it was up to us to get the crowd going.' Only Paul McStay's excellence in midfield was able to lift Celtic's performance above the mediocre, and in some ways the lack of initiative and fire on display made this just as disappointing a result as the one in Switzerland. Celtic had now fallen deep into a steep-sided trough and it would take them another decade before they could climb out of it cleanly.

The appointment of Liam Brady as manager in the summer of 1991 had been a desperate attempt by the then Celtic board to shore up the cracks that were beginning to appear in the Celtic Park superstructure. Brady had an excellent pedigree as a player but it had been a huge gamble to give him his first management job, at the age of only 35, at Celtic and, despite the manager's best intentions, his inexperience had betrayed him badly through his over-estimation of Germinal Ekeren and sudden switch to an apparent under-estimation of Neuchatel Xamax. It was symptomatic of a time when an uncertain Celtic board of directors were searching desperately for a way, any way, forward and were piling one mistake upon another. The emphatic nature of that defeat in Switzerland had been one of the clearest pointers that the only route back to the top in Europe for Celtic would be one that produced a complete change of direction at the club.

THIRTEEN

Deceptive Trends
LIVERPOOL 1997

Henrik Larsson's first goal at Celtic Park was greeted by an awkward silence on the part of the Celtic supporters. It had looked a certainty from the moment he connected with the ball on the edge of the six-yard box and on leaving his boot the ball curved high into the air before dipping dramatically swiftly to nestle neatly in the net. No crowd hysteria or delirium resulted from his effort. Despair was the only response from the Celtic support: Henrik had planted the ball in his own net and had tipped the balance of a finely poised UEFA Cup tie with SC Tirol Innsbruck away from Celtic and back in favour of the Austrian side.

Celtic's followers had been unsure of what to make of Larsson, their new, slightly built, dreadlocked striker, when he had arrived at the club in the summer of 1997 as the first signing demanded by new Dutch head coach Wim Jansen. The more informed members of the support remembered him as a young player who had made sporadic appearances, mainly as a substitute, in the Swedish national side's run to the semi-final of the 1994 World Cup. Others queried why he was leaving Feyenoord for a cut-price fee of £650,000, having exercised a clause in his contract with the Dutch club that allowed him to move on if any other club offered a fee of that amount for him. Larsson had not proved a glowing success in Holland, where he had often played in a withdrawn role behind the front players.

Initial impressions of the striker tended to err on the negative side. Larsson's first appearance for Celtic, as a substitute in the opening Scottish League match of the 1997–98 season, had seen him make a disastrous pass backwards that had led directly to Hibernian's winning goal in a 2–1 defeat for Celtic. Now, later in that August of 1997, the fans were witnessing him marking his home debut in Europe with a spectacular own goal.

It was a moment entirely typical of a time when things were not quite what they seemed, when false indicators were popping up all over the place to mislead and misguide the Celtic support. This was especially true of the supporters' desperate desire for renewed success in European football. That UEFA Cup tie with SC Tirol Innsbruck was watched by a crowd of 47,000, who were entranced and enthralled by a freewheeling second leg that pulsated with excitement. Larsson's own goal had made it 2–2 at half-time, putting the Austrians 4–3 ahead on aggregate, but two goals shortly after the interval put Celtic ahead overall in the tie once more.

Six minutes from time, the Celtic defence failed to cut out a simple cross and were punished when Innsbruck scored through an elementary back-post header. That made it 4–3 to Celtic on the night, but levelled the aggregate at 5–5 and put Innsbruck ahead on away goals. Coach Heinz Peischl, officials and substitutes from the Austrian team danced in delight on the Celtic Park running track to greet the goal, but it was not over yet: two late Celtic goals, from Morten Wieghorst and Craig Burley, gave the Glasgow team a 6–3 win on the night and a 7–5 aggregate victory. The overall aggregate lead in the tie had changed hands no fewer than seven times on the night of that second leg at Celtic Park.

The supporters left the stadium with their emotions wrung dry after a stunning evening's entertainment. It was all too easy to forget that this was August, that this was the second qualifying round of the UEFA Cup, that the game had been littered by basic defensive errors on the part of both sides and that Celtic had been facing a club that had finished sixth in the Austrian League the previous season. Celtic truly were swimming with the minnows of European football at that stage: their attendance for the Innsbruck match was almost three times higher than anything else recorded for the other games in the UEFA Cup second qualifying round that evening. The next best had been the

16,000 who had attended the Spartak Trnava vs. PAOK Salonika match. Unlike Spartak Trnava, Celtic had a rich heritage in European football and when mammoth crowds rolled up to create the type of atmosphere associated with the days of past successes, it was understandable that the Celtic support could get carried away and believe that the great European evenings were already back.

Celtic had hosted Innsbruck in a spanking new, all-seated Celtic Park, which, in the summer of 1997, was a three-sided stadium, with a temporary stand accommodating fans in the west section, where construction of the final part of the stadium was underway. All of this was the product of the overhaul of the club's structure that had begun with the accession to power of Fergus McCann in 1994, when he had ousted an ineffective Celtic board of directors to take control of Celtic Football Club. McCann had quickly gone about the business of starting work on a new, all-seated, 60,000-capacity Celtic Park and he helped put the club on a steady financial footing through a hugely successful share issue that went a long way towards funding the new stadium. Thousands of Celtic fans had invested in this regeneration of their club and it had had the effect of bringing renewed life to Celtic Football Club, with supporters now feeling that they owned a part of that great institution in the shape of their shares. It made the support more desperate than ever to see a successful Celtic. The club also had a new manager that summer of 1997, the third in McCann's three-year spell at the club, and, for the first time in the club's history, team matters were under the control of a continental European, in the person of Dutchman Wim Jansen.

'It was really strange, that game with Innsbruck,' says David Hannah, a midfield player who turned out at right-back for Celtic on the night. 'I think it was quite an open game. We maybe took the foot off the pedal, as it were, when we went in front, and then started to defend too deeply. It was probably too much of an open game, but the crowd helps you along. At Celtic Park you certainly hear the crowd, especially in European games. It seems to be a whole new ball game when you are playing foreign opposition. The fans seem a bit more patient with you.

'Henrik, like any new player who comes in, was obviously going to be a bit apprehensive but, because he had worked with Wim Jansen before, he settled in very quickly. Henrik was quite quiet initially, but he always worked hard in training and he quickly stamped his own personality on the team. I have to say that I can't remember him scoring that own goal but maybe that is why he is better staying out of his own penalty box!'

Celtic had come close to disappearing off the radar in terms of European competition during the 1990s. It was a decade in which they had signally failed to defeat opponents of any standing. The allure of Europe had begun to dim so badly that one Celtic manager, Liam Brady, had even decided to quit in between the first and second legs of a 1993 UEFA Cup tie between Celtic and Sporting Lisbon, even though Celtic were 1–0 up after the first leg, so hopeless did he feel his task to be. The club was, at the time, in turmoil and on the verge of bankruptcy, factors that helped lead to Celtic missing out on Europe for one season before a new manager, Tommy Burns, found himself learning the hard way in European competition.

An encounter with Paris St Germain in the 1995 European Cup-Winners' Cup had seen Burns' Celtic side return from France after a 1–0 first-leg defeat in the Parc des Princes convinced that they had achieved a good result and that the traditional trick of overwhelming teams with pressure at Celtic Park would see them take the tie. They found out that they had been away from the serious business of European competition for too long. Top teams in the 1990s were equally at ease on away turf. Fergus McCann chatted to Archbishop Thomas Winning at half-time about how Celtic were playing well but by then the Parisians were 2–0 ahead. It ended 4–0 to PSG on aggregate, which remains Celtic's biggest loss over two legs in European competition. McCann had demonstrated his grasp of French at the reception for the two clubs on the away trip but, perched in the front row of the Celtic directors' box with fedora on head for the return, he found himself greeted by more earthy language from supporters in the front stand at Celtic Park who turned round to demand that he sort matters out when they found that their seats for the match had been double-ticketed. The teething problems of the new McCann regime were visible on and off the pitch as Celtic softly dropped out of European competition for another season.

'I remember playing Paris St Germain,' says Peter Grant, 'and coming up against guys like Youri Djorkaeff, who is now in the Premiership, Rai, who had won the World Cup, and Patrice Loko, who had cost them a lot of money. That was a great experience. European teams would just play close together and play short five-yard passes or ten-yard passes whereas Celtic would spread out more and go for it.'

Friction between Burns and McCann had made their relationship a heated one from its very beginnings, but the chief executive had allocated funds to the manager to spend on the type of new players necessary to bulk out the playing staff. Burns had the hard task of regenerating the team simultaneously with the ongoing reconstruction of the stadium and the manager's task was the more imprecise, more formidable one, involving as it did working with capricious human beings rather than bricks and mortar. As a man who understood fully Celtic's traditions, Burns had opted to concentrate resources allocated to him on strengthening the team's attacking prowess, a policy that he knew would attract back a support that had become disillusioned with the efforts of the Celtic sides of the early 1990s. Attacking players Paolo Di Canio, Pierre van Hooijdonk, Andreas Thom and Jorge Cadete became the talismanic figures at Burns' new Celtic, but the policy of focusing on fortifying the forward line came undone spectacularly in a UEFA Cup tie with SV Hamburg in 1996.

'The club needed those players,' explains Burns. 'They lifted the team and people enjoyed watching them. If anything, the problem they caused me was trying to play the four of them in the one team. There were some games in which we could get away with that. There were other games, at the top level, where we couldn't get away with it. I think they all had something to offer positively going forward, but it was defensively where playing them caused us a problem. I remember playing Hamburg and playing the four of them. I realised five minutes into the game that that was a mistake because we were already a goal down and Hamburg were causing us all sorts of problems. When they attacked we were four players down. As you go along you realise the need for balance in a team – it is all about getting the right blend.'

Burns' successor, Wim Jansen, as the first continental to select and coach the team, was expected to bring a heightened awareness of tactics to his job that would complement the traditional spirit of a Celtic team that itself was becoming ever more cosmopolitan. Foreign players had flocked to cash-rich British football during the 1990s and Celtic made sure they had their fair share of foreigners: the team that had faced Innsbruck had included Frenchman Stephane Mahé, Dane Morten Wieghorst, the Swede Larsson and the German Andreas Thom. Only Thom – a £2.2 million purchase from Bayer Leverkusen – had cost a sizeable fee. Fergus McCann's policy was to ally prudence with progress.

Even the practical McCann was fully aware of the romance of continental competition. His stated ambition for the club in 1997 was for Celtic once again 'to operate as a major European force in football'. It was, as McCann was aware, what the supporters wished to hear, and when Celtic were drawn against Liverpool in the first round proper of the UEFA Cup, the suporters wondered if it could provide the breakthrough in European competition that Celtic had desired for a decade and a half. The first-leg match would be watched by the biggest crowd for a European tie at Celtic Park for eight years – 48,625 – and both legs would be televised live across Britain.

Some colourful touches suggested that the big European nights were truly back. The young, preening Italian referee, Graziano Cesari, had a deep tan and a stately, coiffured perm that made him look more like a millionaire footballer than the traditionally grey, authoritarian figures who officiated at domestic Scottish games, whilst the Liverpool players who lined up against Celtic were typical of the celebrity footballers who had become ever more high profile in England with the dawning of the lucrative FA Premier League at the beginning of the 1990s.

The Liverpool players even had their own nickname – the Spice Boys – in reference to the playboy culture that had grown up at the club, where the young players of the time were famous for frittering away their riches in the manner of lightweight pop stars. That nickname also had a derogatory edge. Having been borrowed from the Spice Girls pop group, it suggested that the Liverpool players were more about image than substance; better at spending their continually increasing earnings than applying themselves to their work. Their collective nerve would be tested at Celtic Park, where ear-splitting noise greeted the arrival of the teams when they were sighted emerging from the tunnel together. The Celtic players who strode out on to the field were: Jonathan Gould,

Tom Boyd, David Hannah, Alan Stubbs, Stephane Mahé, Jackie McNamara, Morten Wieghorst, Craig Burley, Henrik Larsson, Simon Donnelly and Regi Blinker. Only five of those players – Boyd, Burley, Donnelly, Hannah and McNamara – had been born in Scotland.

'I can remember it as if it was yesterday,' says David Hannah. 'I played in several Old Firm games for Celtic but the atmosphere on the night of the Liverpool match was something else and I will cherish it until I finish in football. The sound of almost 50,000 supporters, including the Liverpool supporters, singing "You'll Never Walk Alone" literally made the hairs on the back of your neck stand up.'

After six minutes Boyd's stray pass into the Liverpool half was collected by Liverpool's Dominic Matteo, who pushed it on to Steve McManaman on the halfway line. A quick, tidy shuffle and flick from McManaman gave Karl-Heinz Riedle the opportunity to send a first-time ball to striker Michael Owen. The speed of the move took five Celtic players out of the game, including Boyd, who had initially been close to Owen but who had then been pulled yards out of position when he had gone to challenge Riedle, with no real chance of getting anywhere near the German. That left Boyd stranded and Owen entirely in the clear when he received the ball. The 17-year-old Liverpool player simply scooped it over goalkeeper Gould for the opening goal.

It was a strange thing, but the Liverpool goal settled Celtic down and Henrik Larsson's footballing intelligence gradually began to exert itself. 'For the first 15 to 20 minutes,' comments Hannah, 'we gave them too much respect – they had names like Fowler, Owen and Ince in their side – and Owen scored quite early, but after 15 minutes we all looked at each other as if to say, "We're just as good as these guys." On the night, thereafter, we were by far the better team.'

Shortly after half-time, a surge by Jackie McNamara down the right flank ended with the wing-back sending a fine, left-footed volley high into the Liverpool net. The goal was greeted with a snatch from the loudspeakers of 'The Celtic Song', Glen Daly's early-1960s accordion-backed homage to 'a grand old team to play for'. It was symptomatic of the Celtic stadium experience, 1990s-style, with a powerful sound system blaring out a snatch of a popular song – a means of prompting the fans that had been borrowed from gimmick-rich American football. It was characteristic of Celtic that the song in question was not some stomping rock anthem but a music-hall-style ditty taken from an era less sophisticated in terms of spectator comforts but one in which the Celtic team on the park had been much more successful. This craving for a connection with the past was vitally important to the supporters – their ultimate desire was to recreate the great Celtic Park atmosphere associated with the 1960s and that desire was felt most keenly on European evenings.

Fifteen minutes from time Henrik Larsson took a tumble over the outstretched arms of David James, the Liverpool goalkeeper. A penalty was awarded and striker Simon Donnelly's kick from the spot kissed the underside of the crossbar on its way into the net. It seemed too good to be true – and so it proved. Two minutes from time, McManaman collected the ball wide on the right inside his own half and was then allowed to make progress from that wide area directly to a central position on the edge of the Celtic penalty area, with only one flimsy challenge having been made on him over a 40-yard stretch. The Liverpool man, now only 20 yards from goal, almost casually bent the ball round Gould for an easy equaliser.

'I had to mark Steve McManaman over the two games,' says David Hannah. 'Wim Jansen pulled me aside and said he wanted me to do a specific man-marking job on him and, although he scored against us in the 89th minute, if you watch the game I was on the other side of the pitch as we were attacking them to try to get the third goal. Morten Wieghorst had picked him up and Morten let Steve McManaman run off him. It was a great individual goal but I've watched the videotape of it and I think Morten would admit he stopped running after the halfway line and let McManaman run on 30 yards. Morten should have maybe challenged him and maybe could have used an ankle-tap and given away a foul instead of letting McManaman run on.

'I think that after the game, in the dressing-room, we felt we should have beaten those guys,' adds Hannah. 'We also knew that, having conceded two goals, it would be hard for us down there. We had competed with one of the top three teams in England and we all wanted to prove we could compete at that level, and I think when we went to Anfield we did that.'

Hannah, who had been signed by Tommy Burns in the 1996–97 season, had carried out an excellent man-marking job on McManaman at Celtic Park, but although he had stuck to that task professionally, he had been made aware that it would not carry any weight in terms of winning a long-term, regular place in Jansen's team. 'The one thing that did surprise me about Wim,' says Hannah, 'was that before the first ball of the season had been kicked he had named his strongest starting 11 and some players found that hard to deal with. I couldn't understand that; it meant that whoever was in that starting 11 would only miss out if they were injured or suspended.

'If a player in the 11 that Wim had named had been out through injury or suspension they would automatically get back into the team once they were fit again or free from suspension. It was strange that when you came in and did well you could then be on the bench again for the next game. You could understand that Henrik would be an automatic choice in any team, but some of those guys in that starting 11 went for a number of games without playing well and would still be in the side. I don't know whether that was a Dutch thing or what. There were a few players who had a really bad season and played game after game after game and guys who were working to get into the team were saying, "What's going on?"' Jansen was Celtic's fifth manager in a six-year period, a turnover of personnel that made for instability and a lack of continuity. A series of new managers introducing new ideas at the start of each season may also have mitigated against success in European competition, which would begin early each season, just as the new man was settling in.

Celtic made two changes for the second leg at Anfield, replacing Boyd with the Italian Enrico Annoni and the injured Blinker with Tosh McKinlay. 'I thought we played really well at Anfield,' says David Hannah, 'and we had a chance when Simon Donnelly tried to chip David James – I think it was after about 11 minutes – but it went just over the bar. We limited them to a few chances over the 90 minutes but with them having the cushion of the away goals they were in a very strong position and defensively they were so hard to break down. Playing against such a good team, you have to take your chances when they come along, but it didn't happen for us. We still came out of it with a fair deal of credit.' Celtic had indeed done a lot better than had been expected, remaining unbeaten over both legs: the Anfield match ended 0–0, a scoreline that sent Liverpool through to the second round.

It was still an encouraging result for Celtic at a time when the club was gingerly being nursed back to full health.

Jansen went a step further when he suggested afterwards that Celtic had shown everyone in Europe that at that time Celtic had a very good team. It was typical of the type of empty myth propagated by some football managers. There had been 32 first-round UEFA Cup ties that week, not to mention a host of Champions League and Cup-Winners' Cup ties. It seemed unlikely that across the continent on the day after Celtic's return match with Liverpool, football followers allowed their morning coffee to grow cold on reading the news that Celtic had been knocked out of the UEFA Cup in the opening round on away goals by Liverpool. That hardly suggested that Celtic were the coming side in Europe. The following round would see Liverpool eliminated by a mediocre French team, Strasbourg, and that threw the match between Celtic and Liverpool into sharp perspective. Touted as the 'Battle of Britain', it had been a bout between the ghosts of two giants. There was still some way to go before Celtic would merit more than a footnote in European football's margins.

FOURTEEN

Giant Steps
JUVENTUS 2001

Robert Prosinecki stood relaxedly chatting and taking in the warm summer air outside the main entrance to Celtic Park. An East End urchin, no more than ten years old, approached the Croatia Zagreb midfielder and boldly asked if Prosinecki could present him with a Zagreb team jersey, gratis, but the Croatian, unable to penetrate the Glaswegian dialect, instead playfully pulled the youngster's ears in affection. Prosinecki's team had just lost the first leg of their 1998 Champions League qualifier to Celtic by 1–0 but it was a match through which the midfielder had strolled casually, and now his happy mood hinted that he was unworried by the prospect of turning the game round when Celtic journeyed to Croatia. A 3–0 victory for Zagreb a fortnight later, masterminded by Prosinecki, who chipped in two of the goals, showed that the experienced Croatian's unworried demeanour had not been out of place in Glasgow.

'I remember the game in Zagreb,' says David Hannah, who watched proceedings from the substitutes' bench. 'I thought they would ask me to do a man-marking job on Prosinecki but they didn't, and he was absolutely out of this world. He basically wasted us over there and they also had Mark Viduka and Maric up front and they gave our centre-halves a really hard night. Prosinecki was just showboating. You could see his touch and vision were second to none, and seeing it at first hand was a joy to watch, even though we were being beaten and were not going to qualify for the Champions League.

'In the Scottish League we had loads of possession of the ball and went forward and scored goals, but in Europe you have to tailor your game. You can't push forward all the time. Also, with the 4–4–2, when you pushed forward with the full-backs you sometimes tended to leave yourself exposed to the counter-attack.'

It had been Celtic's first attempt at making their way into the Champions League and it had been disfigured when, in the days before the match, a dispute between the players and the club over their Champions League bonuses had become public knowledge. Doctor Jozef Venglos, who had been appointed the new Celtic manager just a few weeks beforehand, had to struggle to get the best out of a new set of players, largely unknown to him, whilst also coming to terms with this off-field problem. It did not augur well for Celtic's Champions League prospects.

The Champions League was the new name for the tournament formerly known as the European Cup. UEFA, in 1992, had decided to puff up and expand their premier tournament as a means of maximising income from the 1990s television bonanza. Prior to that decade, the only way for supporters to see home European Cup matches would be to go along to the game; ties were not televised live. Sometimes, away matches would be 'live' but only on a haphazard basis and sometimes only part of a match; perhaps a second half of a key game. Now, a new deal brokered by UEFA meant that all Champions League matches, home and away, would be shown 'live' and in full on television in the home nations of the competing clubs. Football had become fashionable during the early 1990s and the television companies were willing to pour fortunes into the game. That had led UEFA to devise their more television-friendly format for their leading competition. The Champions League, with the core of the competition played on a mini-league and not a knockout basis, meant more games for television, less risk of elimination for Europe's biggest clubs and more money for all involved.

There was even an escape clause introduced in the late 1990s for those clubs who were unlucky enough to lose their Champions League qualifier: entry into an expanded UEFA Cup. Almost simultaneously,

UEFA abandoned the European Cup-Winners' Cup, a tournament that had given great pleasure to millions of supporters for almost 40 years. Cup winners would now join a great swarm of clubs in a swollen UEFA Cup tournament. Celtic's defeat in their 1998 Champions League qualifier in Zagreb meant that the Glasgow club fell into the UEFA Cup safety net but Venglos was still sorting out the team, and in autumn 1998 they were eliminated from that tournament in the second round by Zurich.

Three years would pass after the Zagreb tie before Celtic would win the Scottish League again and enjoy another opportunity to enter the Champions League. Martin O'Neill was by then the Celtic manager, and a haul of 53 goals from Henrik Larsson had won him the Golden Shoe as European football's top scorer in the 2000–01 season and had helped power Celtic to the Scottish League title. Their subsequent qualifying match to gain entry to the lucrative group stages of the Champions League in 2001 saw Celtic again drawn against difficult opponents, this time in the shape of Ajax Amsterdam. It looked a daunting prospect but the confidence that had been injected into the side by O'Neill since his arrival at the club in the summer of 2000 helped Celtic to sweep aside their opponents with a performance of poise and precision in the Amsterdam ArenA. Three goals of stunning quality from Celtic gave the club one of their finest away results in European football against an Ajax side brimming over with talent. O'Neill had instilled a new purposefulness in the side, which was now filled with powerful, pacy players. Everyone looked to Larsson as the source of goals, but it had been three expert finishes from Bobby Petta, Didier Agathe and Chris Sutton that had given Celtic a very useful 3–1 victory in Holland.

'I had two chances against Ajax,' says Henrik Larsson, 'a header that hit the bar, and a shot which was saved, and I thought both were in. I couldn't believe it when the ball didn't go in the back of the net. Luckily, we played really well as a team, and it was very pleasing to get a 3–1 win. It was great to have around 8,000 Celtic fans in the ground making a lot of noise and urging us on. Everyone worked really hard and we moved well and passed well.'

It was Celtic's most impressive result in European competition for two decades, but in the second leg the team suffered the classic dilemma of sitting on a useful lead and not knowing quite whether to defend or attack. Ajax, in contrast, had to look for the win and Celtic's performance on the night of the second leg was as nervy as their approach to the first leg had been nerveless. For long stretches of the match they were outplayed by Ajax and long before the end the Celtic supporters were on edge at the prospect of missing out on a Champions League spot after it had appeared to have been all but sealed. Fortunately, the Dutch managed a mere 1–0 victory, scant reward for them on a night when they had been by far the superior team and when they had been kept at bay only by a series of superb saves from Celtic goalkeeper Rab Douglas. Celtic would, at last, compete in the Champions League for the first time, in the tenth season of that competition's existence.

The Champions League had become a cobbled-together compromise by the early twenty-first century. It was now no longer the exclusive province of champions, and it had never been exclusively a league; instead, it was a hybrid of league and cup competition. At its initial group stage, 32 clubs competed in 8 4-team sections and the top 2 in each group would go on to reach the last 16 and the second group stage. The European Cup trophy, the same prize that Billy McNeill had lifted in Lisbon in 1967, remained in place for the winners, the one major link with the competition's past, providing the new format with status and credibility. UEFA could tinker incessantly with their flagship tournament but as long as that elegant trophy was there for winning the Champions League, it would still be seen as the continuation, in the modern era, of the original European Cup, rather than as a brand-new competition.

The Champions League grated with the traditionalists but it should not have done. Gabriel Hanot, the founder of the European Cup, had first discussed the idea of regular pan-European football during the mid-1930s and he had originally envisioned a European league rather than a cup. His plans had been put on hold because of the events of the Second World War and, when regular football resumed, he compromised in the mid-1950s by proposing a European Cup, a tournament to be played under floodlights and one that, he hoped, would interest Europe's television companies. UEFA, in the 1950s, had initially stated that it would have nothing to do with the organisation of a European Cup and it had only been when the clubs had got together and organised the tournament themselves that UEFA had panicked and decided they had better become involved and bring it under their umbrella. Something similar happened in the 1990s, with frequent threats from Europe's major clubs to break away and form their own competition unless UEFA modified and expanded the European Cup in the manner those clubs desired. UEFA, bowing to those pressures, agreed.

The Frenchman Hanot had been no unworldly dreamer – as a former footballer and a football journalist he fully understood football finance – but even he would perhaps have raised a metropolitan eyebrow at the Champions League, which, with each passing year in the 1990s, became weighted ever more heavily towards the richest clubs in Europe. The competition had soon reached the point where its title had become a complete misnomer; under pressure from Europe's biggest clubs, UEFA had eased the entry restrictions so that not only the champions but three other clubs from each of Europe's major domestic league competitions were allowed entry each season. This expansion meant that there was less room in the group stages of the tournament for clubs from marginalised leagues who played in countries with relatively small television audiences. It meant that clubs such as Celtic, Croatia Zagreb and Ajax Amsterdam had to play in preliminary rounds to win a seat on the Champions League gravy train.

Celtic's two hugely contrasting home and away legs in the tie with Ajax would provide a suitable guide to the pattern that would be drawn by Celtic's Champions League adventures that autumn of 2001. The team would veer from vital victories to demoralising defeats without embracing anything so mediocre as a draw. Celtic were drawn in Group E with Juventus, Porto and Rosenborg Trondheim, and a 3–2 opening-game defeat by Juventus was followed by solid 1–0 home victories over both Porto and Rosenborg. 'Against Porto,' says Henrik Larsson of the home match with the Portuguese that gave Celtic their first victory in the Champions League, 'we started where we left off against Juventus, playing aggressively and taking the game to the opposition. Porto certainly knew how important every match is in the Champions League and weren't content to sit back at Celtic Park. They played really well and we couldn't afford to lose concentration for a second. I was lucky enough to get the goal, but I think everybody in the Celtic team performed well.'

The home victories over Porto and Rosenborg contrasted sharply with Celtic's scatty, patchy performances in the away matches with those two clubs. Both ended in defeat for Celtic. 'Porto scored early against us,' says Larsson as he recalls those two crucial away defeats, 'and Rosenborg also got an early goal. Going a goal down away from home is crucial. The opposition starts filling the midfield and it becomes really tough to break through. You can talk about tactics and players, but if you lose an away goal early in a Champions League match, you have a big hill to climb.'

The 2–0 defeat to Rosenborg in their fifth game in the group meant that Celtic would have to rely on the Norwegian side getting at least a point from Porto in their final match, which would kick off simultaneously with Celtic's concluding fixture, their home encounter with Juventus. Celtic were sitting on six points as they faced Juventus whilst Porto were one point better off.

The defeats in Porto and Rosenborg had been clear-cut, but Celtic's opening-game defeat to Juventus in the Stadio Delle Alpi had been a lot closer. Celtic had been at 2–2 when, in the final minute, the Juventus striker Nicola Amoruso had taken a tumble inside the penalty area when Joos Valgaeren had gone to shadow him. It had been a clear dive by the Italian and so incensed was Martin O'Neill by Amoruso's acting that the Celtic manager was sent to the stand by the referee. Amoruso himself took the penalty to give Juventus a 3–2 victory. Much was made of Amoruso's dive but Valgaeren had been slightly careless in allowing himself to get too close to the Italian and appeared to have brushed Amoruso's shoulders with his hands as they both went for the ball. That had given the Italian the perfect opportunity to feign being fouled.

'As footballers you always learn from your experiences,' says Henrik Larsson of that initial encounter with Juventus. 'The fact that we played well and came away with nothing was a tough lesson. We probably deserved a draw but I, for one, would rather play badly and win. I admit that it did take a while to get over our defeat in Turin. There is no doubt we were robbed of a Champions League point at Juventus by a penalty that was never a penalty. There is no way Joos Valgaeren fouled Nicola Amoruso and, of course, it's never nice to lose like that.

'It's especially not nice to lose like that in such an important game. I thought we had played reasonably well and deserved to have come back to 2–2 after going two goals behind. We showed that we can live with the best sides in Europe. I suppose it's all part of the game that sometimes you find yourself on the end of bad decisions but you just have to hope that it all evens out in the end. There was too much emotion immediately after that game but now we can look back and say that, overall, we did all right. There are world-class players in Scotland, but there are few teams in Europe who can boast the sort of line-up that Juventus can call on.'

Celtic's final group match, the return with Juventus, would be surrounded by unusual circumstances. Juventus had already qualified for the second group stage of the Champions League so, for the first time ever in the history of European football at Celtic Park, the home side would start the match desperate for a win whilst the opposition could afford to lose, knowing that they would still progress to the next stage of the competition. Even if Celtic did win, it might prove worthless because they could only pip Porto for second place in the group if the Portuguese side drew or lost at home to Rosenborg Trondheim. Over the 90 minutes, though, Celtic had no need to concern themselves with such details. They had to go out to get a win; only afterwards would they need to worry about how the cards had fallen.

O'Neill selected a team in his usual 3–5–2 formation to face Juventus. The team was: Rab Douglas, Bobo Balde, Johan Mjallby, Joos Valgaeren, Didier Agathe, Paul Lambert, Neil Lennon, Lubo Moravcik, Bobby Petta, Henrik Larsson and Chris Sutton. The Juventus side featured players of the calibre of Czech midfielder Pavel Nedved and such Italian internationals as centre-back Ciro Ferrara, Alessio Tacchinardi and Alessandro Del Piero, the highest-paid player in the Italian game.

Both sides spent the opening part of the match simply prodding gently at each other in midfield, but 12 minutes in, Juventus were stung when Celtic made the first dent in their defence. Lubo Moravcik burrowed deep into the Juventus half to pelt a tricky, low 20-yard shot goalwards that Juventus' 21-year-old Uruguayan international goalkeeper Fabian Carini twisted round the post.

It was an encounter that grew more engrossing with every move and after 18 minutes Alessandro del Piero was provided with the opportunity to show off his famed free-kick skills when he was felled 20 yards from goal by a combined challenge from Moravcik and Valgaeren. A six-man Celtic defensive wall stood up to the Italian as he prepared to take the kick, but they were reduced to spectators as Del Piero curved a splendid strike high over the wall and into the top corner of the net. Douglas got as close to the ball as he could, but such was the extreme accuracy of Del Piero's aim that the Celtic goalkeeper had no chance of stopping the shot. Even the Celtic supporters had to admire such a display of world-class ability, despite it sending their team 1–0 down. The strength of the celebrations of the Juventus players and their manager Marcello Lippi showed how much they wanted to win this game.

Within one minute of that goal a quick pass from Chris Sutton put Moravcik in on goal with only goalkeeper Carini to beat from 12 yards, but the goalkeeper blocked the ball to send it wide of goal. Moravcik berated himself for the miss but he did not allow it to get him down. Instead, he was hungrier than ever for the ball. The Slovakian, more than anyone, was stretching the Italians with his angled, varied runs from the heart of midfield into the territory around their 18-yard box and it was some Moravcik magic that opened up the Juventus defence once again midway through the first half. Twice he twisted cleverly away from the hawkish attentions of Michele Paramatti on the right wing before clipping a cute cross into the centre of the Juventus penalty area. Joos Valgaeren, supplementing the strike power of the Celtic forwards, flew headlong at the ball to knock a header into the corner of the Juventus net for Celtic's equaliser.

Moravcik was now in his element, dragging the game in whichever direction he chose and displaying his magnificent skills to the full. Seconds before half-time, the midfielder bent a corner into the box and striker Sutton used his muscle to burst past two Juventus defenders to angle a header past Carini and make it 2–1 to Celtic at the break.

It had been Doctor Jozef Venglos who had signed Moravcik back in 1998 and the Slovakian international had earned the affection of the

Celtic support through his tremendous range of sophisticated skills. He was 36 years old by that autumn of 2001 and had been used only sparingly by O'Neill in the 2001–02 season – but to good effect. O'Neill had cleverly kept the player primed for the Juventus match in an effort to extract every ounce of excellence from him, as Lubo explains. 'Before the game against Juventus,' he says, 'Martin O'Neill saw that I would like to play but in the days before the match, he never said anything to me about whether or not I would play. He never said, "Lubo, you will play" or something like that. I was working hard and feeling good about playing in the match and he saw that. He knew we needed to win the game and he gave me the chance. He didn't give me the chance against Kilmarnock or someone because he knew this was the right moment for me, for him, for everybody, and we did well.

'I was feeling that this was my game because it was the last game in the Champions League and Martin knew that I had stayed with Celtic for this competition and I showed my desire to play in this game. I knew one hour before the game that I was in the team: always this is what Martin does, the team is named one hour before the game. Personally, I don't like that. I would prefer to know earlier but for this game it was not important because I was so keen to play, really play with pleasure, and give it everything. Sometimes in a league game you will be missing a little bit of motivation because, you know, when you play many games like that, the small games in the season, you need to know a little bit earlier that you are in the team. That way you can work on your motivation for the game. But for the big game you are always ready.

'Although I knew I was in the team for the match with Juventus only at the last minute, I was really ready to play in that game. Also, I was very good physically. I was really fit and ready to play well. In football, fitness and diet and other parts of preparation are absolutely important, but after that the difference comes through details like concentration and being strong mentally and once you have got confidence and fitness you have to concentrate 100 per cent. Concentration is very important and, for me, the harder the game is, the more you need concentration, because your ability is always there; it always stays the same. So Martin saw how important it was for me to play in the Juventus match and he used that for the benefit of the team. He knew I was ready for it and he knew that if he released me into that game I would do everything I could for Celtic that night.' That decision could, without exaggeration, be said to have tipped the game in Celtic's favour. Moravcik was magnificent that night, producing one of the most dynamic of his many superb performances in a Celtic shirt.

David Trezeguet ambled out confidently as a substitute for Juventus at the start of the second half. The Frenchman, scorer of the goal that had won the 2000 European Championship title for France, was on the field as a substitute for Del Piero, and his more direct style immediately enlivened and refreshed the Juventus attack in the opening minutes of the second period. Five minutes had elapsed when a Juventus passing move, quick as the wind, began on the halfway line and concluded with Nicola Amoruso turning a pass into the path of Trezeguet, who had eased into space on the edge of the Celtic penalty area. The French striker used his first touch to steady the ball with his right foot and with his second touch used his left foot to steer a low, fast, accurate shot into the corner of the Celtic net for a goal of exquisite quality.

The slickness of the Italians' football had looked ominous in the opening stages of the second 45 minutes, but Celtic were determined and driven and soon they had the Italians pinned back deep in their own half yet again. The Juventus players obtained a moment's relief through conceding a corner in the 56th minute but Lubo Moravcik had no sooner taken the kick to send the ball sailing into mid-air when French referee Gilles Veissiere blew for a penalty. Juventus defender Mark Iuliano had blatantly blocked a run by Chris Sutton by tugging and pulling at the Celtic man and making no attempt to even glance in the direction of the ball. Henrik Larsson slipped a sleek penalty low into the left-hand corner of the Juventus net. Marcello Lippi, enjoying one of his customary cheroots on the touch-line, like a man out for an after-dinner stroll, let his smoke drop to the ground where he stubbed it out in a small show of anger.

One minute later Lippi was admonished by the referee to stay silent after the Juventus coach had, from the sidelines, disputed the award of a free kick to Celtic. The Italian coach now appeared to be rapidly losing his famous cool as Celtic pushed forward again and again. Three minutes after the penalty, Celtic should have been given another award when Iuliano clearly handled the ball in mid-air inside the penalty area.

It was an even clearer penalty than the one given, but the referee waved play on. Another incident, one minute later, in full view of the main-stand-side referee's assistant, saw Juventus defender Alessandro Birindelli clearly holding Larsson's jersey inside the penalty area, then using his forearm to slyly smack the Swede across the Adam's apple. Again it should have been a penalty.

The memory of those moments was all but obliterated after 63 minutes when, once again, Moravcik was the pivotal point in an incisive move. He curved a clever free kick from deep on the left wing into the Juventus penalty area, where Bobo Balde flicked the ball backwards and towards Sutton, who was waiting, on his toes, on the edge of the penalty area. Sutton swivelled swiftly to guide a searing volley into the roof of the Juventus net. Moments later, Celtic ripped apart the Juventus defence once again. A long, accurate ball from Moravcik left Larsson with only Carini to beat, but the goalkeeper did well to block the striker's shot on the run and to prevent the score becoming 5–2 to Celtic.

Close to the end of the match, the Celtic defence conceded a sloppy goal when hesitant players failed to clear the ball and Trezeguet was allowed to wriggle past several Celtic men before shooting past Douglas. Celtic tightened up enough after that to hold on strongly to their 4–3 lead and Ciro Ferrara, the tough Juventus central defender, showed his enjoyment of the occasion by applauding the crowd as he trotted off the pitch. The word quickly filtered through that Porto had defeated Rosenborg 1–0 and, as O'Neill stood on the touch-line taking in that harsh news, he looked like a man who had had the breath knocked out of him. That was football, Champions League style, but even the disappointment of non-qualification for the next round of the tournament could not remove the delight of the supporters at having witnessed one of the finest and most enthralling games of football ever seen in Glasgow.

'After the Juventus game everyone was a bit disappointed,' states Larsson. 'We had done everything we could but we weren't expecting Rosenborg to do us any favours and that's the way it turned out. Of course, the performance was good, to score four goals against Juventus, but it wasn't enough in the end. You don't always get what you want in football.'

Once again, Celtic landed in the UEFA Cup safety net, which opens up for clubs who finish third in the first group stage of the Champions League, but it was not a particularly soft landing. Following the testing times they had gone through in the Champions League, Celtic might have expected moderate opposition to ease themselves into the UEFA Cup. Instead, they were paired with Valencia, Champions League finalists six months previously. A heroic performance by Rab Douglas limited Valencia to a 1–0 victory in the Mestalla. The scoreline was reversed at Celtic Park when Henrik Larsson scooped a delicious shot into the corner of the Valencia net. Extra-time yielded no further goals and so, for only the second time, Celtic would be involved in a European tie that would be settled on penalties. Only one of the ten kicks was missed, Celtic's third, and it was Larsson who sent his shot off target to allow Valencia to progress.

'We played better than Valencia,' says Larsson, 'and over the two games we deserved to get through, but unfortunately football doesn't always work out like that. We just couldn't produce the finish to kill Valencia off during the game and when it comes to penalties it becomes a lottery. I fully expected to put my penalty away when I stepped up to take it but I missed, and that happens. I felt terrible afterwards, but there's no use just lying down and crying. If you play football at the highest levels for long enough there are always going to be some big disappointments and the thing is not to let them destroy you. You can argue that penalties are not the way to decide an important game like that but there is no other way when you have played two games and can't be separated. It can mean that the side that deserves to go through doesn't, but that sort of thing happens all the time in football.'

It was one of the strangest exits from Europe in Celtic's history. The supporters had been swept away by the thrill of participation in the Champions League and had used up so much emotion on that, that the exit from the UEFA Cup at the first hurdle seemed, in comparison, almost inconsequential. The ten-match run in European competition had been deeply satisfying; every game had been against opposition of the highest quality and taut with drama. It had been three decades since Celtic had competed at such length and at such a level in Europe and for many supporters it was the first time they had enjoyed the pleasure of seeing Celtic maintain such a sustained run in European competition. The players felt that they had been unlucky with the manner of their exit from Europe for two seasons in a row, but it made them more determined to do even better and go even further in European competition in the 2002–03 season. It was an ambition that they would achieve in style.

FIFTEEN

Seville Thrills
PORTO 2003

Phil Thompson edged himself a few yards forward from the Liverpool dugout to shove his arm in the air and raise a fist triumphantly towards the vast bank of Liverpool supporters. It was seconds after the final whistle of the 2003 UEFA Cup quarter-final first leg between Celtic and Liverpool at Celtic Park, and the game had resulted in a 1–1 draw. Thompson's gesture to the fans away to his right was similar to that which had been employed by Graeme Souness, just five months earlier, when Souness, as Blackburn Rovers manager, had visited Celtic Park with his team. That night too Souness had shuffled forward from his dugout at full-time to punch the air with a fist repeatedly in the direction of the travelling Blackburn supporters.

The gesture by Thompson, Liverpool's assistant manager, was slightly less pugnacious than that of Souness, but the message in both cases appeared to be the same: that the respective English clubs had weathered the storm of the boisterous Parkhead crowd and would finish the business clinically in more conducive surroundings when their team met Celtic at home in the second leg. It was an attitude that was shared by almost all of Celtic's opponents during the Glasgow club's 2002–03 UEFA Cup run – each faced Celtic in Glasgow in the first leg and each left believing they had escaped with a result favourable to them.

Outside Celtic Park after the match with Liverpool, the generally amicable atmosphere between Celtic and Liverpool fans was endangered when one loudmouthed Liverpool supporter, mingling like a bad smell with his Celtic counterparts, let off a stream of goading remarks to the effect that at least the Celtic supporters could console themselves with thoughts of next year in Europe and by making mock enquiries as to whether anyone might care to purchase his ticket for what he saw as a now worthless second leg. It said much for Celtic's newfound optimism in European competition in the early twenty-first century that Celtic fans were quietly confident he would be proved wrong.

Inside Celtic Park, the club's directorate were also pondering the implications of the 1–1 draw with Liverpool, albeit in a more reflective manner. 'Fiscal prudence' was once again the catchphrase in the boardroom that night, after a year in which Celtic had been toiling to reduce a heavy debt. Celtic had been paid a record £1.5 million by Channel Five for the rights to screen the quarter-final with Liverpool, but it was agreed that Martin O'Neill would have to achieve even greater success in Europe – and in UEFA Cup terms that was to be nothing less than progressing all the way to the final – if sizeable funds were to be released to him to buy players. As the return with Liverpool drew nearer, the directors nervously did their sums to work out what winning at Anfield and reaching the semi-finals would mean to Celtic, and a rough calculation placed the figure at £2.5 million. If the club was to go all the way to the final, its total earnings from the UEFA Cup would be anything between £10 million and £15 million.

Cold fog swirled around Liverpool on the afternoon of the return match – landmarks such as Albert Dock and the horizon-hugging model of The Beatles' Yellow Submarine were merely a grey outline. It provided a gloomy outlook for the estimated 14,000 Scottish fans who had left behind unseasonally sunny weather in Glasgow to make the journey to Liverpool. Their optimism remained undimmed, though, and although only 2,700 tickets had been allocated to Celtic supporters through the club, by kick-off approximately 12,000 Celtic supporters were inside Anfield.

David Moyes, Sven-Goran Eriksson and Sir Alex Ferguson were among those who populated the Anfield directors' box for the second leg. A more significant presence in that exclusive section of the ground was El Hadji Diouf, Liverpool's Senegalese international and their premier performer in the first leg at Celtic Park. He had received a two-match ban for an incident late in the first leg when his momentum on chasing a lost ball had taken him into the crowd in the front section of the south stand. A couple of hands had stretched out to palm his shaven head and the African had taken exception to this – a hugely insulting gesture to a Senegalese person; or, indeed, a Scottish person. In response he had, when making his way back on to the pitch, turned and spat into the crowd. It was a gesture that so incensed the Celtic supporters that the next time play took Diouf in their direction, one spectator leapt over the wall towards the player and had to be restrained by half-a-dozen stewards. Diouf was swiftly substituted after the police had had a quiet word in Liverpool manager Gérard Houllier's ear and after the match police could be seen taking statements from those who had been in that part of the stadium.

The result was a two-match UEFA ban for the player, forcing him to miss the second leg, and how Liverpool missed him. In the first leg Diouf had been the most indispensable component of the Liverpool team, holding on to the ball on the right side of their midfield and keeping possession intelligently as the vital link between midfield and attack. Without him at Anfield, Liverpool had no one to act as a brake – a restraining force – on their attacks, and again and again the ball hurtled forward at breakneck pace from midfield to attackers Michael Owen and Emile Heskey. Diouf's indiscipline in the first leg had resulted in an indisciplined Liverpool performance in the return match.

Celtic took full advantage. A topsy-turvy, choppy match turned their way right on half-time when Alan Thompson opted for a daisy-cutting shot from a free kick on the edge of the Liverpool penalty area. The defensive wall, expecting Thompson to loop the ball over them, leapt as one and the ball undercut their efforts, sloping into the unguarded corner of goalkeeper Jerzy Dudek's net. Nine minutes from the end, the burly John Hartson daintily jinked past several Liverpool defenders, like a ballet-dancing bouncer, then powered a magnificent, curling shot high into the top right-hand corner of the Liverpool net.

Liverpool's Kop was in impressive form, staying with their team to the bitter end, but Liverpool were well beaten on the night. An hour after the match, Martin O'Neill could be seen in the atrium to the dressing-room area, knotting his tie whilst trying to cope with the congratulations of all around him. Here was the man who had masterminded one of the longest runs that Celtic have ever undertaken in a season's European competition and he deservedly wore a smile of quiet satisfaction. O'Neill's 3–5–2 system was ideally suited to the type of counter-attacking style that is necessary for away matches in European football, such as that one at Anfield and, as the luck of the draw would have it, every tie Celtic played in Europe in the 2002–03 season had the home leg first and the decisive away leg second.

'It's tremendous that we won it in the manner we did,' says Henrik Larsson of that match with Liverpool. 'We knew that if we played to our ability we could win and that is what happened. Everybody played their part and it was a great team effort. It's great when everyone plays at the top of their game at the same time. When that happens we are a match for anybody. Getting the first goal was really important, since we knew that we were back in front, and even if they scored we could take them into extra-time. They came back at us and there were a few nervous moments until we got the second, which was a tremendous effort from John.'

The progress of Celtic into the last eight of the UEFA Cup had triggered much excited talk about how the club now had the chance to take four trophies in one season and for the first time large numbers of Celtic supporters had begun to believe they had a real opportunity to win the European tournament. Their quarter-final opponents Liverpool had led the FA Premiership table in the early part of the 2002–03 season, although by the time of the tie with Celtic they had tumbled down the table to seventh. They still made a notable scalp for Celtic.

Celtic's European run had begun in August 2002 when Basle had visited Celtic Park for the first leg of a third-qualifying-round match for the Champions League. Basle had been the first club to host a match in a European cup competition, in 1955, and this was the fourth time they had faced Celtic in Europe, making them Celtic's most frequently met opponents in European football. Although Celtic had prevailed each time, the results had become closer and closer with every meeting. The

Swiss club were still dismissed in some quarters as lightweights, but this was a well-run club that stood comparison with Celtic or Rangers in terms of organisation and backing. Basle's 33,000-capacity St Jakob Park stadium is sold out for every match, and their supporters are the most obstreperous and excitable in Switzerland. Club owner Gigi Oeri – whose husband Andreas Oeri is heir to the Roche pharmaceutical fortune – bought 80 per cent of FC Basle in 1999 and her financial backing for the club had helped them capture their first Swiss League title for 22 years in the 2001–02 season.

The draw was greeted with mixed feelings in Basle. A meeting with Celtic brought back memories of the two clubs' encounter in 1974 when Basle had enjoyed their best-ever run in European competition, but when it had been Celtic who had halted the run by defeating the Swiss in the European Cup quarter-finals. A pulsating game at Celtic Park in August 2002 saw Basle striker Christian Gimenez infiltrate the Celtic defence in the opening seconds to put the Swiss side ahead, but by the end of the 90 minutes, despite Henrik Larsson missing a penalty, Celtic were 3–1 ahead in the tie.

'Anyone who says Basle aren't a good side doesn't know what they're talking about,' says Henrik Larsson. 'The gap that used to exist between the top European sides and the rest just isn't there anymore. European sides are getting tougher and tougher all the time and Basle were a team who passed the ball really well. Conceding a goal so early in the first leg at Celtic Park was annoying and it put us on the back foot straightaway, especially with the away goals rule. I was really glad we got the opportunity to get a goal back soon and after that we started to get on top and managed to restrict the amount of chances they had. When they did manage to get through, Rab was great for us, and by the second half we pushed on a bit more and started to get the upper hand.'

Three days from the end of that August of 2002, Martin O'Neill could be found indulging in some spectacular histrionics on the St Jakob-Park touch-line as Celtic succumbed to a 2–0 defeat in Basle. The Celtic manager appeared ready to bite the Swiss turf in despair, as he kneeled, doubled up in emotional agony, head buried in hands and face down on the ground. That result meant a 3–3 aggregate that put Basle into the lucrative group stage of the Champions League on the away goals rule. O'Neill had begun the away match with Basle playing four men at the back, a departure from his 3–5–2 policy as rare as it was risky. It failed to solidify the defence and, with the players unfamiliar with the demands of a 4–4–2 after two seasons of non-stop 3–5–2, a shaky Celtic had conceded both goals in the early stages. A reversion to 3–5–2 for the second half reinvigorated the team and made it a more even match, but Basle held out for the win on a costly evening for Celtic.

'We didn't play well enough to go through to the Champions League,' says Larsson. 'I really don't have a clue why we didn't perform, and I'm not sure you can look at anything in particular and say that it is the reason. Sometimes you have nights like that where you don't play well and you don't get any lucky breaks.'

Once again, the UEFA Cup safety net caught Celtic but it seemed, in the late summer of 2002, meagre consolation for the Champions League capitulation to have been parachuted into UEFA's secondary competition. That was reflected in the attendance at Celtic Park for the first-round UEFA Cup tie with Suduva of Lithuania, when a crowd of 37,000 turned up for the occasion. It was a measure of how complete Celtic's regeneration had become by the early twenty-first century that that was regarded as a relatively small crowd. The new, 60,000-capacity Celtic Park would be packed to the gunnels for each and every home Scottish League match and for matches with the bigger names in European football. With 54,000 captive season-ticket holders, the club was guaranteed a massive annual income and that huge audience had been tapped into to draw lucrative sponsorships to the club and to market pricey merchandise at the supporters. It all combined to make Martin O'Neill the most handsomely remunerated and best-resourced manager in Celtic's history. Celtic now had a wage bill the equal of that of Bayern Munich, Champions League winners in 2001, and only Manchester United in Britain had a higher average attendance. Thanks to that great block of season-ticket holders, Celtic were now the eighth-best-supported club in Europe, a standing that seemed well out of proportion for a team playing in the Scottish League but one that reflected the passion and devotion of the Celtic support.

The Celtic players that faced Suduva featured 11 different nationalities and had cost close to £30 million in total. Most were on five-figure weekly wages, with the best-paid earning anything between £30,000 and £40,000 per week. That placed them amongst the highest earners in any profession in the country and bought them a lifestyle far removed from that of most supporters. Celtic players could now be found living at Glasgow's best addresses, frequenting the finest golf courses in the country and happily hanging out at exclusive enclaves such as the Gleneagles Hotel. The importation of so many non-Scottish players and supplying them with bulging bank balances made this a Celtic team like no other in history, but Martin O'Neill's alchemy had fused them together into a team that forgot the fripperies once they got on to the field of play, where the dominant features of the team were pace, aggression and hard work, together with scoops of skill from such individuals as Henrik Larsson, Paul Lambert, Stilian Petrov and Alan Thompson.

It proved all too much for Suduva, their modest opponents from impoverished Lithuania. Celtic scored an easy eight goals against Suduva, including two excellent ones; the first, from Larsson, saw him expertly sweep, first time, a low cross high into the net; the other was a spectacular flying volley from Stilian Petrov. 'Of course we were really happy with the 8–1 result,' says Larsson, 'and with the way the whole team played. We had done a bit of homework on them, but we still didn't know exactly what to expect from the game. We were all really eager to get a good start to the match, and I think we did that from the first whistle. We put pressure on them and played the ball around nicely. I know a lot of people will say they were not top-quality opposition, and that might be true, but you still have to go out there and be professional and do the job that is expected of you. If you relax at all you can get tripped up and make a bad mistake.'

The emphatic home win over Suduva made the return match in the Baltic state little more than a training exercise and O'Neill duly drew on the extensive squad of players available to him to put out a largely second-choice team for the return, which Celtic won comfortably by 2–0. That low-key entry into the UEFA Cup was followed by a much-hyped encounter with Blackburn Rovers for which the 'Battle of Britain' epithet was brought out and dusted down by those who like that kind of thing. It seemed to be something of a dated concept: both Celtic and Blackburn Rovers fielded multinational teams for the first leg, although there was a more parochial dimension to the tie in the return of Graeme Souness to Glasgow as the Blackburn manager; his first visit to Glasgow for a competitive match since leaving Rangers more than a decade previously. Souness' subsequent career in charge of various clubs in England and on the continent had been less than successful but he appeared to have righted himself, finally, at Blackburn in the early 2000s. A tumult of abuse was expected to pour down upon his head on his appearance at Celtic Park but the Blackburn manager neatly deflected that by delaying his entrance to his dugout until the match had been underway for a few minutes; then made a point of offering a handshake to Martin O'Neill. The occasional jeer still found its way towards Souness but, as the match wore on, the Celtic supporters had much more with which to concern themselves.

Souness had offered views in advance of the match, in that annoyingly pseudo-superior way of his, that English football was stronger than the Scottish game and that the UEFA Cup was a mere distraction for his team. Although he had been a much-capped Scottish international, Souness appeared to have an ambivalent attitude towards his homeland. He stated that survival in the Premiership, rather than UEFA Cup progress, was Blackburn's priority. It seemed that his own Blackburn team took his views less than seriously as they worked and moved and shifted the ball around at speed in the early stages of the match at Celtic Park. It was their best performance under Souness and at times in the first half of the game it was embarrassing how easily they kept the ball away from the Celtic players – passes were spun out in a web from Blackburn midfielder David Thompson and the Celtic players were as immobile as trapped insects as the Blackburn players sped here and there. The Celtic defence had been opened so wide at times that it made the Grand Canyon look like a crack in the pavement and by half-time the English side had had four top-notch chances to build up a clear lead and, even at that early stage, kill the tie. They had, however, failed to put any of those chances away. Even so, Souness was out on the pitch at half-time, congratulating his players; it was the type of gesture seen more often from managers at full-time after a significant victory. Blackburn had been good in the first half but this seemed bizarrely excessive with only one quarter of the tie having been played and was particularly puzzling after Souness having downplayed the importance of the match.

The English side continued to look good in midfield as the second half began and they now began indulging in fancy flicks and tricks, as if they were playing lower-division opposition in a pre-season friendly. Celtic could find some encouragement in Rovers' front two, Dwight Yorke and Andy Cole, having appeared to have formed a two-man branch of strikers anonymous. As the half continued, Celtic seeped slowly back into the game, clamping down hard on Blackburn's midfield activities and with 15 minutes remaining, Martin O'Neill made a smart substitution, withdrawing Paul Lambert and pushing on a third striker in the shape of John Hartson, to take advantage of a Blackburn defence that appeared to be tiring. Five minutes from time, Hartson met an Alan Thompson corner with a header that Brad Friedel, Blackburn's American goalkeeper, could only parry and Henrik Larsson pounced on the chance like a gimlet-eyed magpie to shuffle the ball over the line.

It ended 1–0 to Celtic but they knew they would have been behind in the tie had it not been for a couple of world-class saves by Rab Douglas in each half – one from David Thompson and one from David Dunn – that had prevented the away goal. Their task in the second leg looked a considerable one, but there was some hope in that Blackburn had looked a team very much in the image of Souness as both player and manager: skilful, combative, a tad arrogant and, yes, a bit complacent. Minutes after the match, the word got out that inside the Blackburn dressing-room, the game was being described as having been 'men against boys'; this despite Blackburn's defeat.

'You can't take anything away from Blackburn,' says Henrik Larsson of that first leg, 'they played well and passed the ball well, especially in the first half, when we had to defend. They had a few chances but we managed to get tackles in when they were needed and Rab Douglas did really well when he was called into action. We were defending and did not have as much possession, so because of that I was trying to drop a bit deeper and go looking for the ball. That is what you have to do as a striker sometimes. We had more of the ball in the second half and put a few moves together, but they were always dangerous and you have to make sure you are defending as well. In matches like that you have to ride your luck a little bit and take your chances when they come along, and we were able to do that. For the goal I saw the ball come over and realised I wasn't going to get to it. I saw John Hartson was going to make contact and just tried to get into the right place in the event that there was a rebound. Luckily, that's what happened and I was able to score.'

O'Neill produced another surprise with his line-up for the return match in Blackburn. Hartson, far from a regular starter since arriving at the club in the summer of 2001, began the match alongside Larsson, with Sutton dropping back into an advanced midfield position, in place of Paul Lambert. The presence of the aggressive Sutton and the energetic Petrov in midfield would allow Blackburn's playmakers David Thompson and Tugay Kerimoglu less time on the ball than they had enjoyed at Celtic Park.

Only quarter of an hour had passed when a sweet, simple, geometrically precise move from Celtic had the tie spinning 180 degrees on its axis. Bobo Balde found Didier Agathe wide on the right and the wing-back poked the ball diagonally forward to Chris Sutton, who first-timed it in the direction of Hartson, but both he and his marker, Craig Short, slipped simultaneously on the rain-soaked surface, missing the ball entirely, and, as it slithered forward, Henrik Larsson streaked on to it, then, exuding calm and cool, took one touch to stun the ball before clipping it over Friedel and into the net. The tie had begun with Blackburn looking in a favourable position to claim qualification, but Larsson's goal meant that the Ewood Park side now needed three goals to go through.

Blackburn threatened sporadically after that, but they found Rab Douglas in flawless form yet again whilst Yorke and Cole, Souness' multi-million-pound partnership, enjoyed only a distant relationship with the ball. Midway through the second half, a clever corner from Stilian Petrov was met by Sutton just in front of the near post and his sharp, angled header made it 2–0 to Celtic on the night and put the game thoroughly beyond Blackburn's reach. Long before the end, swathes of empty blue and red seats had become visible as the packed Blackburn stands emptied rapidly of home supporters. The English club had made £1 million from their home tie with Celtic – perhaps the Blackburn board might have questioned how such a lucrative competition could be so undervalued by their manager. Such questions would be even more pertinent in the light of the English club's lack of progress past that point.

A succinct summing-up by Henrik Larsson, captain on the night, shows the strength of feeling among the Celtic players on hearing the comments of some Blackburn players after the first leg, 'We wanted to show that we are a better side than you would think from a lot of comments that we heard from different Blackburn players. They should learn a lesson: never talk until the game's finished.' Souness had failed to find success in Europe with Rangers and everywhere else he had gone as a manager; Celtic had now had the pleasure of extending his joyless run in European competition.

'It was a great result to beat Blackburn,' says Larsson. 'It wasn't difficult to turn in a better performance than we did in the first leg at Celtic Park, when we know we played badly and snatched a good result. We were probably a bit lucky not to concede a goal in the first game and that gave us the chance to come out and put some good football together at Ewood Park. By the second game we also had a clearer idea of the sort of team we were up against. It sometimes takes a bit of time to get to know your opponent. It was important to get that first goal at Ewood Park, as it always is, and that allowed us to relax a bit and play with a bit more confidence. I think it was a great team effort but I have to say that Chris Sutton played brilliantly in that role just behind John Hartson and me. He closed Tugay down all game and that was really important for us, allowing us to have a bit of space in midfield.'

The nature of the second-leg victory over Blackburn had been hugely impressive and it had been the first time since the 1980s that Celtic had been able to cruise relaxedly through the final minutes of a second-leg match against major opposition knowing that their lead was so great that there was no danger of them losing the tie. The subsequent tie, against Celta Vigo of Spain, would offer Celtic the opportunity of another breakthrough. If Celtic were to win the tie, it would be the first time that they would have knocked Spanish opposition out of European competition. The matches with Blackburn had been open, rollicking affairs, with plenty of chances coming and going at either end of the field. The matches with Celta Vigo, challenging for the Spanish title at the top of La Liga, promised to be more tentative in nature.

It did not seem like that when, after 12 seconds of the first leg at Celtic Park, Celta Vigo's Gustavo Lopez flashed in to the Celtic penalty area to hit a low, left-footed shot that the alert Rab Douglas did well to hold. From then on, both sides had sporadic chances to score, although it was Celtic who got the only goal of the game after 52 minutes. A Steve Guppy corner was headed down into the six-yard box by Bobo Balde and when the ball flew up off the ground, Henrik Larsson bounced bravely into the air between two Spanish defenders to head Celtic into the lead.

The referee for the match, Frenchman Claude Colombo, had signalled clearly that he was somewhat eccentric when, at the beginning of the game, he had awaited Celtic fans completing a rendition of 'You'll Never Walk Alone' before allowing the match to kick off. The 90 minutes had been punctured throughout by his odd decisions and, two minutes from time, the referee sent Martin O'Neill to the stand from the dugout for disputing the latest in a long list of strange calls. The feeling at the finish was relief that Celtic had managed to escape with a 1–0 victory on an evening when the referee had been almost as difficult to contend with as the Spanish opposition. As in the return with Blackburn, Celtic headed into the away leg needing a big performance if they were to go through.

'I was pleased to get the goal,' says Henrik Larsson, 'which was the result of a nice bit of play and a great ball down to me. It was one of those occasions when you just have to throw yourself into the fray, and I was lucky to get there first. I was definitely very happy to see the ball go over the line.' It had, in fact, been a marvellous goal, a rich blend of timing, skill and courage; an opportunity to score that few strikers would have seen, followed by a brilliant execution from a position where the opposing defenders had looked sure to get to the ball first. It would prove vital for Celtic.

Celta, a side packed with Spanish and Argentinian internationals, began the second leg brightly but Celtic looked strong, confident, well organised and disciplined in defence. The Celtic players were quick to get behind the ball when Celta were in possession but Larsson and Hartson always looked likely to make good use of anything that might come their way up front. The outlook began to become more gloomy midway through the first half when midfielder Jesuli deceived Sutton inside the Celtic penalty area and slipped past the Celtic man for a shot that Rab Douglas appeared to have covered until a vital deflection off Celtic defender Ulrik Laursen defeated the Celtic goalkeeper.

This Celtic side was made of strong stuff, though, and they kept their nerve despite Celta consistently spitting, diving inside the penalty area and persistently noising up the Celtic players. Ten minutes from half-time, a petty foul on Bobo Balde by Celta's Benni McCarthy gave Celtic a free kick deep inside their own half. It was taken by Ulrik Laursen and his left-footed, lofted strike travelled 60 yards to Chris Sutton, again acting as an advanced midfielder, who headed it down diagonally into the path of John Hartson. The Welsh striker, 20 yards out and directly in front of goal, used his muscle to hold off and fell Celta centre-back Eduardo Berizzo before turning to power a shot low into the corner of the Celta net. It was a goal entirely characteristic of Celtic's direct, no-nonsense style under Martin O'Neill.

It meant that Celta needed two more goals to win the tie but the gloom descended on Celtic again shortly after half-time, when a low cross from the excellent Gustavo Lopez was whisked into the Celtic net by South African international McCarthy. Celtic lived dangerously at times as the second half unfolded but, vitally, they kept the game stretched, with the tireless Henrik Larsson working like a demon to keep pressure on the Celta defence. That ensured that the Spaniards could not pour all of their resources into attack. One last, desperate attack from Celta in the last minute ended with a goalbound shot being deflected narrowly wide of Douglas's right-hand post. Celtic had made it through, but it had been a close thing. The Celta manager Miguel Angel Lotina had been less than complimentary about Celtic after the first leg; now he could join Graeme Souness in watching from afar as the rest of that season's UEFA Cup competition unfolded.

'It was great to get the result against Vigo,' says Henrik Larsson. 'They may have been critical about Celtic but we didn't care what they said. It wasn't about them, it was about us, and we showed them over two legs that we could knock them out. To beat them over the two legs was no mean achievement. We knew from the start that we couldn't throw people forward and with the state of the pitch, which was very heavy, it would be difficult to play flowing football. What we did was to sit tight and absorb the pressure. After John Hartson scored we just had to contain them and, despite a couple of scares, we did just that. Towards the end they were throwing everybody forward and had about seven players in attack. We had to get hold of the ball and hold it whenever we could. We didn't panic and played an intelligent game. It was tough because they were looking for every decision, but that is the way they play.'

Winning that tie kept Celtic in European competition after Christmas for the first time since the 1979–80 season and, as they faced VfB Stuttgart in the fourth round of the UEFA Cup, Celtic's target was to reach the quarter-finals of a European competition for the first time since their European Cup meeting with Real Madrid in 1980. The match with Stuttgart would prove to be a classic – the two-legged tie in Celtic's 2002–03 UEFA Cup run that would provide button-popping, lung-bursting, unrestrained excitement from start to finish.

Celtic were without Larsson, the victim of a broken jaw, and he was joined in the directors' box for the Stuttgart match by Martin O'Neill, banished there after his touch-line conflagration with referee Claude Colombo at the end of the first leg with Celta Vigo. Shaun Maloney, a baby-faced 20-year-old making only his tenth start for the club, and Chris Sutton would be Celtic's front two. Stuttgart, as with Celta Vigo and Blackburn, were a side peppered with internationals and in the German club's case these were Greek, Bulgarian, Croatian, Belarussian and, of course, German. Under coach Felix Magath, Stuttgart were the most improved side in Germany during the 2002–03 season and were chasing Bayern Munich for the Bundesliga title.

O'Neill twitched uncomfortably in the stand as the action flew by and little more than quarter of an hour had gone when two masterful first-time passes, from Chris Sutton then Shaun Maloney, sent Stilian Petrov speeding towards goal. A desperate challenge from Marcelo Bordon sent Petrov crashing to the ground and, having prevented a clear goalscoring opportunity, the Brazilian defender was dismissed instantly by Italian referee Pierluigi Collina. It proved a decisive moment in the tie. Magath had to reshuffle his team, substituting the pacy Greek attacking player Ioannis Amanatidis with defender Steffen Dangelmayr, but Stuttgart continued to probe at Celtic and, with 27 minutes gone, Krassimir Balakov crossed for striker Kevin Kuranyi to run from behind Joos Valgaeren, leap in front of the Celtic defender and direct a precise, angled header down and past Rab Douglas. The German team were more muscular and direct than the silky Celta Vigo, but it was refreshing, after the niggling approach of Celta, to find Celtic facing a strong but sporting side again.

An equaliser, stunning in its simplicity, arrived for Celtic when Jackie McNamara crossed into the penalty area, Petrov chested the ball into the path of Paul Lambert and the midfielder, using expert technique, whipped a low, bending shot into the net. The supporters were still glowing from the excitement of that excellently executed goal when a cross from Alan Thompson flew off the shins of Dangelmayr and Shaun Maloney preyed on the mistake to bounce a shot off the ground and into the net to make it 2–1 to Celtic at the break.

The second half found Stuttgart hanging back and hoping to hold on to the 2–1 defeat – even striker Kuranyi was spending an inordinate amount of time inside his own half – but another piece of exceptional play from Celtic scuppered the Germans' battle plans. Petrov prodded the ball to Sutton, who eased it to Paul Lambert, on the right side of midfield. Petrov had continued moving and had stayed onside by running along the Germans' back line. Now, as Lambert nudged the ball forward, Petrov broke into the box, collected the ball and, with a wonderful piece of skill, sent a low, hard, surprise, disguised shot, on the turn, between goalkeeper Timo Hildebrand and the German's near post. It was only Celtic's fourth shot on target and three of them had produced goals.

It was a record-equalling ninth successive home win in Europe for Celtic, and their 100th victory in European competition, but that would count for little unless they could build on their first-leg lead to take the tie. Their chances of doing so appeared to have been aided by the twin suspension of Stuttgart's first-choice centre-backs Fernando Meira and Marcelo Bordon for the return but the opening minutes in the Gottlieb-Daimler Stadium were enervating for Celtic as Stuttgart twice came within inches of scoring.

Celtic survived to surge into an early lead. Didier Agathe crossed, John Hartson flicked the ball on with his head and Alan Thompson carefully judged the flight of the ball before nipping in front of Christian Tiffert to dive and head the ball back across goalkeeper

Hildebrand and into the net. Stuttgart were still shaking from the shock of losing that goal when Celtic struck again. Again Agathe raced up the right wing. This time his cross was a low, fast one that whirred past Hildebrand and into the six-yard box, where Sutton rushed past two defenders before sidefooting the ball high into the Stuttgart net. That quick burst of goalscoring meant that Stuttgart now required five goals to take the tie, although the Germans did manage to put a more respectable veneer on the scoreline at half-time when Tiffert headed Heiko Gerber's cross past Rab Douglas.

It was in the second half in Stuttgart that Celtic began to miss Henrik Larsson badly. Playing with Hartson and Sutton up front, the team had no one with the mobility and willingness of Larsson to harry defenders and stretch the game in the manner in which the Swede, so vitally, had done in Vigo. In Stuttgart, Celtic did not have the capacity to chase and worry opposition defenders when the Germans were in possession. It meant that Stuttgart felt free to chase the game by switching to a three-man defence for the second period and that that back three could push up to the halfway line to begin attacking moves.

With 15 minutes remaining, and Celtic still 2–1 to the good, the Scottish side appeared to be coasting home. Then Aliaksandr Hleb started and finished a clever move that saw him cut a swathe through the Celtic defence to make it 2–2. The dangerous Hleb then hit a post with a left-footed strike and the upright was still reverberating when Hleb made a surgically precise pass into the heart of the Celtic penalty area that allowed substitute Michael Mutzel to crack the ball past Rab Douglas and make it 3–2 to Stuttgart on the night. Now Stuttgart's required target had been halved and Stuttgart needed two goals in the remaining seven minutes to go through. Within seconds of Mutzel's goal, Douglas had to race clear of his penalty area to clear after Stuttgart had again threaded the ball through a wobbly Celtic defence. A Jochen Seitz shot screeched over the bar before Celtic could finally rest easy on hearing the referee's whistle for the end of the 90 minutes.

There had been worrying moments in defence during those closing minutes. Celtic had played intelligently at times in Germany but for much of the second half they had invited the Germans to come on to them and it had been fortunate that Stuttgart had not accepted the invitation skilfully enough to find the net until the closing stages of the match. Of particular concern had been the manner in which the back three had been pulled around and out of position to allow Stuttgart the space in which to attack. O'Neill might also have introduced Shaun Maloney as a substitute at half-time, rather than later in the match, to perform the harrying role that Henrik tended to carry out to perfection.

The two legs with Liverpool proved a tactical triumph. An even game at Celtic Park that ended in a 1–1 draw may have convinced the English side that they were in command of the tie, but at Anfield Celtic were masterful in drawing their opponents on to them and breaking swiftly into attack. The 3–1 aggregate victory was fully deserved and took Celtic into their first European semi-final since 1974, where they would face Boavista of Oporto, the Portuguese club with the quirky checkerboard shirts. The importance of the occasion was underlined when Boavista's centre-back Paulo Turra could be seen looking to the heavens and offering up a silent prayer seconds before kick-off in the first leg at Celtic Park. The rays of the setting springtime sun could be seen glistening off the walkways in between the seats of the Lisbon Lions Stand as the ball rolled into action and that was a pleasant reminder of how unseasonal it was to find Celtic in European competition at that late stage.

Celtic had never previously lost the home leg of a European semi-final and that record looked in little danger of being broken against a very ordinary Boavista side who offered little other than defence in depth. Their strikers looked less than competent and it was soon clear that, semi-finalists or not, Boavista were the least able of Celtic's opponents in European competition during the 2002–03 season, with the exception of Suduva. The Portuguese still did a solid containing job on Celtic – O'Neill's side are at their best against teams that want to play enterprising football – and Boavista even enjoyed a wild break of the ball shortly after half-time when Valgaeren deflected a cross-shot into his own net. A quick equaliser from Henrik Larsson looked like spurring Celtic on to go for the winner. They had had the shock of conceding the own goal; now, surely, they would have to try to build a lead for the second leg.

With an hour gone and the score 1–1, Neil Lennon decided to pass the ball all the way back to his goalkeeper, Rab Douglas, from just inside his own half. That negative piece of play found Lennon being instantly booed by some Celtic supporters. They wanted Celtic to push forward and look to score and, with no Boavista player in his vicinity, believed that it had looked just as easy for Lennon to have pitched the ball forward rather than bump it back. The supporters' voicing of their displeasure saw Martin O'Neill round on those Celtic followers seated in the front stand behind his dugout and begin berating them for the booing of Lennon. Supporters leapt to their feet to bite back at O'Neill in the way that only Glasgow fans can, before the manager was finally dragged away by his assistant John Robertson. It was one of the most bizarre episodes ever seen in a European game at Celtic Park. The match finished at 1–1.

'If Neil Lennon has no alternatives,' stated O'Neill in the aftermath of the match, 'then if he feels the best way to keep possession is to play it back, then I'm sorry, we'll live with that. An education is definitely needed and that doesn't mean that everyone who pays their money shouldn't go and form an opinion.' It seemed unfair for O'Neill to castigate the support and to suggest they required an 'education'. Had he cast his mind back, he might have recalled how in previous European ties Celtic supporters had shown true tolerance of the passback as executed by Lennon. During the Champions League match with Juventus at Celtic Park in October 2001, for example, Lennon had sent a pass back to Rab Douglas from well inside the Juventus half and no one had objected; Celtic had been 4–2 ahead and set for a win. Against Celta Vigo, earlier in the 2002–03 season, Lennon had passed back from the same position as against Boavista without receiving the same reaction. It was the particular circumstances of the backpass in the match with Boavista, in that it had come at a time when Celtic were needing goals, that had upset the supporters. The backlash against the backpass, as used by Lennon, had been smouldering for a long time and the Boavista game had found certain supporters unable to contain themselves any longer.

'It was disappointing not to get the win at Celtic Park,' says Henrik Larsson. 'I think we played all right in patches, but we didn't get much luck, and we gave away a silly goal. We got back to equalise quite quickly, and the game was there for us, but Boavista are a hard-working team and frustrated us. They were trying to slow the game down as much as possible but it was still up to us to take it to them. There were a few chances that on another day would have gone in and, of course, I missed a penalty. That's just one of the things that happen in football; occasionally you're going to miss penalties, and it's never good when it happens in a match as important as that.'

For the return with Boavista, Celtic were issued with a mere 2,515 tickets. Boavista's Estadio do Bessa was undergoing reconstruction in advance of Portugal hosting the 2004 European Championships and, in spring 2003, it would accommodate a crowd of little over 10,000 for the match with Celtic. By then, Celtic were the last surviving British team in European competition following Manchester United's elimination by Real Madrid in their Champions League quarter-final the previous evening. It proved to be a fraught night in Portugal, with Celtic stuttering along in second gear for much of the match, creating few chances and occasionally looking exceptionally jittery in defence. Boavista were ahead on away goals and the second leg looked like petering out in a 0–0 draw when, with 12 minutes remaining, Celtic got the ball into the Boavista box. The ball rebounded from a defender and into the path of Henrik Larsson. A piece of brilliance from the Swede saw him swiftly change feet as he prepared to strike the ball and his left-footed shot floated inches past the right-hand of goalkeeper Ricardo, who had been deceived by Larsson's sleight of foot. The goalkeeper, suspended in mid-air, almost got a flailing glove to the ball but it eluded him by inches and crept gently into the corner of the net. That single goal was all Celtic needed to ease into their first European final for 33 years.

'Scoring the goal that gets your team through to a major cup final is the sort of thing you dream about as a kid,' says Larsson. 'We've been unlucky a number of times in Europe since I've been at the club. We have gone out when we have been the better side over the two games, but you do learn from those experiences. We were good at home and played cleverly away in our two-legged UEFA Cup ties. We scored goals away from home and if you do that in Europe you always have a chance of going through. Sometimes you are playing ties home and away, with only a week in between, and that is a lot with which to cope.

'We knew we were the better team after playing the first leg against Boavista, but you still have a tough task to travel away and get a win.

They made things difficult because they weren't interested in going forward. Of course they were timewasting in the second leg when they were ahead on away goals, but we always knew that we had to score and although we weren't making many chances we all knew we just had to keep battling away. There was always the chance that we could create an opportunity and sneak a goal, and that's what happened. In a way it was tough going there knowing we had to win but it also made it a quite straightforward task.

'We were playing three up front, so I was playing slightly wider on the right and when John Hartson got the ball I started to make my run. When it reached me on the edge of the area I tried to slip it through to John but the defender slid in. I could see as he intercepted the ball that it would break back to me, so I kept going. When the ball came back I took one touch and then hit it and hoped there would be enough on it to take it into the goal. There wasn't much time because I could feel a challenge coming in. Luckily I was able to get enough on it and it was a great feeling to see it go in. It was a good time to score because they didn't have much time to get one back and suddenly had to start playing football. It would have been difficult if we had scored earlier and had had to soak up loads of pressure. As it was, they had no time and we defended strongly to hold them out.

'There are always people who have doubts about Scottish football and perhaps even about Celtic Football Club, but I think we may have started to make a few of the doubters think again. At least it would be nice to think so. The further you go in a tournament the more there is at stake, but we never cracked and that shows a lot of character in the team. When we play the football we know we can, we are a match for anyone. We were always confident that we could go all the way if we got the breaks and didn't make any stupid mistakes. Perhaps our biggest strength, though, is our work rate. We never give up and we battle right to the end. We never believe that a game is over until the final whistle.'

Boavista's limited abilities were reflected in their finishing tenth in the Portuguese League in 2002–03 but Celtic's other opponents in their UEFA Cup run finished in positions in their leagues that reflected their pedigrees and the degree of difficulty that Celtic had had in defeating them. Blackburn Rovers and Liverpool would go on to finish sixth and fifth respectively in the 2002–03 FA Premiership; Celta Vigo would finish fourth in La Liga and VfB Stuttgart would end the season second in the Bundesliga.

Paul Lambert, as he ascended the stairs in the North Stand at Hampden for the 2002 European Cup final, would little have considered the possibility that he would be involved in his second European final only one year later and six years after winning the European Cup with Borussia Dortmund. Few, indeed, would have countenanced Celtic's chances of reaching the UEFA Cup final after their defeat by Basle in their Champions League qualifier. The unexpectedness of Celtic's arrival in the final after a 33-year absence from such an advanced stage of European competition helped fuel a desperate scramble for tickets to witness the concluding episode in Celtic's terrific run in that season's UEFA Cup.

Those lucky enough to be allocated a ticket from the club found themselves in a queue at Celtic Park that snaked under the stands and that took two hours to negotiate until the precious, colourful briefs for the final in Seville were in the hand. For others, the weeks in advance of the final would induce an anxiety-ridden search for tickets by all means possible. Tickets for the final, with a face value of £21, were being sold at £350 five weeks before the match and, as the game drew near, the price of £1,000 began to be regularly quoted. This being the twenty-first century, people were auctioning tickets via the internet and tales of fraud and of the circulation of forgeries were legion.

Celtic's final home league match of the 2002–03 season, against Dundee, saw beach balls incessantly tumbling down the stands and onto the Celtic Park turf. At one point O'Neill pleaded with the stewards to stem the flow of beach balls as the team was chasing goals in the tightest title race involving Celtic for almost two decades. Prior to the game, flamenco dancers had turned and twisted in front of the Lisbon Lions Stand, bringing touches of gaudy colour to a chilly Scottish spring evening whilst 'Y Viva Espana', a cheesy pop hit from the 1970s, was given a new lease of life as it received repeated airings. Another indicator that the fans were looking forward to holidaying in the south of Spain at the time of the final with Porto was the numerous sombreros that could be seen dotted around the crowd as the fans warmed up for the heat of Seville.

During the weeks before the final, the subject of Seville permeated almost every conversation in every corner of Glasgow and the estimated number of Celtic supporters that descended on the Spanish city for the final was anything between 50,000 and 80,000. It would have been the largest travelling support for a match in the history of the game of football, except that many of these supporters did not have tickets for the match – only 17,000 tickets had been allocated to the club. Some 8,000 other tickets had been procured by optimistic supporters early in 2003 from UEFA's website and some fans would pay extortionate prices on arrival in the Spanish city. One local 'tout' could be found preying on increasingly ticket-desperate Celtic fans in the city centre of Seville as kick-off approached. He had on offer a cleaner's pass for the stadium, with which he was willing to part for 1,500 Euros. It beggared belief that a Celtic supporter was expected to turn up at the gate in full regalia and pass themselves off as a cleaner.

At the Stadio Olimpico, the venue for the match itself, out on the Isla de la Cartuja, across the Guadalquivir River, and several miles north-west of the city centre, it was unusual to see a Spaniard in the vicinity of the stadium; the chance to sell tickets at a high price had proved too tempting for all but a handful of the locals and on the evening more than three quarters of the stadium had been taken up by Celtic supporters with only the blue-and-white Porto end preventing the stadium's stands being flooded completely by a sea of green.

The Celtic players had missed much of the build-up through being based in Jerez, and had instead trained gently and had enjoyed relaxing with CDs, DVDs and PlayStations at their remote base, 40 miles from Seville. Their hotel itself was far from palatial and a lack of suitable air-conditioning on the bus that took the team to the stadium had players perspiring and removing clothes in an effort to keep cool.

The rear of the Stadio Olimpico was a vast, faceless, dun-coloured slab of concrete on the outside with only the occasional slit in the façade and nothing to suggest it was a place for football. It could just as easily have been an anonymous, forbidding office block. Supporters approaching the end allocated to Celtic had to climb over two crash-barrier-type obstacles before reaching the entrance to the stadium. It was a struggle, particularly for some female supporters, to clamber over those obstructions. All of that external ugliness belied the Olimpico's graceful interior, where the sheer, cliff-like terraces afforded fans all around the ground a useful view of the action despite a running track separating the pitch from the spectating areas.

Celtic's travelling support to Lisbon in 1967 had been distinguished by one or two outlandish characters who stood out from the rest, but the supporters in Seville were much more garish. The steep, angled terraces of the Stadio Olimpico were pasted with followers of Celtic wearing green and white hooped replica shirts, the mass-marketing of which had begun in earnest during the 1990s. Those who stopped at that were the more conservative among the crowd. Others would not have been out of place in the film *Apocalypse Now*, such as a writhing, cadaverous individual with an emerald-green mohican who looked as though his mind had been transported anywhere but the match; others wore Zapata moustaches; a number went in fancy dress as Arabs. Again, beach balls bounced down the terraces and in Seville they landed at the feet of truncheon-ready Spanish police, who stood impassively, unsmilingly, in reaction. Alcohol had been the only poison for Celtic supporters at the 1967 European Cup final; at Seville, the occasional marijuana joint could be seen dangling openly from the fingers of some Celtic supporters as casually and practisedly as from the hand of a 1967 Keith Richards.

Inside the stadium, Euro-pop blasted the ears and cold hot-dogs offered scant sustenance for the fans in advance of kick-off. Flamenco dancers displayed some local colour on the running track. The Carlsberg cheerleaders from Copenhagen appeared for the fans' entertainment, wearing green and white corporate colours – it didn't look exactly neutral but nobody in the Porto section seemed too bothered. Then the rubber-limbed Spanish pop group Ketchup wiggled and wriggled to the tune of that trio's summer hit 'The Ketchup Song'. A Celtic club crest incorporated into the design of an Andalucian fan was spread out behind the Celtic goal as Ketchup's stage was cleared, the UEFA Cup was wheeled out, thunderous music was piped over the sound system and the two teams emerged. Finally, it was time for the final.

Unlike some of Celtic's opponents in previous rounds, Porto featured several instantly recognisable names, such as Ricardo Carvalho, the central defender with a shock of wild, frizzy hair who had played so well in the Champions League ties between the clubs; Portuguese international centre-back Jorge Costa; goalkeeper Vitor Baia, once of Barcelona; the talented but unpredictable wide player Nuno Capucho, who had damaged Celtic badly in their Champions League meetings with Porto; and Porto's newest superstar, the Brazilian-born Deco, now a naturalised Portuguese. Only four of this Porto team had lined up against Celtic in their second Champions League match in October 2001: Carvalho, Costinha, Deco and Capucho. The Portuguese side's new manager, José Mourinho, had introduced his own, young, hungry players after his appointment in January 2002 and had retained only the very best from the previous regime. Celtic, in contrast, featured only one change from the line-up for that match in Porto in 2001: Chris Sutton rather than John Hartson would play in the final. The Welshman missed the match through a debilitating back injury. The Celtic team was: Rab Douglas, Johan Mjallby, Bobo Balde, Joos Valgaeren, Didier Agathe, Paul Lambert, Neil Lennon, Stilian Petrov, Alan Thompson, Henrik Larsson and Chris Sutton. Every one of those players had been born within a 30,000-mile radius of Glasgow. It was manager Martin O'Neill's 31st European tie with Celtic in his three years with the club and there, on the touch-line, O'Neill could be spotted in his familiar black sweatshirt and jogging pants, prowling like a cat round and round his technical area.

Celtic did not have to wait long to discover how threatening Porto could be. Three minutes into the match a low shot from Porto's Maniche bisected six Celtic players and went hurtling through the opened legs of striker Derlei. Rab Douglas, playing his first match after nearly one month out through injury, did well to get down low to his left to save a ball that travelled through a crowd of players and that he did not see until it was almost upon him.

The weather was unseasonably hot even for the south of Spain, which was experiencing a heatwave, and the temperature in Seville on the afternoon of 21 May had peaked at 38 degrees Centigrade, although by kick-off that had declined to nearer 30 degrees. Celtic were still feeling the heat of the night and of the occasion. As the sun set, the sultry evening sky was framed by the oval roof of the Stadio Olimpico.

This made the setting picturesque but in those early stages Celtic's play was less than easy on the eye, littered as it was with misplaced passes. They could find no rhythm and they struggled to contain the elusive Portuguese. This was reflected materially in Joos Valgaeren's eighth-minute booking for a foul on Deco, who, even at that early stage, was already beginning to dominate the midfield.

Celtic, in that first half, were simply being left behind in terms of close-quarters deception and anticipation and Porto's tactical formation was designed to pull Celtic all over the place. Striker Derlei was on his own as an advanced player, with three Porto players dropping off him – Dmitri Alenitchev, Deco and Nuno Capucho – and that meant that Celtic's back three were constantly tempted forward and out of position to snap at that tricky trio. The most encouraging aspect of the occasion was the firm handling of goalkeeper Douglas who dealt efficiently with everything that was thrown at him.

It took until midway through the first 45 minutes for a chink of optimism to split the gloom that had been gathering over Celtic's performance when a 20-yard, angled free kick from Henrik Larsson sped round Porto's defensive wall to be held low by Vitor Baia. It was only a brief hint of daylight – before long Deco and Capucho were nibbling away at Celtic's defence again and, worryingly, the Portuguese side were being given vast amounts of space in the midfield in which to weave their magic. Stilian Petrov was failing to spark in the advanced area of the midfield and playmakers Maniche and Deco had plenty of room within which to boss the game. Celtic, in contrast, looked too wooden, too inflexible.

Celtic still managed to hold out for most of that first half, despite their defensive jitters, although four minutes before half-time, a magical flick, twist and turn from Deco allowed him to go zipping clear into the Celtic penalty area as far as the corner of the six-yard box. His swiftness had left Lennon, trying to keep pace with him, trailing like a puffed-out Sancho Panza, and the Brazilian now had only Douglas to beat. It looked a certain goal, but Douglas stood up to the challenge brilliantly and used his feet to deflect the ball past the post for a corner.

Having enjoyed that narrow escape, the first half even appeared to be ending on an upbeat note for Celtic when Didier Agathe's cross from the right was only just reached by Vitor Baia for him to punch clear from Larsson. The resultant scramble on the edge of the Porto penalty area saw Celtic denied a clear free kick 20 yards from goal, with Slovakian referee Lubos Michel perhaps mistakenly playing the advantage to allow Paul Lambert a shot at goal from further back than from where the free kick would have been taken.

Three minutes of time added on for stoppages at the end of the first half was indicated by the fourth official and nearly one minute of that had passed when Deco again loomed ominously close to the Celtic penalty area. As he played the ball in towards Derlei, Johan Mjallby, the right-sided marker in Celtic's back three, was dragged towards the striker to help deal with the danger. It meant there were now four Celtic players attending to Derlei on the left side of the Celtic box and no cover on the right side where neither Mjallby nor wing-back Agathe were present. When Derlei, under pressure, managed to stab the ball back to Deco, the playmaker was able to use his wonderful skill and awareness to instantaneously lift the ball into that unguarded right side of the penalty area to find the Russian international Dmitri Alenitchev racing, all alone, on to the ball. The Russian immediately jabbed a left-footed volley goalwards. The ball was blocked by Douglas but went spinning behind him and across the face of goal for Derlei to sidefoot it into the net as the Celtic defenders stood ballwatching.

Derlei raced behind the goal to the chagrin of the huge Celtic support and, after goading them, moments later went one better when he aggravated the Celtic players by viciously hammering the ball into Didier Agathe's midriff to win a throw. As the referee indicated half-time, angry Celtic players advanced on Derlei, sparking off a scrum that involved local police, the Porto backroom staff and players, and Martin O'Neill. A nasty atmosphere was now hanging over the game. When Celtic returned to the pitch at the start of the second half, the Porto players decided to hang back in the tunnel to make their opponents stew a bit longer in the heat. Some Porto players had even advanced towards the pitch when they were summoned to return to the mouth of the tunnel to try to irritate their opponents. The Celtic players appeared to have barely noticed this petty con-trick, and they kicked off the second half with what appeared to be fresh vigour.

The Porto manager José Mourinho had told his players at half-time to calm the game, to concentrate on making short passes to one another so that they would slow the match down, sit on their lead, hold possession and keep the ball away from Celtic. His words appeared to have fallen on deaf ears. Porto began the second half by playing long, inaccurate balls deep into the Celtic half and when they did have the ball the Portuguese were quickly hustled out of possession by their opponents.

Celtic made good use of their new-found momentum. Two minutes after the break, Didier Agathe received the ball wide on the right wing. There was space behind the Porto left-back into which he could have accelerated to hit the touch-line but instead Agathe opted to take half-a-dozen delicate touches on the ball and manoeuvre himself forward gradually until he was almost at the corner of the penalty area. He then swung a high cross beyond Porto goalkeeper Vitor Baia's back post. Henrik Larsson anticipated the flight of the ball beautifully and stole swiftly away from his marker, Ricardo Costa. As the ball travelled across the box, Larsson, showing great presence of mind to win himself the necessary space, veered backwards to the midway point of the white line that marked the side of the six-yard box. Ricardo Costa floundered backwards, a hazy shadow of the Celtic man, and, as his defender flailed in his wake, Larsson soared into the air to meet the ball firmly with his forehead and steer it back across the face of goal, leaving Vitor Baia stranded underneath the ball as it made its reverse journey. The ball dropped out of the air perfectly to clip the inside of the Porto post and go skipping into the back of the net. It was the type of goal that only a world-class player such as Larsson could have plotted in his head in a few seconds before executing it to pure perfection. It was a glorious way for Larsson, who considered the UEFA Cup final to be the biggest game of his life, to score his 200th goal for Celtic.

The teams were not level for long. Seven minutes after Larsson's goal, Joos Valgaeren went diving into an attempted tackle on Deco on the fringes of the Celtic penalty area, only to find both player and ball elude him embarrassingly. The Porto man glided inside Valgaeren and into a central position a few yards outside the Celtic penalty area. From there, he spotted a run being made by Alenitchev and a precise, disguised pass from Deco bisected Johan Mjallby and Paul Lambert, leaving Alenitchev, again unchecked and unmarked, free to streak on to the ball at speed and send it flashing past Douglas. Alenitchev dashed behind the Celtic goal to share his joy with the Porto support and was soon joined there by his teammates. The Porto goal celebrations lasted one and a half minutes and that had Martin O'Neill spitting fury at the fourth official in frustration at the referee allowing the love-in between the Porto players and fans behind the goal to go unchecked.

It had taken Larsson's equaliser to spur the Porto players into regaining the initiative but, on going 2–1 up, Porto again looked less than comfortable at being in the lead. Within two minutes of their goal, an Alan Thompson cross from the left wing induced panic in defender Nuno Valente and the Portuguese man headed the ball only narrowly over his own crossbar, despite there being little pressure on him from Celtic attackers. Thompson himself took the corner, swinging the ball from the right towards the same back post at which Larsson had scored his first goal. This time, as the ball was in flight, Larsson initially feinted to move towards goal but instead swiftly stepped a couple of feet out and away from goal to rid himself of his marker, this time Paulo Ferreira. Porto had marked up well enough in defence but, as at the first goal, the swiftness of Larsson's movement and the precision with which he judged the speed and height of the ball, meant the defender had no chance of staying with him and that allowed Larsson the time and space in which to connect cleanly and freely with the ball. He headed firmly down and past the outstretched arm of Vitor Baia to send the Celtic support delirious with joy for the second time in ten minutes. That 57th-minute goal was the Swede's 44th of the season.

It signalled the best period of the game, which now became a classic contest, with play roving from end to end, but gradually tiredness and the extreme heat caught up with the players, overwhelmed them and, as a result, there were few clear scoring chances in the remainder of the ninety minutes. Eighteen minutes from the end of the second half, Celtic brought on Ulrik Laursen for the injured Joos Valgaeren, who had suffered a gash to his cheekbone in a mid-air collision with Nuno Capucho and, with 15 minutes remaining, the tiring Paul Lambert was replaced by Jackie McNamara. Ten minutes from time, Balde was booked, correctly, for a challenge on Deco, after the Celtic man had appeared to try to shred Deco's legs into tiny pieces. A dozen figures from the Porto bench had piled on to the pitch in protest at the severity of the Celtic defender's challenge and Capucho had, using gestures, questioned Balde's sanity in making such a lunge.

The superfit Larsson was still expending energy at an admirable rate, often dropping deep into midfield to prompt attacking moves by pushing perfect passes into the paths of his teammates or easing into exactly the right position to receive the ball. Celtic's most penetrative moves from midfield came from Larsson rather than from the midfielders themselves. The problem was that whenever Larsson started a move in midfield he could not then also be inside the penalty area to finish the move off.

Four minutes of stoppage time had been added on to the regulation 90 by the referee, and in the fourth of those minutes the 53,000 inside the Stadio Olimpico held their breaths as McNamara tried to play a square ball across the front of the Celtic penalty area only to give the ball away to Alenitchev. This time the Russian's shot veered off target. Alenitchev pulled up with cramp as soon as he had made his strike but the pain of knowing he had just missed the perfect opportunity to finish the game in its dying seconds must have cut him even more deeply.

Extra-time meant that the teams now entered the 'silver goal' period, an innovation from UEFA that meant that if either team had the lead by the end of the first half of extra-time, they would be the winners of the UEFA Cup. Neither side was able to establish much fluidity in their play at the beginning of extra-time, but after five minutes of the additional period, Celtic suffered a severe blow. Balde went in late on Derlei, crashing into the striker from the side, missing the ball and sending the Brazilian shooting into the air like a human cannonball. It was inevitable that Balde would be dealt a second yellow card and an automatic dismissal. Now, with ten tiring men, Celtic would be at a real disadvantage as they tried to prevent Porto from seeping through their patched-up defence. McNamara dropped into the back three to make up for the absence of Balde.

The Celtic supporters chanted Balde's name as he left the field, which was nice of them, but Balde might have served the support and his teammates better by staying on his feet rather than rushing into such a reckless challenge. Derlei had, at the time of Balde's foul on him, taken possession of the ball in an advanced midfield position but there was not enough of a significant danger from the Brazilian for Balde to have made such a risky, desperate challenge on the player.

Celtic spent the remainder of the first half of extra-time penned deep inside their own half, terrified of conceding the dreaded 'silver goal'. Porto, now adhering carefully to their manager's instructions, were holding possession, hoping to wear down Celtic's resistance. Despite their dominance, Porto were still unable to get a shot on target before the end of the opening 15 minutes of extra-time, and neither were Celtic.

It was going to be a struggle for Celtic to hold out till the end of 120 minutes with ten men but four minutes into the second period of extra-time they were lucky not to be reduced to nine. Alan Thompson was extremely fortunate to remain on the field after a high challenge on Ricardo Carvalho as the Portuguese defender drifted up Porto's right wing with the ball. Celtic's English midfielder simply barged into Carvalho, leading dangerously with his arm, and knocked the Portuguese off his feet and on to the running track. It was a piece of blatantly violent conduct and Celtic could have had no complaints had Thompson been sent off. Instead, referee Michel, perhaps apprehensive about sending off a second Celtic man so soon after Balde's dismissal, did not even show Thompson a yellow card, despite giving a free kick to Porto for the foul on their player. There would be much comment afterwards from Martin O'Neill about how the referee looked a bit too young to be handling a game of such magnitude and insinuations that he had allowed the Porto players to get away with too much. The referee actually had a fair match but his failure to take action against Thompson for that challenge was his biggest error of the evening. Had he acted, it would almost certainly have sentenced Celtic to defeat there and then. In that instance, Michel had appeared to lose the nerve to make a second big, game-changing decision.

Celtic almost took advantage of that narrow escape, going close to taking the lead. Shaun Maloney, a 105th-minute replacement for Stilian Petrov, showed sharpness, swaying away from two Porto defenders on the edge of the Portuguese team's penalty area and carving out a precise centre for Henrik Larsson. This time, Nuno Valente got his head to the ball to clear from the Celtic striker just as Larsson, directly in front of the Porto goal, was craning his neck in preparation to nod the ball past Vitor Baia for a third time. Within seconds, Maloney again found the space to serve up an almost identical cross for Larsson but once again Porto were able to clear the ball.

The match had entered its 115th minute when a long clearance from

Jackie McNamara was propelled forward by Carvalho and a clever pass from just inside the Celtic half drilled a hole in the Celtic defence to leave Porto substitute Marco Ferreira chasing the ball towards goal. Rab Douglas got to the ball before him but it squirmed away from his body and directly into the path of the one man on the field to whom Celtic would not have wished the ball to have fallen: Derlei. McNamara showed swift reactions to snap into a sharp tackle on the Porto man but the Brazilian quickly sidestepped the Celtic player before cracking a low, hard shot towards goal from just inside the Celtic area. Douglas had recovered well enough from his initial dive for the ball to get his hands to Derlei's shot but he could only slow, not stop, its progress. Laursen, on the line, got a foot to the ball but he could not prevent it squeezing into the net. Celtic were 3–2 down with four minutes remaining. The entire Porto backroom staff piled on to the pitch at the third goal, displacing the Porto players, who left the pitch to go and celebrate behind the goal with their supporters.

Desperate measures were now employed by both sides. Celtic pushed forward, with even Rab Douglas supplementing the attack at times, but the Porto goalkeeper Vitor Baia clutched a high ball safely. Laursen then clearly, and entirely needlessly, tripped the Portuguese, presenting him with the opportunity to go rolling around the turf, timewasting in mock agony. Vitor Baia's reaction was clearly out of proportion to the foul but Laursen's pointless act had provided the goalkeeper with the perfect opportunity to indulge in his own personal floor show.

Nor could Celtic complain that the referee failed to take account of such incidents: referee Michel added on four minutes of additional time at the end of the second fifteen-minute period and during those four minutes he dismissed Nuno Valente after the Porto left-back had scythed down Alan Thompson by using one of the most obvious and violent professional fouls seen on the night. The resultant free kick offered Celtic one final opportunity to create a scoring chance. Maloney used the kick to attempt a cross into the box, but instead of the ball dropping into the heart of the Porto penalty area, it instead drifted high and wide of their goal. That signalled the end for Celtic and they could only watch, hearts sinking, as Michel blew his whistle for the end of the match and the Porto players rushed to their supporters to celebrate wildly with them yet again.

As the Porto players began to move round the stadium before being presented with their medals they were greeted with extreme hostility and booing on the part of the Celtic supporters. The Porto men sensibly decided to proceed no further than the halfway line. O'Neill would comment afterwards, 'Porto are a very talented team but you saw the reaction they got from our fans, who are as fair-minded as any fans in Europe.' It seemed strange to find O'Neill now calling on the good judgement and good sense of the Celtic supporters. This, after all, was the same O'Neill who had suggested that those same supporters required 'an education' after the first leg of the semi-final with Boavista.

Porto's supposed timewasting tactics had had a negligible effect on the flow of the match. Referee Michel had fully compensated for their timewasting by adding on the requisite extra minutes at the end of every period of the match. Indeed, at the end of the first half of injury time O'Neill had even appeared to be signalling to the official to blow his whistle a couple of minutes before he was due to do so; at that point Celtic were one man down and under pressure from Porto. Porto's excessive goal celebrations were another source of complaint from O'Neill, but their extensive celebrations at their second goal had served only as a prelude for Celtic's second goal; Porto themselves had appeared to struggle to regain the rhythm of their game after their over-indulgent celebrations.

It seems second nature for modern Latin players such as those of Porto to stay down on the ground to try to win free kicks; Celtic should not have been surprised by this and it can be offered as no real excuse for Celtic's defeat. It is as futile to complain about such gamesmanship as to complain about the sun rising in the morning and nothing that Porto did had any real effect on the game. None of the Celtic players seemed to be as put out by it as O'Neill, despite being equally, if not more, disappointed in defeat as their manager.

'Football is all about the highs and the lows,' says Henrik Larsson, 'and when you have been in the game as long as I have, you learn to take the disappointments and move on. I hate to lose, especially in a match like this. It was certainly one of the biggest, if not the biggest, game I have ever played, and so afterwards I was very down. After the match it was tough on everybody, but we have a great spirit and that helps you get through it.

'We worked really hard to get to that final in Seville, and although you can say we did brilliantly to make it that far, we know we didn't really achieve anything because we didn't win the Cup. There always has to be a winner and a loser and I can tell you that when you are a loser it is very hard to find anything positive about the game. Of course people might take a bit more notice of Scottish football, and that's great, but it's not what you are thinking about when the final whistle goes.

'All the way to the final we had shown our battling spirit and the fact is that this team will never give up so long as there is any chance of winning. We worked hard in the game against Porto and there was always a chance we could win it but when we went down to ten men it became very difficult. It was so late in the game that it didn't give us much time to reorganise and losing a goal shortly afterwards meant there simply wasn't the chance to come back again. We still never gave up, and we did create a few opportunities in extra-time, but Porto obviously had the advantage at a crucial stage of the match. You can say what you like about the way that Porto played the game but the fact is that they won no matter how it was achieved. I'm sure none of the Porto players is too worried about how they won the Cup; they will have no regrets. Winning is everything at this level.

'I don't see anything positive about my own performance in the final. Scoring two goals in the final doesn't mean anything if you lose. All I wanted was for Celtic to win the Cup. That is what we were in Seville for, and anything else was not important. We wanted to win it badly for ourselves, for the club, and for the supporters who were magnificent yet again. I would obviously rather not have scored and Celtic had won. We played quite positively, and tried to get the ball forward as much as possible but it was never going to be a game with a hatful of chances. It was an amazing atmosphere to go out and play football in, and the sea of green and white was fantastic to see. Of course we want to get to a European final again. After a disappointment like that you want to get the chance to put it right.'

Weeks after the UEFA Cup final, with the dust having finally settled on the events of that evening, José Mourinho, the Porto coach, settled down in his office to look back over the match in relaxed fashion. The cicadas were humming outside and the Portuguese summer was at its height, but the man who had taken the trophy back to Oporto was happy to cast his mind back to replay the events of that hot spring evening in Seville.

'Before the match,' he says, 'I would say that both ourselves and Celtic had an equal chance to come out on top in the UEFA Cup final. I would not say that either side were favourites to win the game. Both teams had followed a fantastic path to the final and picking a winner before the match was difficult.

'After my team had gone 1–0 up in the 45th minute, I told my players at half-time that they should play the ball short; that they should try to keep possession as much as possible, to hold on to the ball for as long as they could; I suggested to them that the first ten to fifteen minutes of the second half could be of great importance to the final result.

'Our intention in the match was to be winning and keeping the ball for as long as we could; we wanted to pass and move the ball as much as possible and to change possession from one player to another more often than we actually did on the night. We wanted to keep the ball moving but the high temperature on the evening didn't allow us to put into practice our intentions. I believe that it was the same for Celtic, that they were affected in the same way.

'Before extra-time my players were exhausted but again I told my players that they should play the ball shorter and keep their concentration. It was the same message as at half-time: I wanted them to keep possession and conserve their energies. I was not happy with the playing surface on the day before the match and, on the night of the game, I have to say that the pitch was as bad as the day before.

'I have to say that FC Porto is a team that has a better technical quality than Celtic, but the match was a very balanced one and after the score had become 2–2, Celtic had better chances to score than FC Porto. Then, of course, in the extra-time period, when the silver goal came into play, we knew that anything could happen. Celtic played at a very high level on the night of the final; it was not easy at all to beat Celtic. For us, it was easier to play against Lazio, with all their big players, in the semi-final.'

With regard to the complaints after the match from the Celtic manager Martin O'Neill that Porto had been guilty of timewasting, Mourinho is of the opinion that this is almost an irrelevance. 'I would say simply that FC Porto did what Celtic would have done if they had been in our position,' he comments. 'Celtic would have done the same thing if they had been ahead at that stage in extra-time; by then, there was not the energy available for more than that and we needed to win time for ourselves at that point in the game.' Anyone who doubted that only needed to think back to the closing minutes of the second leg of Celtic's semi-final with Boavista when the Celtic players had clearly indulged in timewasting. It was of a different nature to that employed by the Portuguese; Celtic had simply kicked the ball destructively into touch as often as possible rather than rolling around in mock agony, but it was still timewasting. Porto had also been much less irritating in their behaviour than Celta Vigo, whom Celtic had defeated in the third round; the Spanish side's players had tumbled, under no challenge, several times inside the penalty box and had spat slyly on Celtic players.

Henrik Larsson's two goals against Porto were his 28th and 29th in Europe for Celtic, making him by far the highest scorer in Europe in the club's history. It is an inescapable fact that his all-round excellence was the major driving force behind Celtic's run to the 2003 UEFA Cup final. Martin O'Neill had shaped into existence a team that would compete robustly, but Henrik was the vital spark that fired Celtic's performances into brilliance. His genius and his teammates' teamwork had re-established the reputation of Celtic as a club that could compete with the elite of European football. It was where the club belonged.

CHAPTER SIXTEEN

Spain Again
BARCELONA 2004

There were only ten short weeks between the 2003 UEFA Cup final and Celtic's next entry into Europe. Memories of that gaudy night in Seville remained fresh as Celtic travelled to Lithuania to face Kaunas in a second-round Champions League qualifying match but this was an outing that contrasted severely with the fiesta of football that the Celtic supporters had enjoyed in southern Spain. That ten-week period was the shortest gap ever between European matches in successive seasons for Celtic but playing in Kaunas' ramshackle stadium underlined heavily that, after the heights of the 2003 UEFA Cup final, Celtic really were starting all over again.

Tragedy tinged the tie. Three days prior to Celtic's match with Kaunas, the Lithuanian club's leading goalscorer, Audrius Slekys, was killed in a car crash. His funeral took place the day before the first leg in Lithuania and although Martin O'Neill, the Celtic manager, stated that he would have been amenable to a postponement, the Lithuanians decided that the match should go ahead as scheduled. There were only 2,500 present in Kaunas that late July evening to witness Celtic's first competitive fixture of the 2003–04 season and Celtic ran up a simple 4–0 win, notable chiefly for a first goal for the club from 22-year-old Irish midfielder Liam Miller and for Henrik Larsson's 30th goal in Europe for Celtic.

If the match was a straightforward affair, the return journey was more problematical. An insect had built a nest inside Celtic's Britannia Airways jet, which put the Boeing 757's air-speed indicator out of action. It was only when the plane was thundering down the runway in Kaunas that the pilot was alerted to the problem and applied the brakes, bringing the Boeing screeching to a halt. The Celtic players were forced to disembark from the malfunctioning aircraft and return to their hotel at 3.00 a.m. A replacement aeroplane was sent out to Kaunas and late on the Thursday afternoon the players finally arrived back in Glasgow.

The return with Kaunas at Celtic Park was part of the club's annual season-ticket package for 2003–04, consequently drew a 48,000 crowd, and elicited a unique complaint from Celtic supporters: many who attended the second leg could be heard complaining of the boredom of watching their side obtain the formality of a 1–0 victory and stroll through into the third qualifying round of the Champions League. This was a first: boredom among the fans at seeing Celtic progress through to the next round of a European competition. The third qualifying round produced almost a mirror image of the tie with Kaunas. Celtic were drawn against MTK of Hungary but this team was a pale image of the one that had dealt Celtic such a severe blow back in the 1964 Cup-Winners' Cup semi-finals. The first leg, in Budapest, saw Celtic stroll to another easy 4–0 victory before completing the job by winning 1–0 at Celtic Park, again with a season-ticketed crowd of supporters bemoaning how tedious it all was.

The contrast between those soporific qualifying ties and the group stages of the Champions League was like transferring from a jacuzzi into a bath of ice. Celtic plunged into their group games through an encounter with Bayern Munich, champions of Germany, who featured midfielder Michael Ballack, Germany's Footballer of the Year for the second successive season, and a player praised highly by Franz Beckenbauer, the Bayern president. 'Sooner or later, Ballack will be king of European football. He is five years younger than Zidane but he is more dangerous around goal.' The Bavarian club also fielded Dutch striker Roy Makaay, who had won the Golden Shoe as Europe's best goalscorer for his 29 goals with Spanish club Deportivo La Coruna in the 2002–03 season. Bayern had pursued Makaay for two months over the summer of 2003 and, after a series of complicated negotiations, had won his signature at a cost to the club of a record £13.6 million transfer fee.

'We will fight tooth and nail in the six games to try and have a corner to defend,' was Martin O'Neill's backs-to-the-wall declaration prior to the approaching Champions League sequence. At the Olympiastadion, Bayern had more possession and carved out the better goalscoring opportunities but neither they nor Celtic had managed to get a serious scoring effort on target until, after 57 minutes, Henrik Larsson touched the ball away from Bixente Lizarazu to Didier Agathe, whose high cross arced from the right wing to the corner of the six-yard box where Alan Thompson dived to head the ball into the net off Bayern goalkeeper Oliver Kahn's right-hand post. Late in the game, a clearing header from Stanislav Varga, Celtic's centre-back, dropped on to the right boot of Makaay and although the Dutchman, 20 yards out, failed to catch his shot cleanly, it was still good enough to beat Magnus Hedman, Celtic's Swedish goalkeeper. Worse was to follow. A left-footed cross from Makaay, deep on Bayern's right wing, looped high and long into the Celtic penalty box where Hedman allowed the ball to curl into the net to gift Bayern a lucky winner.

'It was always going to be a tough first game for us,' says Henrik Larsson, 'and for a long time it looked like we were going to get something from it. We played pretty well, especially in the first half, and although we might not have created too many chances we were competing in every area of the pitch. I don't think you can lay the blame anywhere in particular for us conceding the two goals.'

Next up were Olympique Lyon, champions of France, and skill seeped from every part of their side, which included such players as Edmilson, a World Cup-winner with Brazil in 2002, and Giovanne Elber, joint-top goalscorer in Germany in 2002–03, but sold on by Bayern Munich to Lyon after the arrival of Roy Makaay at the Olympiastadion. Elber made a lot of noise pre-match about how Henrik Larsson had failed to prove himself as a striker because he was 'only' scoring goals in Scotland. The best possible answer came on the night when Henrik showed such exquisite skills that the epithet 'world-class' seemed too well worn to describe the player's ability to lift his team and his teammates to special levels of performance.

There had been a difficult backdrop to the game. Martin O'Neill had suggested beforehand that Celtic might have to get used to being in the 'slow lane' of football again with the club having failed to buy any players in the summer of 2003 and the club's chairman Brian Quinn stressing the need for financial prudence above all else. There had been rumours that O'Neill was wanted by Tottenham Hotspur for their vacant manager's job, and some had even warned that O'Neill might depart the club if Celtic were to lose to Lyon. The Celtic support shrugged it all off to hit boisterous form on the night. As the teams took to the field, with the mock-classical Champions League music trumpeting their arrival, the supporters let out a great collective roar. The little mascot holding captain Jackie McNamara's hand looked up at the Celtic captain in shock and awe at the noise and McNamara had to do his best to provide reassurance that some great natural calamity had not occurred.

Celtic had in 2001 been feeling their way in the Champions League but after the run to the final of the 2003 UEFA Cup, there was a confidence about the team that they could take on and beat the best at the top level in Europe. Lyon quickly showed why they were deserving of their place among Europe's elite, moving the ball around with subtlety and style, but Celtic's more direct style, laced with plenty of individual skill, was equally potent and five minutes from half-time, Stilian Petrov's clever, diagonal ball into the Lyon penalty area disoriented Anthony Reveillere, who sent a header into the air that only placed him in further trouble. As he and Larsson went for the ball inside the penalty area, Larsson took a tumble and a penalty was awarded. Many supporters could not bear to look: Celtic had missed numerous penalties in the previous season; most notably Henrik had missed against Basle in the Champions League in 2002 and against Boavista in spring 2003. Their fears were proven correct as Gregory Coupet, the Lyon goalkeeper, sprang from his line like a panther to block Alan Thompson's kick to keep the score 0–0 at half-time.

The Champions League remained distinctly different. At the beginning of the second half the referee had to delay the kick-off for one minute until a TV-connected figure, as if in a studio, had counted him down, second by second, from the touchline to synchronise kick-off with the demands of 'live' television. During the half-time break O'Neill fired the team up, telling them to go out and tear into Lyon who, for all their skill, failed to match the manner in which the Celtic players chased and harried their opponents all over the field. It paid off after 69 minutes. Henrik Larsson took possession of the ball wide on the left wing and as he scanned the scene in front of him he saw six Lyon players strung out in a straight line across the penalty area. Larsson still managed to pick out, with extreme precision, Liam Miller, who had entered play only five minutes earlier as a substitute for John Hartson. A sharp, firm, downward header from the young Irishman, directed expertly between Coupet and the Frenchman's left-hand post, put Celtic ahead. Eight minutes later, Larsson repeated the feat, curving a cross on to the head of Chris Sutton for his co-striker to head home from the same spot on the edge of the six-yard box as Miller. 'What a ball!' said Sutton to his provider as he and Larsson embraced after the goal.

Late in the match, manager Martin O'Neill had become so obsessed with how matters were progressing that he had strayed into the Olympique Lyon technical area. So oblivious did he appear to anything but the action, that he appeared unaware he was standing alongside the more stationary, more contemplative figure of Lyon manager Paul Le Guen, who gently pushed O'Neill away.

Lyon had been the better side for long periods of the game and there had been some nerve-racking moments for Celtic but the French had gradually been worn down by Celtic's desire. It had been yet another magnificent night at Celtic Park; one for the connoisseur of European football. Long after the end, two of the French club's fans sat bemused in a near-deserted south stand at Celtic Park and gazed at the pitch as if to try to work out just what had hit their team, animatedly going over what had happened and where. Henrik Larsson comments, 'The win over Lyon was very important after we'd failed to get anything from our first Champions League match. It's a tough competition and if you start to get behind it is very difficult to catch up. It was essential that we got the points to keep us in touch and to keep our fate in the tournament in our own hands.' Musing on the personal comments from Lyon prior to the match, Larsson says determinedly, 'I do not need to prove anything to anyone. I have scored goals in World Cups and European Championships. I know how good I am.'

It had been an evening when all the best things about Martin

O'Neill's Celtic had been on display. Powerful running and tackling had provided a platform on which players such as Larsson and Petrov could use their skills to best effect. The euphoria lingered long enough for Petrov to state, prior to the meeting with Anderlecht in Celtic's third Champions League group fixture, that Celtic were looking to brush aside the Belgian champions in Brussels and leave Anderlecht sidelined as serious rivals for one of the top two spots in the group. It was a comment that reeked of over-confidence and, on the night in the Stade Constant Vanden Stock, Celtic struggled badly despite Anderlecht having captain and centre-back Glen de Boeck dismissed early in the match. O'Neill's innate caution appeared to have determined the team's tentative tactics on the night and after the positive push for victory against Lyon there was something almost lethargic about Celtic as they went down to a 1–0 defeat.

It made the return with Anderlecht a fortnight later another match in which victory would be vital and, yet again, Celtic were at their best at home. Fireworks whizzed and cracked outside the ground that Guy Fawkes night and it was the same inside as Celtic exploded into action in a match in which Anderlecht were ripped apart in the first half. After 12 minutes, Henrik Larsson's expertly flicked header from Didier Agathe's cross had Celtic ahead. Liam Miller made it 2–0 with a nerveless strike; high in the stands, the onlooking Sir Alex Ferguson, manager of Manchester United, would have been suitably impressed. They were 3–0 up and cruising towards the three points long before the half-time whistle signalled relief for the beleaguered Belgians.

Bayern Munich visited Celtic Park on competitive business for the first time on 25 November 2003. There on the touchline, for this gilt-edged occasion, was the great Franz Beckenbauer, the Kaiser himself, gazing imperiously out across Celtic Park. On the field with the players was Uli Hoeness. Both men had been World Cup winners with West Germany and European Cup winners with Bayern during German football's glory days of the 1970s. Celtic knew that a win against a Bayern side that had been in uncertain Champions League form would put them out of reach of Bayern and would leave Celtic on the verge of qualification for the knockout stages. A draw would leave Celtic too much at the mercy of fate in their final match, away to Lyon.

The match proved to be an enthralling tactical battle, with Bayern having the two clearest-cut scoring chances in a 0–0 draw. The German side were as skilled as any Celtic had faced in Europe during the 2000s. As it turned out, Anderlecht defeated Lyon on the same night to leave Celtic top of their topsy-turvy Champions League section and needing only a draw in Lyon to go through to the knockout stages. 'I think we played reasonably well against Bayern,' says Larsson, 'but we didn't really get that little bit of luck that you sometimes need in games like that.'

A traumatic night in Lyon saw the prized point come within Celtic's grasp as they went a goal behind twice, equalised twice and went careering towards the end of the game with the score at 2–2. Four minutes from the end, Bobo Balde, the Celtic centre-back, leapt for a ball with Lyon forward Peguy Luyindula. Balde positioned his arm in such a way as to make sure that the ball would strike it and not get past him as he went to make his aerial challenge inside the Celtic penalty area. The ball did, indeed, strike his arm and Urs Meier, the Swiss referee, awarded a penalty. There had been no discernible reason why Balde should take such action; although the ball was in the penalty area Luyindula was not directly threatening the Celtic goal and if Balde had left the ball it would have bounced towards Hedman or out of play. Juninho prodded the penalty into the Celtic net and went high-stepping towards the Lyon fans, aware that that dramatic end to each club's sixth-group game would send Lyon through and Celtic tumbling out of the Champions League. Martin O'Neill raged against the referee's decision on the night, but Balde says of that match in Lyon, 'I know I touched the ball. When the ball hit me, I saw the referee's reaction and he gave a penalty. You cannot argue because he was so close and he saw I jumped with my arm out. When he gave the penalty, he would never change his mind so there was no point in arguing about it. I know it was a big disappointment for everyone at Celtic but making mistakes is part of life.'

On the following Saturday, against Dundee, there were signs that players were exasperated with Balde, regardless of O'Neill's railing against the referee. A mishit pass from the defender would see teammates turning and letting off steam in his direction to the point where he ceased attempting difficult passes and instead focused on doing the simple thing. That rash hand-ball brought back memories of

Balde's needless sending-off against Porto in the 2003 UEFA Cup final; a second unforced error in seven months had again been hugely costly to Celtic.

Almost three months passed between Celtic's early-December elimination from the Champions League and their opening fixture in the UEFA Cup, into which teams placed third in their Champions League group parachuted during the 2003–04 season. The disappointment at the Champions League exit had by then dissipated and with it came fresh excitement at being involved in the UEFA Cup, a tournament in which, from late February onwards, the successive rounds would arrive staccato-style in the weeks before the final in Gothenburg, Sweden. Celtic could also, by that point, look forward to direct entry into the 2004–05 Champions League, thanks to their having wrapped up the Scottish League title, in effect, with their emphatic 3–0 victory over Rangers on 3 January 2004. It meant the team could focus fully on the UEFA Cup.

Teplice, Celtic's Czech opponents at the third-round stage, had been weakened by the sale in January 2004 of 21-year-old striker Jan Rezek, who had scored in Teplice's impressive away victories over Feyenoord and Kaiserslautern, whom they had eliminated in earlier rounds of the competition. They had, though, replaced him with Jiri Kowalik, from 1 FC Synot, who had been the Czech League's top scorer in 2002–03. Celtic's principal goalscorer, Henrik Larsson, would also soon be on the move as he had pledged that 2003–04 would be his final season with the club. He had proven himself one of the greatest of all Celtic players in his seven-year career at Celtic Park but a mysterious midwinter slump in 2004 had onlookers wondering whether he could again find the form that had inspired Celtic to the final of the UEFA Cup in 2003, especially as the cast of clubs that they could face in the UEFA Cup during 2004 looked considerably stronger than it had done the previous season and included Benfica, Barcelona, Valencia, Internazionale, Roma, the wintertime Serie A leaders, PSV Eindhoven and Olympique Marseille.

Teplice appeared likely to succumb to the type of onslaught with which Celtic had punished so many visitors during the O'Neill era. The Czech team had sold eleven players during the transfer window of January 2004 and had brought in nine replacements. With a first-team squad of only 14 players, it meant that Celtic's opponents were unrecognisable from the side that had won through to the third round of the UEFA Cup and the Czechs had had only two domestic games to enable their new players to become familiar with one another before being exposed to the searing heat of Celtic Park. Celtic, in contrast, appeared a model of stability. On the Sunday prior to the tie, O'Neill's side had set a new Scottish League record of 24 successive victories in a season and were unbeaten at home for 70 games; the 1–0 reverse to Ajax in August 2001 being their then most recent defeat at Celtic Park.

It proved a curious evening when Teplice came to Celtic Park – Sepp Blatter, secretary of FIFA, was on the pitch at Celtic Park beforehand, grabbing the microphone from Celtic's on-pitch announcer and glad-mouthing the Glasgow fans by launching into a stream of platitudes in their direction before presenting a FIFA Fair Play award for the fans' sporting behaviour at the 2003 UEFA Cup final in Seville. Celtic, similarly, flattered to deceive despite starting on fire. Larsson and Sutton each hit the net within the opening 12 minutes as the two Teplice centre-backs melted under Celtic pressure, but after 20 minutes the game simply went flat and Celtic did not really pick up the pace again until the closing minutes. There appeared a lack of urgency, a sense of caution, throughout the team as they faced opponents who were by far their inferiors – O'Neill's Celtic appear to require their opponents to be as committed as them so that Celtic can spark off them for inspiration. The Czechs even had a couple of good chances to score that would have made the second leg a close affair but Henrik Larsson's second goal, in the final minute, had the fans on their feet to provide the perfect crescendo to an oddly low-key evening. The 3–0 victory all but guaranteed Celtic's progress into the next round.

'We got off to a good start and we were happy to go into half-time 2–0 up,' says Larsson, 'but it's tough to keep going forward in search of goals because the last thing you want to do in Europe is concede a goal at home. Obviously, you want to attack but you always have to be careful and make sure that you are not leaving any gaps. Even after getting the early goal there was no way we were going to do anything silly and try to notch up a load of goals. It was great to get a start like that but it was still a matter of playing a tight game and being patient. I never thought for a moment that it was going to be a high-scoring game, but perhaps we were a little bit too careful in the middle section of the game. It was good to get that third goal right at the death. At 2–0 they were definitely still in the tie but 3–0 made it very tough for them.'

A tepid Celtic performance in Teplice saw them concede a goal shortly before half-time when Stanislav Varga's clearing header was quickly controlled and half-volleyed high into the Celtic net by Jiri Masek. Fear of a second goal led to some nervy moments but the eventual 1–0 defeat saw Celtic shuffle into the next round.

Teplice, a town of 50,000 inhabitants and a club who were novices on the European stage, could not have provided a greater contrast than with Barcelona, Celtic's opponents in the fourth round. Eight-times trophy winners in European competition, Barcelona's Nou Camp is the biggest stadium in Europe, holding 98,000, and by 2004 they had made the greatest expenditure of any club in the world during the four years of the twenty-first century, with a total outlay of £200 million since 2000. Marc Overmars alone had cost £25 million of that sum, but such were Barcelona's resources that he would spend most of the two legs with Celtic sitting on the substitutes' bench. It was a club that demanded success but it had been five years since Barca had won a trophy of any sort and the UEFA Cup represented their final chance of a trophy in the 2003–04 season. Their team was crammed with stylish players such as creative Spanish midfielder Xavi Hernandez Creus, Brazilian forward Ronaldinho, whose cheerleaders claimed him to be the world's best footballer, Carlos Puyol their energetic and expert centre-back, and Argentinian striker Javier Saviola. On Barcelona's arrival in Glasgow for the first leg in March 2004, the Barcelona president, Joan Laporta, suggested that they wished to add another stellar name to their team of talents: he was, he said, keen to sign Henrik Larsson for the 2004–05 season.

Barca, prior to the first leg with Celtic, had strung together nine successive victories to recover from a fitful start to the season but that run had been due in large part to the tenacious qualities of Edgar Davids, the Dutch midfielder who had been signed on loan from Juventus in January 2004 and he was cup-tied, having played for the Italian club in the Champions League earlier in the season. Barca were also without the injured Patrick Kluivert, their Dutch international striker, and Giovanni van Bronckhorst, once of Rangers. That helped to even up the injury difficulties Celtic were experiencing. During the previous fortnight the strikers John Hartson, Chris Sutton and Shaun Maloney had all been counted out of the Barcelona tie, leaving Martin O'Neill with only two front players: Larsson and Craig Beattie, an untested 20-year-old.

The encounter with Barcelona sparked a frenzy for tickets and anyone with a Celtic connection found themselves besieged by people requesting briefs in the days prior to the match. Former Celtic players who took little to do with the club audaciously began placing calls with Celtic's ticket office to seek seats; some of those ex-players had not even been seen near Celtic Park in the years since they had left the club.

Anticipation of the match was tangible in Glasgow, although the first leg against Barcelona took place only eight days after the return with Teplice. That made the build-up seem rather hurried. Matters were complicated by Celtic having to play a Scottish Cup quarter-final against Rangers four days prior to their game with Barca. Celtic won the Old Firm encounter 1–0 but even that was not a complete distraction from the Barcelona match. Players admitted that their minds had strayed towards the Thursday evening's UEFA Cup tie despite the habitual intensity of the Glasgow derby. The tie with Barcelona was formidable in itself but UEFA had, in the 2003–04 season, also drawn the quarter-finals and semi-finals simultaneously with the draw for the fourth round. That left Celtic with the most difficult route possible to a second successive final: if they could defeat Barcelona they would face Roma or Villareal and then, in the semi-finals, possibly Valencia, who were en route to winning Spain's La Liga. Such speculation was shifted aside as Barcelona alighted at Celtic Park on the freezing evening of 11 March.

For a second time that 2003–04 season, Celtic found themselves in a European encounter tinged with tragedy. On the morning of the match, more than 200 people had been killed after terrorist bombs had been detonated on trains in the environs of Madrid, the capital of Spain. FC Barcelona, with the full backing of Celtic, had requested of UEFA that the match be postponed but the Spanish government, desperate to appear strong in advance of a general election three days later, specified that all four UEFA Cup matches involving Spanish clubs should go ahead, preceded by one minute's silence. It seemed strange that an entire programme of Champions League and UEFA Cup matches had been postponed in the wake of New York's 11 September tragedy in 2001 but that European ties would still go on after a large-scale terrorist outrage on UEFA's home continent. It made for a sombre atmosphere at Celtic Park before the game.

The Celtic players who filed out under the floodlights that night were: Rab Douglas, Didier Agathe, Bobo Balde, Stanislav Varga, Jackie McNamara, Neil Lennon, Alan Thompson, Stephen Pearson, Stilian Petrov, Craig Beattie, Henrik Larsson. Of those players only Larsson, in 2004, had a reputation that extended to any great extent internationally and they found their illustrious opponents overshadowing them in the early part of the match. Neil Lennon, in particular, appeared almost static as lithe, athletic Barcelona players shuttled the ball around him in midfield. On reaching half-time, Celtic had competed well and had tested the Barcelona defence but, equally, could have had no complaints if Barcelona had gone in 2–0 or 3–0 ahead. Saviola and Ronaldinho had squandered two clear openings on goal and on half-time, only a superb goal-line clearance from Jackie McNamara had prevented what had looked a certain goal for Barcelona.

The 15-minute half-time interval proved to be the turning point in the match. A tunnel scuffle as the players made their way towards the dressing-rooms resulted in Rab Douglas, the Celtic goalkeeper, and Thiago Motta, Barcelona's left-sided midfield player, being red-carded in the referee's room. Twenty seconds before the interval, Motta had sneakily stretched out his left arm to punch Balde on the mouth as the two players had jumped for the ball and the Celt had taken issue with this in the tunnel, leading to a commotion in which a racial taunt was reportedly used. Supporters stood shuffling themselves warm in the cold south stand, unaware of all the drama taking place beneath them, but when Celtic re-emerged for the second half they could see that Douglas had been replaced by David Marshall, Celtic's 19-year-old goalkeeper, appearing in only his second match for the club, and that both Celtic and Barcelona were down to ten men. The madness continued into the opening minutes of the second half when Saviola whacked Thompson on the leg, an action that saw the Argentinian instantly dismissed by Wolfgang Stark, the German referee.

Barcelona, minus their striker and down to nine men, hung in bravely after that but on the hour a precise ball into the box from Petrov allowed Larsson to steal in between markers Carlos Puyol and Michael Reiziger to guide the ball down beautifully for the unmarked Thompson who, with a side-on scissors-kick in mid-air, hit the ball sweetly past Victor Valdes, the Barcelona goalkeeper. A teasing, angled shot from Larsson almost made it 2–0 for Celtic but after a testing, traumatic night, on which Celtic had had luck heavily on their side, few could quibble with a 1–0 victory; a result to be prized.

The evening's events left Frank Rijkaard, the Barcelona manager, with plenty of problems. Saviola would be suspended for the return, leaving Rijkaard, the Dutchman, with a striking problem. Motta had been subtly influential in midfield for Barcelona and his automatic absence meant that Barcelona faced the second leg missing five key players. As with the first leg, those enforced absences from Barcelona's starting line-up were amply matched by those that faced Celtic. Bobo Balde had collected a booking in the first leg, leaving him suspended for the match in the Nou Camp, along with Douglas. O'Neill would be forced to play Marshall in that intimidating arena. He also had a rush on to get Chris Sutton fit for the return. Beattie had played in the first half against the Spaniards at Celtic Park but he had looked too raw a player to have been thrown in at that level, had been exposed badly and had been substituted at half-time.

'The Barcelona game was very tough and did take a lot out of us,' says Henrik Larsson. 'There is little doubt in my mind that Barcelona are the best side we faced in Europe at Celtic Park. It's a great experience to line up against players that you see playing at the highest level on TV. You don't have to lift yourself for those games because they are the ones you dream about when you are a young player.'

Phillip Cocu, the straight-backed, elegant, Dutch midfielder who was Barca's captain at Celtic Park, was surprised by the way in which O'Neill had set out his team to play in the first leg, when Celtic had lined up at home in a 4–5–1 formation. 'We played a very good game at Celtic Park,' says Cocu. 'We created lots of chances – the only thing missing for us was a goal. Celtic are very well organised and a strong, powerful team. They made things very difficult for us in the first leg but also tried to play good football as well. I have to say, though, that they played a bit more defensively in the game than I would have expected.

Although there were three red cards in the game at Celtic Park, for me it was not a bad-tempered or aggressive match. It was a good game without too many problems for the referee to sort out.'

An appeal from Celtic to UEFA to rescind Douglas' red card failed. Douglas' usual deputy, Magnus Hedman, had been sent on loan to Ancona of Italy for the second half of the season and at the time of the Barca ties was recovering from an operation. Danny Milosevic, an experienced Australian goalkeeper, had been signed from Leeds United as emergency cover for the on-loan Hedman on a six-month contract in late January 2004 but had been instantaneously allowed the freedom to take time off away from the club to deal with some personal problems. He was still, surprisingly, away when, in mid-March, O'Neill, struggling for goalkeepers, contacted him to see if he might return to help out with the goalkeeping situation. Milosevic, whose fitness after two months away from Celtic must have been in question, responded in the negative and Celtic immediately tore up his contract.

Another member of the squad for Barcelona was Liam Miller, the young Irish midfielder who had made a huge impression after being introduced to the team on a regular basis early in the 2003–04 season and who had scored key goals and turned in impressive performances against Anderlecht and Lyon earlier in the season. He had stunned the Celtic support in January 2004 when it had been announced by Manchester United that Miller had agreed to join them in summer 2004 once his contract had expired with Celtic. O'Neill, in his quirky way, stated, after the news of Miller's pending departure had broken in early 2004, 'I spoke to his agent, Fintan Drury, in the summer about an extension to Liam's agreement. There was no talk of Manchester United at that time and there wasn't a rush to sign Liam for any other club. He had wanted a fair crack of the whip where first-team football was concerned and Liam had surpassed our expectations on the pre-season tour in America. But then his agent went on holiday in late August.' Miller was thus left free to leave in 2004. He would double the wage offered to him by Celtic when he signed up at Old Trafford and Celtic would receive no transfer fee for him.

O'Neill had, prior to the match with Teplice, stated that the UEFA Cup final with Porto was becoming a fast-fading memory, yet a few days prior to the match in Barcelona, he could still be found harping on about, in his opinion, the theatrical diving of the Porto players on the night of that match. Porto, a club less wealthy than Celtic, and their crafty manager José Mourinho were meanwhile progressing smoothly towards capturing the European Cup to add to the UEFA Cup: proof that ingenuity could still count in the big-money age of football.

Barcelona's injury problems, with first-choice striker Saviola ruled out and Kluivert also eliminated from the tie through injury, meant that the experienced Spanish international Luis Enrique, who had enjoyed his best days in the 1990s, would lead their patched-up attack. With a third-choice striker in place and key supporting players out, Barca would rely heavily for invention on Ronaldinho, the cheekily skilful Brazilian. In the first leg he had shown much trickery but had failed to employ his abilities to best advantage for the team; the question now was whether he could adjust his game to adapt to the extra responsibility that would fall on his shoulders through his teammates being injured.

Chris Sutton came back into Celtic's forward line but the Barca match would be his first for a month. Celtic looked the team best equipped to cope with absentees: it was one of the more positive quirks of O'Neill's management that he was able to instil such a strong team spirit in his players that almost anyone's absence could go unnoticed and, whatever permutations might mutate the starting eleven, the line-up would include the great Larsson, the one irreplaceable member of the side. These Celtic players trod on to the inviting expanse of turf at the Nou Camp: David Marshall, Didier Agathe, John Kennedy, Stanislav Varga, Jackie McNamara, Neil Lennon, Alan Thompson, Stephen Pearson, Stilian Petrov, Chris Sutton and Henrik Larsson.

The tie was beautifully poised at 1–0: any away goal in the Nou Camp would tilt it hugely in Celtic's favour but there was still little doubt in Catalonia that it would be Barcelona that would go through. Johan Cruyff, long retired as Barcelona manager but living in luxury in the city, always had an opinion on everything Barca-related and offered that Barca would do better at home than on what he described as Celtic's 'potato patch' pitch. Hristo Stoichkov, a Barcelona striker when Cruyff had been manager during the 1990s and now on the club's coaching staff, mouthed off, as was his wont, that Barca had to win 4–0 to emphasise what he saw as the gulf in quality between the clubs. It all mattered very little once Domenico Messina, the Italian referee, had sounded his whistle for kick-off and the two sets of opponents began their tussle to see who would take the quarter-final place that would be the prize after the evening's exertions.

A mere 20 seconds had expired when Jackie McNamara's loose back-pass forced David Marshall to concede the first corner of the match. It was half-cleared by Celtic but Carlos Puyol dispossessed Chris Sutton, threaded his way past three Celtic players and fed Ronaldinho, whose quick, slick pass was played between Stanislav Varga and Didier Agathe to put the running Lopez Gerard one on one with Marshall. It looked a certain goal but Marshall stuck out a left arm and scooped the ball away from Gerard's left foot for a sumptuous save; the goalkeeper's timing had been so precise that in palming the ball clear he had clean nutmegged the Barcelona forward.

Only 55 seconds had passed but the pattern had already been set for the night. Eight minutes later, Ronaldinho crossed, Gerard headed firmly down and Marshall dived low to his right again to prevent Barcelona taking the lead. Three minutes on, Luis Garcia's dipping cross from the left wing dropped over Marshall's head but, tumbling backwards, he pushed the ball behind his goal. From Xavi's corner, Ronaldinho angled a header into the six-yard box where Luis Enrique knocked a first-time shot towards goal. Marshall instantaneously twisted swiftly to his right to deflect the ball off target and followed that up by ushering Luis Enrique away from goal after the rebound had fallen to the Spaniard. Ronaldinho was the centre of attention, where he liked to be, after 20 minutes as he made a diagonal run into the penalty area that was cut short by John Kennedy, the 20-year-old Celtic centre-back, The Brazilian took a tumble after that tackle and appealed for a penalty but Kennedy had timed his thumping intervention with maximum precision. Soon, Barcelona began to run out of inventiveness. They had had more than 70 per cent of the ball in the first half but too often their passing had been sloppy and imprecise and their creative players had been hounded at every turn by Celtic midfield players and defenders.

Celtic had fluttered around the fringes of the Barcelona penalty area on occasion but not once in the first half had they managed a shot on target. They went one better in the second half, when, after 62 minutes,

Henrik Larsson managed Celtic's only shot on target in the entire match but it was a limp, left-footed, wan effort from the edge of the Barcelona penalty area that barely troubled Valdes, the Barcelona goalkeeper. That moment apart, the match reverted to type, with all 11 Celtic players spending much of the second period deep inside their own half.

Barcelona had, after half-time, again appeared slightly sluggish but they were prodded from their somnambulent stroll through the match after 68 minutes when Ronaldinho took possession of the ball in midfield and showed it briefly to Neil Lennon before leaving the Irishman trailing like a piece of discarded litter in his wake, went outside Kennedy, inside Agathe and rounded off his run by flashing an angled shot at goal that Marshall turned round the post for a corner. Ronaldinho concluded that silvery sliver of skill by exhorting the sleepy Barcelona crowd to get behind their team. He also appeared to have roused his teammates. The corner was cleared by the Celtic defence but quickly played back towards goal by Barcelona, allowing Garcia Gabri the opportunity of a 25-yard shot on goal that was beaten away by Marshall.

Two minutes later, an exquisite, angled, lofted pass from Xavi into the penalty area found Luis Garcia, whose run had not been picked up by Alan Thompson. That left Luis Garcia on his own inside the area, perfectly positioned to meet the ball on the penalty spot and volley it high towards the top corner of the Celtic goal. It produced the pièce de résistance of the evening from Marshall, who made a leap to twist on to the ball and turn it over the bar. Head in hands, Luis Garcia could not believe he had been denied. There were 20 minutes remaining and one more fine Marshall save to come: a low dive to his left to push away a 25-yard shot from Sergio Garcia. That was the Spanish side's final real scoring opportunity and Celtic had eliminated Barcelona from the UEFA Cup. It had not been pretty but it had been pretty effective.

'Barcelona must have felt before the game that they still had a good chance and would have fancied themselves at home,' says Henrik Larsson, 'but I'm sure they didn't underestimate us in any way. They will have been well aware of what Celtic are capable. They played really well. They are a great team with loads of talent but we put in a solid defensive performance. We ended up having to play a more defensive game than an attacking one because of the way Barcelona took the game to us. That meant the midfield had to get behind the ball and Chris Sutton and I had to do our bit in tracking back and trying to deny Barcelona space. We were trying to break out and we were looking for any opportunity to push forward but they squeezed us so tightly that it forced us to play further back than we would have liked. You have to defend as a team and attack as a team, and if we couldn't move forward as a unit we couldn't move forward. It wasn't one of my best attacking performances but I was quite pleased with my defensive game. It was one of those occasions where you have to assume a slightly different role and I'm happy with that.' Marshall, in contrast to Miller earlier in the season, was immediately offered a contract extension, with an increased wage, that he duly signed.

Celtic had defeated the only club to have competed in every season of European competition since it had begun in the mid-1950s. Their quarter-finals opponents would be Villareal, a club from further down the north-eastern coast of Spain but one, in complete contrast to Barcelona, enjoying their first season in European football. Villareal were, when drawn against Celtic, sitting ninth in the Spanish League in a classic mid-table position, equidistant from leaders Real Madrid and bottom club Murcia and separated by 22 points in each case. Those statistics proved deceptive. Villareal may not have boasted the household names to be found at the Nou Camp but their performance in the first leg of the quarter-final at Celtic Park was one of excellence as they propelled the ball around the field with stunning speed, accuracy and skill and took the lead after nine minutes. Their quick, clever movement in midfield was rewarded when Moreno Berdu Josico stole into the Celtic penalty area to glide a header past Marshall. The Celtic midfield, with Lennon as its fulcrum, looked static in comparison with that of Villareal and twice in the opening 15 minutes Villareal passed up good opportunities to go further ahead. It helped Villareal that the Celtic Park 'potato patch' had been dug up and relaid; the new sward of turf allowed the ball to move unerringly, and speedily, across the playing surface. Thompson hit the Villareal post as the first half drew on but early in the second half Villareal had clear opportunities to put the tie beyond Celtic. Sonny Anderson, the striker, one on one with Marshall, saw his low shot well saved by the goalkeeper; then a swerving strike from Sebastian Battaglia slapped against the Celtic crossbar.

One minute later, Henrik Larsson charged down a clearance from the goalkeeper to send the ball flying into the Villareal net. The ball had appeared to strike his arms, which had been raised to his chest to protect himself from the blow of the ball but it looked unlikely to have been deliberate handball. That, though, was the ruling from the referee, Kyros Vassaras, of Greece, and Celtic remained one goal down. That decision looked especially harsh when, within seconds, a Stanislav Varga header struck Fabrizzio Coloccini on the arm inside the penalty area, just as it had done Larsson, but this time the referee waved play on. The referee could do little to deny Celtic an equaliser when, in 63 minutes, Larsson climbed high inside the penalty area to head cleanly into the Villareal net for his 35th goal for Celtic in European competition.

'We were obviously a bit disappointed that we conceded a goal in the first leg at Celtic Park,' says Larsson. 'Keeping a clean sheet at home is a crucial aspect of success in Europe but they caught us out early in the game. We kept calm and tried to be patient in looking for the equaliser, which I thought we'd got when I charged a clearance down. I was really surprised when the referee disallowed it for handball. That was a big decision. The ball hit me in the chest from point-blank range. I could have understood the decision if it had hit my arm away from my body but it didn't. It was so important to get the goal back that we knew we couldn't let that decision affect us, so we didn't panic and kept looking for an opening. It was a real relief to score the equaliser.'

Celtic had salvaged some pride on the night but in Villareal the following midweek a hesitant Bobo Balde and Marshall allowed Sonny Anderson to smooth his way in between them and head the Spanish side into an early lead. Further sluggishness, on the part of Joos Valgaeren, the centre-back, allowed Garcia Roger to slam home a second goal for Villareal in the second half and Celtic, after two disjointed quarter-final performances, were out of Europe. 'I would have loved to have had a run all the way to the final again,' says Henrik Larsson,'but it wasn't to be. Football is like that. It only takes one game to see a lot of hard work come to an end. There is no doubt that we missed players like Chris Sutton, John Hartson and Alan Thompson. No matter what level you play at, whether it's the Swedish fifth division, or the UEFA Cup quarter-final, you want to go out with your first-choice team. Injuries and suspensions meant that simply wasn't possible against Villareal.

'Villareal are a very good side. They played fast, skilful football and on the night we came off second best. It was tough going a goal behind early again because you're then in a situation where you know you have to score more than once and not concede again. Unfortunately, in the second half we did let another goal in and then there was a mountain to climb. As a team, we didn't do enough to get the result we wanted.'

Celtic's European adventures had begun beside the orange groves of Valencia in 1962 – now things had come full circle with a UEFA Cup campaign that ended beside the orange groves of Villareal, a town that was a short hop from Valencia along the north-eastern coast of Spain. Celtic's next entry into Europe was sure to produce sights and sounds to be savoured as much as those experienced throughout the four vibrant decades in European competition that had separated Celtic's first visit to Valencia from their trip to Villareal.

Appendix
CELTIC IN EUROPE – GAMES, GOALS AND SCORERS

Inter Cities Fairs Cup 1962–63
First Round
Valencia (Spain) 4 (Coll 2, Guillot 2): Celtic 2 (Carroll 2)
Celtic 2 (Verdu own goal, Crerand): Valencia 2 (Guillot, Waldo)

European Cup-Winners' Cup 1963–64
First Round
Basle (Switzerland) 1 (Blumer): Celtic 5 (Divers, Hughes 3, Lennox)
Celtic 5 (Johnstone, Divers 2, Murdoch, Chalmers): Basle 0
Second Round
Celtic 3 (Chalmers 2, Hughes): Dinamo Zagreb (Yugoslavia) 0
Dinamo Zagreb 2 (Lamza, Zambata): Celtic 1 (Murdoch)
Quarter-final
Celtic 1 (Murdoch): Slovan Bratislava (Czechoslovakia) 0
Slovan Bratislava 0: Celtic 1 (Hughes)
Semi-final
Celtic 3 (Johnstone, Chalmers 2): MTK Budapest (Hungary) 0
MTK Budapest 4 (Kuti 2, Vasas, Sandor): Celtic 0

Inter Cities Fairs Cup 1964–65

First Round

Leixoes (Portugal) 1 (Esteves): Celtic 1 (Murdoch)

Celtic 3 (Chalmers 2, Murdoch): Leixoes 0

Second Round

Barcelona (Spain) 3 (Zaldua, Seminario, Rife): Celtic 1 (Hughes)

Celtic 0: Barcelona 0

European Cup-Winners' Cup 1965–66

First Round

Go Ahead Deventer (Holland) 0: Celtic 6 (Lennox 3, Hughes, Johnstone 2)

Celtic 1 (McBride): Go Ahead Deventer 0

Second Round

AGF Aarhus (Denmark) 0: Celtic 1 (McBride)

Celtic 2 (McNeill, Johnstone): AGF Aarhus 0

Quarter-final

Celtic 3 (Gemmell, Murdoch 2): Dynamo Kiev (Soviet Union) 0

Dynamo Kiev 1 (Sabo): Celtic 1 (Gemmell)

Semi-final

Celtic 1 (Lennox): Liverpool (England) 0

Liverpool 2 (Smith, Strong): Celtic 0

European Cup 1966–67

First Round

Celtic 2 (Gemmell, McBride): Zurich (Switzerland) 0

Zurich 0: Celtic 3 (Gemmell 2, Chalmers)

Second Round

Nantes (France) 1 (Magny): Celtic 3 (McBride, Lennox, Chalmers)

Celtic 3 (Johnstone, Chalmers, Lennox): Nantes 1 (Georgen)

Quarter-final

Vojvodina Novi Sad (Yugoslavia) 1 (Stanic): Celtic 0

Celtic 2 (Chalmers, McNeill): Vojvodina Novi Sad 0

Semi-final

Celtic 3 (Johnstone, Wallace 2): Dukla Prague (Czechoslovakia) 1 (Strunc)

Dukla Prague 0: Celtic 0

Final – Lisbon, Portugal

Celtic 2 (Gemmell, Chalmers): Internazionale (Italy) 1 (Mazzola)

European Cup 1967–68

First Round

Celtic 1 (Lennox): Dynamo Kiev (Soviet Union) 2 (Pusach, Byshovets)

Dynamo Kiev (Byshovets)1: Celtic 1 (Lennox)

European Cup 1968–69

First Round

St Etienne (France) 2 (Keita, Revelli): Celtic 0

Celtic 4 (Gemmell, Craig, Chalmers, McBride): St Etienne 0

Second Round

Celtic 5 (Murdoch, Johnstone 2, Lennox, Wallace): Red Star Belgrade (Yugoslavia) 1 (Lazervic)

Red Star Belgrade 1 (Ostojic): Celtic 1 (Wallace)

Quarter-final

Milan (Italy) 0: Celtic 0

Celtic 0: Milan 1 (Prati)

European Cup 1969–70

First Round

Basle (Switzerland) 0: Celtic 0

Celtic 2 (Hood, Gemmell): Basle 0

Second Round

Celtic 3 (Gemmell, Wallace, Hood): Benfica (Portugal) 0

Benfica 3 (Eusebio, Graca, Diamentino): Celtic 0

(Celtic won the tie on the toss of a coin)

Quarter-final

Celtic 3 (Auld, Carpenetti own goal, Wallace): Fiorentina (Italy) 0

Fiorentina 1 (Chiarugi): Celtic 0

Semi-final

Leeds United (England) 0: Celtic (Connelly) 1

Celtic 2 (Hughes, Murdoch): Leeds United 1 (Bremner)

Final – Milan, Italy

Celtic 1 (Gemmell): Feyenoord (Holland) 2 (Israel, Kindvall)

European Cup 1970–71

First Round

Celtic 9 (Hood 3, Hughes, McNeill, Johnstone, Wilson 2, Davidson): Kokkola (Finland) 0

Kokkola 0: Celtic 5 (Wallace 2, Callaghan, Davidson, Lennox)

Second Round

Waterford (Ireland) 0: Celtic 7 (Wallace 3, Macari 2, Murdoch 2)

Celtic 3 (Hughes, Johnstone 2): Waterford 2 (McNeill own goal, Matthews)

Quarter-final

Ajax Amsterdam (Holland) 3 (Cruyff, Hulshoff, Keizer): Celtic 0

Celtic 1 (Johnstone): Ajax Amsterdam 0

European Cup 1971–72

First Round

Boldklubben 1903 Copenhagen (Denmark) 2 (Johansen 2): Celtic 1 (Macari)

Celtic 3 (Wallace 2, Callaghan): Boldklubben 1903 Copenhagen 0

Second Round

Celtic 5 (Gemmell, Hood 2, Brogan, Macari): Sliema Wanderers (Malta) 0

Sliema Wanderers 1 (Cocks): Celtic 2 (Hood, Lennox)

Quarter-final

Ujpest Dozsa (Hungary) 1 (Horvath): Celtic 2 (Horvath own goal, Macari)

Celtic 1 (Macari): Ujpest Dozsa 1 (Anton Dunai)

Semi-final

Internazionale (Italy) 0: Celtic 0

Celtic 0: Internazionale 0

(Internazionale won the tie 5–4 on penalties)

European Cup 1972–73

First Round

Celtic 2 (Macari, Deans): Rosenborg Trondheim (Norway) 1 (Wirkola)

Rosenborg Trondheim 1 (Christiansen): Celtic 3 (Macari, Hood, Dalglish)

Second Round

Celtic 2 (Dalglish 2): Ujpest Dozsa (Hungary) 1 (Bene)

Ujpest Dozsa 3 (Bene 2, Fazekas): Celtic 0

European Cup 1973–74

First Round

Turun Palloseura Turku (Finland) 1 (Andelmin); Celtic 6 (Callaghan 2, Hood, Johnstone, Connelly, Deans)

Celtic 3 (Deans, Johnstone 2): Turun Palloseura Turku 0

Second Round

Celtic 0: Vejle Boldklub (Denmark) 0

Vejle Boldklub 0: Celtic 1 (Lennox)

Quarter-final

Basle (Switzerland) 3 (Hitzfeld 2, Odermatt): Celtic 2 (Wilson, Dalglish)

Celtic 4 (Dalglish, Deans, Callaghan, Murray): Basle 2 (Mundschin, Balmer)

Semi-final

Celtic 0: Atletico Madrid (Spain) 0

Atletico Madrid 2 (Garate, Abelardo): Celtic 0

European Cup 1974–75

First Round

Celtic 1 (Wilson): Olympiakos (Greece) 1 (Viera)

Olympiakos 2 (Kritikopolous, Stavropoulos): Celtic 0

European Cup-Winners' Cup 1975–76

First Round

Valur Reykjavik (Iceland) 0: Celtic 2 (Wilson, MacDonald)

Celtic 7 (Edvaldsson, Dalglish, Pat McCluskey, Hood 2, Deans, Callaghan): Valur Reykjavik 0

Second Round

Boavista (Portugal) 0: Celtic 0

Celtic 3 (Dalglish, Edvaldsson, Deans): Boavista 1 (Mane)

Quarter-final

Celtic 1 (Dalglish): Sachsenring Zwickau (East Germany) 1 (Blank)

Sachsenring Zwickau 1 (Blank): Celtic 0

UEFA Cup 1976–77

First Round

Celtic 2 (MacDonald, Dalglish): Wisla Krakow (Poland) 2 (Kmiecik, Wrobel)

Wisla Krakow 2 (Kmiecik 2): Celtic 0

European Cup 1977–78

First Round

Celtic 5 (MacDonald, Wilson, Craig 2, McLaughlin): Jeunesse D'Esch (Luxembourg) 0

Jeunesse D'Esch 1 (Giulana): Celtic 6 (Lennox, Glavin 2, Craig, Edvaldsson 2)

Second Round

Celtic 2 (Craig, Burns): SW Innsbruck (Austria) 1 (Kreiss)

SW Innsbruck 3 (Welzl, Stering, Oberacher): Celtic 0

European Cup 1979–80

First Round

Partizani Tirana (Albania) 1 (Murati): Celtic 0

Celtic 4 (MacDonald, Aitken 2, Davidson): Partizani Tirana 1 (Sneddon own goal)

Second Round

Celtic 3 (MacDonald, McCluskey, Burns): Dundalk (Ireland) 2 (Muckian, Lawlor)

Dundalk 0: Celtic 0

Quarter-final

Celtic 2 (McCluskey, Doyle): Real Madrid (Spain) 0

Real Madrid 3 (Santillana, Stielike, Juanito): Celtic 0

European Cup-Winners' Cup 1980–81

Preliminary Round

Celtic 6 (McGarvey 3, McCluskey 2, Sullivan): Diosgyeori Miskolc (Hungary) 0

Diosgyeori Miskolc 2 (Gorgei 2): Celtic 1 (Nicholas)

First Round

Celtic 2 (Nicholas 2): Politechnica Timisoara (Romania) 1 (Adrian)

Politechnica Timisoara 1 (Paltinisan): Celtic 0

European Cup 1981–82

First Round

Celtic 1 (MacLeod): Juventus (Italy) 0

Juventus 2 (Virdis, Bettega): Celtic 0

European Cup 1982–83
First Round
Celtic 2 (Nicholas, McGarvey): Ajax Amsterdam (Holland) 2 (Olsen, Lerby)
Ajax Amsterdam 1 (Vanenburg): Celtic 2 (Nicholas, McCluskey)
Second Round
Real Sociedad (Spain) 2 (Satrustegui, Uralde): Celtic 0
Celtic 2 (MacLeod 2): Real Sociedad 1 (Uralde)

UEFA Cup 1983–84
First Round
Celtic 1 (Aitken): AGF Aarhus (Denmark) 0
AGF Aarhus 1 (Scheepers): Celtic 4 (MacLeod, McGarvey, Aitken, Provan)
Second Round
Sporting Lisbon (Portugal) 2 (Jordao 2): Celtic 0
Celtic 5 (Burns, McAdam, McClair, MacLeod, McGarvey): Sporting Lisbon 0
Third Round
Nottingham Forest (England) 0: Celtic 0
Celtic 1 (MacLeod): Nottingham Forest 2 (Hodge, Walsh)

European Cup-Winners' Cup 1984–85
First Round
Ghent (Belgium) 1 (Cordiez): Celtic 0
Celtic 3 (McGarvey 2, McStay): Ghent 0
Second Round
Rapid Vienna (Austria) 3 (Pacult, Lainer, Krankl): Celtic 1 (McClair)
Celtic 3 (McClair, MacLeod, Burns): Rapid Vienna 0
(Celtic's home leg was subsequently declared void by UEFA and ordered to be
    replayed)
Second Round Second Leg Replay at Old Trafford, Manchester
Celtic 0: Rapid Vienna 1 (Pacult)

European Cup-Winners' Cup 1985–86
First Round
Atletico Madrid 1 (Setien): Celtic 1 (Johnston)
Celtic 1 (Aitken): Atletico Madrid 2 (Setien, Quique)

European Cup 1986-87

First Round

Shamrock Rovers (Ireland) 0: Celtic 1 (MacLeod)

Celtic 2 (Johnston 2): Shamrock Rovers 0

Second Round

Celtic 1 (Johnston): Dynamo Kiev (Soviet Union) 1 (Yevtushenko)

Dynamo Kiev 3 (Blokhin, Yakovenko, Yevtushenko): Celtic 1 (McGhee)

UEFA Cup 1987-88

First Round

Celtic 2 (Walker, Whyte): Borussia Dortmund (West Germany) 1 (Mill)

Borussia Dortmund 2 (Dickel 2): Celtic 0

European Cup 1988-89

First Round

Honved (Hungary) 1 (Fodor): Celtic 0

Celtic 4 (Stark, Walker, McAvennie, McGhee): Honved 0

Second Round

Celtic 0: Werder Bremen (West Germany) 1 (Wolter)

Werder Bremen 0: Celtic 0

European Cup-Winners' Cup 1989-90

First Round

Partizan Belgrade (Yugoslavia) 2 (Milojevic, Djordjevic): Celtic 1 (Galloway)

Celtic 5 (Dziekanowski 4, Walker): Partizan Belgrade 4 (Vujacic, B Djordjevic, Djurovski, Scepovic)

(Partizan won on away goals)

UEFA Cup 1991-92

First Round

Celtic 2 (Nicholas 2): Germinal Ekeren (Belgium) 0

Germinal Ekeren 1 (Schmoller): Celtic 1 (Galloway)

Second Round

Neuchatel Xamax (Switzerland) 5 (Hossam Hassan 4, Bonvin): Celtic 1 (O'Neil)

Celtic 1 (Miller): Neuchatel Xamax 0

UEFA Cup 1992-93

First Round

Cologne (Germany) 2 (Jensen, Ordenewitz): Celtic 0

Celtic 3 (McStay, Creaney, Collins): Cologne 0

Second Round

Borussia Dortmund (Germany) 1 (Chapuisat): Celtic 0

Celtic 1 (Creaney): Borussia Dortmund 2 (Chapuisat, Zorc)

UEFA Cup 1993-94

First Round

Young Boys Berne (Switzerland) 0: Celtic 0

Celtic 1 (Baumann own goal): Young Boys Berne 0

Second Round

Celtic 1 (Creaney): Sporting Lisbon (Portugal) 0

Sporting Lisbon 2 (Cadete 2): Celtic 0

European Cup-Winners' Cup 1995-96

First Round

Dynamo Batumi (Georgia) 2 (Machutadze, Tugushi): Celtic 3 (Thom 2, Donnelly)

Celtic 4 (Thom 2, Donnelly, Walker): Dynamo Batumi 0

Second Round

Paris St Germain (France) 1 (Djorkaeff): Celtic 0

Celtic 0: Paris St Germain 3 (Loko 2, Nouma)

UEFA Cup 1996-97

Qualifying Round

Kosice (Slovakia) 0: Celtic 0

Celtic 1 (Cadete): Kosice 0

First Round

Celtic 0: SV Hamburg (Germany) 2 (Baron, Schupp)

SV Hamburg 2 (Baron, Breitenreiter): Celtic 0

UEFA Cup 1997-98

Preliminary Round

Inter Cable Tel (Wales) 0: Celtic 3 (Thom, Johnson, Wieghorst)

Celtic 5 (Thom, Jackson, Johnson, Hannah, Hay): Inter Cable Tel 0

Qualifying Round

SW Tirol Innsbruck (Austria) 2 (Mayrleb 2): Celtic 1 (Stubbs)

Celtic 6 (Donnelly 2, Thom, Burley 2, Wieghorst): SW Tirol Innsbruck 3 (Mayrleb, Larsson own goal, Krinner)

First Round

Celtic 2 (McNamara, Donnelly): Liverpool (England) 2 (Owen, McManaman)

Liverpool 0: Celtic 0

(Liverpool won on away goals)

Champions League 1998–99

First Qualifying Round

Celtic 0: Saint Patrick's Athletic (Ireland) 0

Saint Patrick's Athletic 0: Celtic 2 (Brattbakk, Larsson)

Second Qualifying Round

Celtic 1 (Jackson): Croatia Zagreb (Croatia) 0

Croatia Zagreb 3 (Maric, Prosinecki 2): Celtic 0

UEFA Cup 1998–99

First Round

Vitoria Guimaraes (Portugal) 1 (Geraldo): Celtic 2 (Larsson, Donnelly)

Celtic 2 (Stubbs, Larsson): Vitoria Guimaraes 1 (Soderstrom)

Second Round

Celtic 1 (Brattbakk): Zurich (Switzerland) 1 (Fischer)

Zurich 4 (Del Signore, Chassot, Bartlett, Sant'Anna): Celtic 2 (O'Donnell, Larsson)

UEFA Cup 1999–2000

Qualifying Round

Cwmbran Town (Wales) 0: Celtic 6 (Berkovic, Tebily, Larsson 2, Viduka, Brattbakk)

Celtic 4 (Brattbakk, Smith, Mjallby, Johnson): Cwmbran Town 0

First Round

Celtic 2 (Larsson 2): Hapoel Tel Aviv (Israel) 0

Hapoel Tel Aviv 0: Celtic 1 (Larsson)

Second Round

Olympique Lyon (France) 1 (Blanc): Celtic 0

Celtic 0: Olympique Lyon 1 (Vairelles)

UEFA Cup 2000–01

Qualifying Round

Jeunesse d'Esch (Luxembourg) 0: Celtic 4 (Moravcik 2, Larsson, Petta)

Celtic 7 (Burchill 3, Berkovic 2, Riseth, Petrov): Jeunesse d'Esch 0

First Round

Celtic 2 (Larsson 2): HJK Helsinki (Finland) 0

HJK Helsinki 2 (Roiha 2): Celtic 1 (Sutton)

Second Round

Girondins de Bordeaux (France) 1 (Dugarry): Celtic 1 (Larsson)

Celtic 1 (Moravcik): Girondins de Bordeaux 2 (Laslandes 2)

Champions League 2001–02

Third Qualifying Round

Ajax Amsterdam (Holland) 1 (Arveladze): Celtic 3 (Petta, Agathe, Sutton)

Celtic 0: Ajax Amsterdam 1 (Wamberto)

First Group Stage

Juventus (Italy) 3 (Trezeguet 2, Amoruso): Celtic 2 (Petrov, Larsson)

Celtic 1 (Larsson): Porto (Portugal) 0

Celtic 1 (Thompson): Rosenborg Trondheim (Norway) 0

Porto 3 (Clayton 2, Mario Silva): Celtic 0

Rosenborg Trondheim 2 (Brattbakk 2): Celtic 0

Celtic 4 (Valgaeren, Sutton 2, Larsson): Juventus 3 (Del Piero, Trezeguet 2)

(Celtic finished third in their four-team Champions League group and qualified for the UEFA Cup)

UEFA Cup 2001–02

Third Round

Valencia (Spain) 1 (Vicente): Celtic 0

Celtic 1 (Larsson): Valencia 0

(Valencia won 5–4 on penalties)

Champions League 2002–03

Third Qualifying Round

Celtic 3 (Larsson, Sutton, Sylla): Basle (Switzerland) 1 (Gimenez)

Basle 2 (Gimenez, Murat Yakin): Celtic 0

(Basle won on away goals)

UEFA Cup 2002–03

First Round

Celtic 8 (Larsson 3, Petrov, Sutton, Lambert, Hartson, Valgaeren): Suduva (Lithuania) 1 (Radzihevicius) 1

Suduva 0: Celtic 2 (Fernandez, Thompson)

Second Round

Celtic 1 (Larsson): Blackburn Rovers (England) 0

Blackburn Rovers 0: Celtic 2 (Larsson, Sutton)

Third Round

Celtic 1 (Larsson): Celta Vigo (Spain) 0

Celta Vigo 2 (Jesuli, McCarthy): Celtic 1 (Hartson)

(Celtic won on away goals)

Fourth Round

Celtic 3 (Lambert, Maloney, Petrov): VfB Stuttgart (Germany) 1 (Kuranyi)

VfB Stuttgart 3 (Tiffert, Hleb, Mutzel): Celtic 2 (Thompson, Sutton)

Quarter-final

Celtic 1 (Larsson): Liverpool (England) 1 (Heskey)

Liverpool 0: Celtic 2 (Thompson, Hartson)

Semi-final

Celtic 1 (Larsson): Boavista (Portugal) 1 (Valgaeren own goal)

Boavista 0: Celtic 1 (Larsson)

Final – Seville, Spain

Celtic 2 (Larsson 2): Porto (Portugal) 3 (Derlei 2, Alenitchev)

Champions League 2003-04

Second Qualifying Round

Kaunas (Lithuania) 0: Celtic 4 (Larsson, Sutton, Maloney, Miller)

Celtic 1 (Gvildys own goal): Kaunas 0

Third Qualifying Round

MTK Hungaria (Hungary) 0: Celtic 4 (Larsson, Agathe, Petrov, Sutton)

Celtic 1 (Sutton): MTK Hungaria 0

Group Stage

Bayern Munich (Germany) 2 (Makaay 2): Celtic 1 (Thompson)

Celtic 2 (Miller, Sutton): Olympique Lyon (France) 0

Anderlecht (Belgium) 1 (Dindane): Celtic 0

Celtic 3 (Larsson, Miller, Sutton): Anderlecht 1 (Dindane)

Celtic 0: Bayern Munich 0

Olympique Lyon 3 (Elber, Juninho 2): Celtic 2 (Hartson, Sutton)

Celtic finished in third place in their group and qualified for the UEFA Cup

UEFA Cup 2003-04
Third round
Celtic 3 (Larsson 2, Sutton): Teplice (Czech Republic) 0
Teplice 1 (Masek): Celtic 0
Fourth round
Celtic 1 (Thompson): Barcelona (Spain) 0
Barcelona 0: Celtic 0
Quarter-final
Celtic (Larsson) 1: Villareal (Spain) 1 (Josico)
Villareal 2 (Anderson, Roger): Celtic 0

Index